05. JUN 03

08 JUN 2013

R CITIZENS

STUDIES IN MODERN HISTORY

General editors: John Morrill and David Cannadine

This series, intended primarily for students, will tackle significant historical issues in concise volumes which are both stimulating and scholarly. The authors combine a broad approach, explaining the current state of our knowledge in the area, with their own research and judgements; and the topics chosen range widely in subject, period and place.

Titles already published

POOR CITIZENS
The State and the Poor in Twentieth-Century Britain

David Vincent

Longman
London and New York

LONGMAN GROUP UK LIMITED,
Longman House, Burnt Mill, Harlow,
Essex, CM20 2JE, England
and Associated Companies throughout the world.

*Published in the United States of America
by Longman Inc., New York*

© Longman Group UK Limited 1991

First published 1991

British Library Cataloguing in Publication Data
Vincent, David
 Poor citizens: the state and the poor in
 twentieth century Britain. - (Studies in modern
 history)
 I. Title II. Series
 362.50941

 ISBN 0-582-08451-2
 ISBN 0-582-49469-9 pbk

Library of Congress Cataloging in Publication Data
Vincent, David, 1949-
 Poor citizens : the state and the poor in twentieth century
 Britain / David Vincent.
 p. cm. -- (Studies in modern history)
 includes bibliographical references and index.
 ISBN 0-582-08451-2 (cased). -- ISBN 0-582-49469-9 (paper)
 1. Poor--Great Britain--History--20th century. 2. Public welfare--
Great Britain--History--20th century. 2. Public welfare--policy. 4. Welfare
state. I. Title. II. Series: Studies in modern history (Longman (Firm))
 HV4086.A3V56 1991
 362.5'8'094109048--dc20
                                                            90-27394
                                                                 CIP

Set in Bembo
Produced by Longman Singapore Publishers (Pte) Ltd.
Printed in Singapore

Contents

Preface

In a discussion of historical approaches to social welfare written nearly two decades ago, Asa Briggs identified two requirements of future work in the field. Firstly, it was necessary to pay critical attention to the influential analysis of T.H. Marshall: 'His argument that within an inegalitarian money economy there was being established an increasingly egalitarian system of "citizenship", carrying within it full and equal "membership" in the modern community, needs re-examination.'[1] Secondly, in approaching the problem of poverty, it was important not to be deflected by the abstract explanatory categories surrounding the subject: 'We must try to get behind words to the human relations which make up the stuff of social history.'[2]

These twin observations form the point of departure for this brief survey of relations between the poor and the state in the twentieth century. What follows is an attempt to bring together what have in the past all too frequently been discrete subjects of study. The great strength of Marshall's insight was that he recognised that the modern welfare reforms formed part of a much longer sequence of changes which were gradually widening the meaning of citizenship. He was aware that there were tensions between the legal, political, economic and social categories, but much subsequent research has concentrated on one element of these to the relative exclusion of the others. With the growing engagement of academic researchers in political pressure-group activity and its associated media campaigns, there has been increasing movement across the boundaries, and some of the best work on contemporary Britain, such as Mack and Lansley's *Poor Britain*, has made a real attempt to explore the dynamics of both government policy and the experience of deprivation. What is lacking, and what this book seeks to provide, is a longer-term survey of the problem since the linked emergence at the beginning of this century of the modern democratic state and new ways of thinking about and dealing with deprivation. It is argued here that the strategies of the poor and the state cannot be studied in isolation, that their interaction became increasingly complex as the period wore on, and that the fate of the poor as social citizens was throughout intimately connected with their fate as political citizens.

In many different ways, the quality of the forms of citizenship available to the least prosperous sections of society was determined by their capacity to participate in the relevant structures of activity. There has been a tendency in even the most careful and sympathetic studies of the subject to see poverty as a condition, to identify the poor in terms of a definable list of possessions whose absence leads to measurable forms of material hardship. These issues are of course important, but in essence poverty was not a condition but a practice. It was, as Briggs observed, a matter of human relationships which were conducted in a series of contexts from the family outwards. Even the most hopeless pursued intricate strategies of survival which embodied complex normative and material aspirations and involved elaborate negotiations with a wide range of individuals and agencies. At all times, the fewer the resources, the more thought and energy that had to be expended in their use. The task for the historian is to try to identify the components of these strategies, and to explore the ways in which their outcome was shaped and reshaped by the complex political, economic, social and cultural changes of the period.

The implementation of this task presents considerable problems of organisation. There has to be a broad chronological structure as the account moves from the beginning of the first decade of the twentieth century to the conclusion of the first decade of Mrs Thatcher's Government, but the pattern of developments and interactions is too complex to be reduced to a simple Act-by-Act narrative. The solution adopted here has been to divide the period into four broad blocks, the first concluding with the ending of Liberal England, the second with the ending of peace in 1939, the third with the ending of the post-war boom in the mid-sixties, and the final one as near to the present day as the process of revision and publication will permit. Each chapter contains an introductory and concluding discussion and separate sections on the strategies of the state and the broader political processes in which they were embedded, and the strategies of the poor and the forces which shaped them. The last section of each chapter takes the form of a concluding discussion of the relationship between the strategies in the period the chapter covers.

It is hoped that such an approach will clarify the dynamics of change, but the reader coming to the subject for the first time may still find it difficult to keep track of the technicalities and terminology of the legislation and organisations which mediated relations between the state and the poor during the period. For this reason a substantial Glossary has been attached to the book. This provides chronological lists of the major acts and their basic provisions organised by theme, spells out the many abbreviations, and gives brief definitions of important technical terms.

I have been greatly helped in writing this book by the students I have taught at Keele, many of whom have had a more direct engagement with straightened circumstances than they might have wished. I am particularly grateful to Penny Fisher, Paul Johnson, Christine Lapping, Andy Miles and Mike Savage for taking the time to read the chapters, and, once more to Charlotte Vincent for doing her best to keep me on the straight and narrow path of plain writing.

Keele and Shrawardine
August 1990

REFERENCES

1.   A. Briggs, 'The History of Changing Approaches to Social Welfare', in *Comparative Development in Social Welfare* (London, 1972), p. 20.
2.   *Ibid.*, p. 21.

To the memory of

Mary Hannah Kirkham
Warden Vincent
Martha Rebecca Lynn
Percy Samuel Heath

CHAPTER ONE

Strategies of Poverty 1900 – 14

INTRODUCTION

The new century began with a 'thunder-clap', the publication, according to the journalist and Poor Law Guardian, C.F.G. Masterman, of 'one of the most important pieces of detailed social investigation ever undertaken'.[1] Seebohm Rowntree's study of the outwardly prosperous cathedral town of York revealed that 27.84 per cent of the inhabitants 'were living in poverty'.[2] It now appeared that London, which had been the subject of Charles Booth's extensive survey a decade earlier, was more typical than had been assumed. As a consequence of his research, Rowntree argued, 'we are faced by the startling probability that from 25 to 30 per cent of the town populations of the United Kingdom are living in poverty'.[3] This was a problem, concluded Masterman, 'which if only definitely realised in its squalid immensity is surely enough to stagger humanity'.[4]

Poverty: A Study of Town Life was, as Masterman recognised, first and foremost a challenge to the imagination of the Edwardian public. What had to be grasped was the totality of the suffering which lay beneath the surface of the country's prosperity. In the book, case histories were presented only as illustrations of general conditions. Disaggregation of the poor into individual families with unique failings was an evasion of the problem. The political reverberation of a text which scrupulously avoided political prescription was a product of its attempt to force new ways of thinking about the subject of its title.

There were two aspects to the reassessment which Rowntree demanded. Firstly the scale of the problem had to be recognised; secondly the underlying causes had to be identified. These were separate objectives, requiring different conceptual tools, and Masterman was only to be the first of a long line of critics, both sympathetic and hostile, to have difficulty with the difference between them.[5] 'What does Mr Rowntree mean by "Poverty"?', he asked, and in reply summarised the calculation of the 'minimum of physically healthful existence',[6] which he misleadingly termed the 'poverty line'. In fact the line that divided the poor from the non-poor in York was drawn not by nutritional science but by general observation. 'The investigator', explained Rowntree, 'in the course of his house-to-house visitation, noted down the households where there were evidences of poverty, i.e. obvious want and squalor.'[7] The numbers in 'secondary poverty', which comprised about two-thirds of the poor, were derived by subtracting families in 'primary poverty' – those whose income could not meet the standard of physical efficiency – from the total of those whose appearance and behaviour separated them from the rest of the community.

Whilst Masterman was content to accept the overall figure as a true measure of the extent of poverty in early twentieth-century Britain, other contemporary observers quickly dismissed the category of secondary poverty as the product either of inadequate procedure by the observers, or inadequate behaviour by the observed. Rowntree himself was partly responsible for the ease with which, for instance, *The Times* was able to conclude that the larger proportion of poor 'were miserable mainly from their own fault'.[8] After the parade of scientific data and arithmetical calculation which introduced the concept of primary poverty, his wider measure seemed dangerously impressionistic. He gave hostages to his enemies by suggesting in the book that the descent into deprivation by those whose income would otherwise keep them out of primary poverty, 'would appear to be mainly due to the following immediate causes, namely – Drink, betting, and gambling. Ignorant or careless housekeeping, and other improvident expenditure',[9] and in the ensuing public debate still further compromised his case by redefining primary as 'economic' and secondary as 'preventable' poverty.[10] Subsequent research, particularly by A.L. Bowley, and later by Rowntree again, abandoned the category of secondary poverty altogether as being unworkable and indefensible, yet it can be argued that of the two ways of approaching the issue, it bore much the closest approximation to the world in which the mass of the population lived.

As a careful reading of *Poverty* makes clear, the concept of primary poverty was essentially a heuristic device, introduced to clarify the dynamics of the problem. Rowntree emphasised that he had omitted from his calculation 'expenditure needful for the development of the mental, moral, and social sides of human nature',[11] and even at the purely physical level, he was aware that his minimum diet 'would require considerable changes in established customs, and many prejudices would have to be uprooted'.[12] The statistician A.L. Bowley, whose study in 1915 employed both Rowntree's primary poverty line and a refined version of his own, accepted that 'all such standards' were 'abstract and arbitrary' in relation to the actual behaviour of the poor.[13] Helen Bosanquet's gibe that the poverty line was 'nothing but a picturesque way of talking',[14] was harsh, but contained an element of truth.

By contrast, the investigator who surveyed the appearance of families and their homes in York at the turn of the century, was seeking to identify poverty in terms that the poor themselves would understand. However much it might offend the sensibilities of those anxious to ground the young discipline of social science on the firm foundations of fact rather than the shifting sands of opinion, there was something to be said for asking the neighbours who they thought was poor, or accepting that 'the pinched faces of the ragged children told their own tale of poverty and privation'.[15] Such an approach recognised that the struggle for existence amongst the working class embodied a complex mix of material and normative aspirations in which outward show was at once a consequence of deprivation and a concern in its own right. The battle began to be lost when it became impossible to conceal the physical results of malnutrition, or the shaming devices which had been adopted to avoid total destitution. Families became poor when they could no longer keep their stories private.

At the heart of such narratives were strategies for survival, which were pursued week in and week out until death or the workhouse finally intervened. Rowntree's invention of the poverty line achieved its intended effect of drawing attention to the essential impossibility of the campaigns which were being waged in so many households. The reality highlighted by the artificial calculation of average dietary requirements was that a substantial section of the population was faced every day with a set of irreconcilable objectives. Whereas the non-poor could specify a set of minimum physical and psychological needs and at least in the short term hope to achieve them, the defining characteristic of those in poverty was that the attainment of any one basic goal always involved the loss of another. If a particular member of a family was adequately fed, the others were not; if the fire was burning well, the table was ill-provided; if cultural hunger was diminished, bodily malnutrition was increased; if short-term respite was supplied by a money-lender, long-term recovery was postponed; if recourse to the poor law prevented physical extinction, nevertheless it destroyed social standing. For the most practical reasons the schemes of the poor were always impractical.

In a sense therefore, it may be misleading to borrow the metaphor of strategy from the military sphere. Men at war devise elaborate plans which result in either victory or defeat over a finite period of time. Families in poverty patched together no less intricate designs which were mutually contradictory and ended in nothing better than survival. Yet the concept remains appropriate in that it directs attention to a range of issues central to the evolving relationship between the state and the poor in this period.[16]

It encourages first of all a search for the rationality of behaviour which too frequently seemed a negation of planned activity. Whilst it appeared to many contemporaries that the more powerless the social group, the more incoherent were their struggles, it may be argued that the reverse was the case. Those with the fewest resources required the most sophisticated strategies to exploit them. It required endless invention and adjustment to reconcile the profound conflicts between choice and constraint which dominated their lives. Strategies were formed as a means of coping with outside forces over which there was little prospect of direct control. And whilst it was often assumed that the poorer the group, the more narrowly material were their preoccupations, it is evident that the interaction between physical and normative pressures was nowhere more complex than amongst the dispossessed. No matter how far it had sunk into Masterman's 'Social Abyss', each family was engaged in a relentless campaign in which physical goals and obstacles coexisted and competed with values and sanctions set by the community in which it lived. If the basic equation of income and household size conditioned every step that was taken, the range of devices adopted to maximise resources and minimise expenditure could never be reduced to a simple balance sheet. The ways in which money was raised and used were determined as much by social convention as by market forces or bodily needs.

At the same time the concept demands a sensitivity to the ways in which individuals lived and worked in groups. It will be argued in what follows that the household was the principal unit for devising and implementing strategies for survival, yet as will be made clear, there were variations of outlook and endeavour within the home, and its members, particularly the women, were at the same time capable of forming overlapping strategies with others in the community. Such neighbourhood support networks were dependent on shared needs and common values, but were in turn riven with jealousy and mistrust.

The complexity of the shifting patterns of co-operation and conflict was a consequence of the intensity of the pressures under which life had to be conducted. The strategies of the poor were formed not in isolation, but in relation to the strategies of others. Over time, the intentions and devices of government have become of increasing relevance to the formation and outcome of the plans of the poor. Whilst Rowntree's calculation of minimum weekly food costs owed much to the accumulated expertise of workhouse managers, his poverty line was his own, and he used it to illuminate a way of life strikingly independent of official rules and organisations. In the modern world, however, we have become accustomed to defining the poor in relation to the state. Despite occasional attempts to devise fresh, independent measures of poverty,[17] most observers base their line on the government's current welfare benefit levels. Depending on the point of view, the poor are those whom the state ought to help adequately but does not, or who ought to help themselves but instead rely on the state.

In 1901, by contrast, the great majority of the households falling into primary or secondary poverty conducted their affairs without any reference to the regulations and officers of national or local bureaucracies. As a casual labourer and his wife struggled from day to day and from week to week to keep the family afloat, the state was a distant and irrelevant entity. For the most part it existed only to punish the failure of the strategies for survival, as in the nearly one and half million plaints for debt taken out annually against working men, or the disenfranchisement imposed on them by the Poor Law. Only in the field of education was there extensive interaction between public and private endeavour. Within a few years of Rowntree's report, and partly as a consequence of it, the strategies of the poor and of the state and its agencies began to impinge upon each other in ever more complex ways.

POOR STRATEGIES

For every social investigator of the period, the study of the poor meant the study of poor families. Amidst the arguments over methodologies and prescriptions there was general agreement that the strategies for coping with poverty were founded on the needs and resources of households and not individuals. Surveys often turned up a scattering of single men and women, but these were mostly widows and widowers for whom the workhouse was likely to be the enforced alternative to the families they once had raised. Bowley's sample study in 1913 pointed out that the contemporary nuclear family of two parents and three children 'is itself quite rare',[18] yet few of his population were living by themselves, and fewer still had never lived with other relatives since leaving childhood. At the same time it was common ground that within the family the experience of hardship, and the steps taken to alleviate it, differed sharply according to age and gender. Deprivation did not standardise suffering, neither did it break down long-established divisions of responsibility and power.

At no level of society was the doctrine of separate spheres more rigidly observed than amongst those consigned to the outer reaches of civilised living. Families whose appearance and pastimes outraged every canon of polite behaviour nonetheless maintained distinctions of role and status which in their way were as complex and unbending as those practised in the highest circles. The division between husband and wife was observed by the dock labourer's daughter, Grace Foakes, as she grew up in East London before the First World War: 'Mother was the central figure in our home. Father worked when there was work available, and was head of the household.'[19] The difference between being at the centre and at the head of the endlessly overcrowded tenement was fundamental. Inadequate and unreliable though his wages may have been, Grace's father retained the status of the supporter of his family, the ultimate source of its well-being and fount of all authority over its members. However, his involvement in the maintenance of the household ended at the point at which he handed over his pay packet, having in most cases first deducted a small sum for his private use. The day-to-day drama of expediency, compromise and sacrifice that was required to keep the domestic unit going, was directed entirely by his wife. Another East London child, Walter Southgate, recalled his mother as 'the linchpin of the family wheel. Nothing was done without mother being consulted.'[20] Any understanding of the strategies which were adopted to cope with poverty, and the costs which they entailed, has to begin with those around whom everything seemed to revolve.

The first priority of a poor man's wife was to put herself last. Shoes, and other clothing if it could be afforded, were bought for her husband, then for her children, then for herself.[21] Food was distributed on the same basis. The head of the household had the biggest portion, and the first call on any meat if it was available; the children were fed according to their size, and whether they had themselves started work;

then the mother had what was left, remaining at the end of the line even if she herself had some form of part-time employment.[22] During the week she was usually deprived of the basic privilege of sitting down to the table with the rest of her family. When ill-health made its frequent appearance, a doctor might be summoned in an attempt to keep the bread-winner on his feet, or to save the life of a small child, and money might be laid out on medicine for them. Such decisions were made by the wife and mother, who would rarely permit similar expenditure on her own ailments. Margaret Llewelyn Davies surveyed the cumulative impact on her of this ordering of the household's pattern of consumption: 'It is on the whole an impression of perpetual over-work, illness and suffering.'[23]

At the best of times it was a tiring life. 'My mother too', remembered Bert Coombes, '– like all women of her class – her work never finished . . . . No holiday, week-day or Sunday, and no other prospect but to get greyer and weaker with the years.'[24] What did most to turn weariness into physical destruction was the absence of any respite during pregnancy and the early months of nursing. There was no addition to the insufficient diet, and no relief from the burden of heavy labour about the home whilst the baby was being carried. If she avoided involuntary miscarriage, which ended at least 15 per cent of pregnancies, or a still-birth, which accounted for another 6 per cent,[25] and if she herself survived the continuing high rates of maternal mortality, she would be back on her feet after no more than a fortnight's rest, and often less, faced with all her old tasks, in addition to the loss of sleep and energy which feeding and caring for a new-born baby entailed. The combination of prolonged physical strain and inadequate medical attention led to an accumulation of persistent and often acutely painful conditions, such as breast abscesses, prolapsed wombs, bad backs and varicose veins. In such circumstances, life might continue, but youth was destroyed. As the Birmingham slum child, Kathleen Dayus, observed, 'They were worn out and old women at forty.'[26]

Such a decline was so visible and inevitable as to raise questions about the readiness of daughters to become mothers in their turn. As Grace Foakes commented:

> Considering all things, I think it was the women of my generation who had the hardest times. For what with child-bearing, poor housing and unemployment, and the constant struggle to make both ends meet, their lot was not an enviable one. Yet surprisingly enough it was the aim of every girl to get married, and those who did not were looked upon with pity and were said to be 'on the shelf'.[27]

The answer lay partly in the mixture of convention and necessity which rendered marriage and motherhood the only perceived means of achieving any sort of emotional and material security over a lifetime, and partly in the sense of satisfaction yielded by playing the key role in the survival of the household. Richard Hoggart stressed that there was more to a mother's lot than the endless hardship and frequent sorrow: 'Behind it, making any vague pity irrelevant, is pride in the knowledge that so much revolves around them.'[28] At the heart of this sense of self-worth was the sheer complexity of the calculating and decision-making which pervaded every waking moment of the day.

Firstly there was the question of whether and how the mother was to make her own contribution to the family's income. The range of employment available to married women varied greatly according to the nature of the local economy. Even where there was a long tradition of female labour, such as in the textile and pottery industries, full-time work was usually given up at marriage or the first pregnancy, and not resumed unless the family turned out to be very small and very poor. For reasons of both status and concern for her own physical well-being, an artisan's wife would hope to stay out of the labour market in which most jobs still involved considerable physical toil, but the further down the income scale, the more likely it was that some part-time labour would be added to the range of tasks undertaken by the mother. Such employment was not easy to identify or quantify, but Rowntree calculated that the size of a wife's financial contribution to the family economy varied in inverse proportion to its prosperity, ranging from an average of 5s 8d when the household was living on less than 18s a week, to 1s 3d when it had 30s or more at its disposal.[29]

Many of the tasks, such as child-minding, taking in lodgers, washing or sewing, making food or drink, or running a small shop, could be conducted in the home, or as an extension of its activities.[30] During the nineteenth century the growth of factories and of state regulation in areas such as school teaching had curtailed some opportunities, but especially in the towns the expansion of the consumer market for food and clothing, and the introduction of new technology such as sewing machines, had created fresh possibilities of earning a few shillings a week without leaving the house. In many ways Isaac Singer's invention typified the kind of economic freedom open to the poor man's wife. Providing the family was not totally destitute, it was just about possible to contemplate diverting enough money from other necessities to buy a machine on a readily available instalment system, and once acquired, it might both pay for itself and make a crucial difference to the family economy. At the same time the work, particularly if it took the form of making up garments on piece rates for a wholesaler, was grossly underpaid, involving long hours of labour in poor light. And whilst it reduced the vulnerability of the household to financial collapse, it increased the prospect of exploitation by the notional head of the family. 'The reason he never gave her regular wages', wrote Albert Jasper of his father, 'was he knew my mother could always earn a few shillings with her machine.'[31]

There were sufficient prospects of part-time employment to ensure that a housewife could never be certain she was doing all that she could, but not enough to resolve the endless difficulties of making the family's income cover its basic needs. Once she had received her husband's contribution, and added her own and those of any of her children old enough to earn, she could begin the immensely complex series of calculations which faced her every hour of every day. Lonely decisions had to be taken on a wide range of financial issues, as Margaret Loane observed: 'Money matters are left almost entirely to the wife; it is she who decides whether an increased rent can be paid, or an article of furniture bought, whether a boy shall be apprenticed or must take what work he can find, and what insurance clubs, etc., shall be found.'[32] By this period, almost all the younger women had received some formal schooling, but the kind of functional numeracy which running a household required bore little relation to the abstract exercises once undertaken in the classroom. Although few were at ease doing sums on paper, as investigators seeking household budgets soon discovered, they were forced to become, as Mrs. Pember Reeves noted, 'curiously efficient in a kind of mental arithmetic'.[33]

The financial strategy of a poor man's wife was based on a number of apparent paradoxes. Firstly, the more destitute the family, the greater the number of luxuries in its budget. When times were hard, the range of absolutely necessary items of expenditure was remarkably small. During a given week, almost any purchase could be substituted or postponed. Clothing, virtually all household items except coal, and most forms of food and drink except bread, potatoes, tea and margarine, could be dispensed with.[34] Here, as in many other instances, the poorer a family became, the more its way of life retreated in time. Under pressure, the proportion of income spent on food rose and the diet was increasingly dominated by loaves, now much more often bought than baked. 'Gradually we sank lower and lower into poverty', recalled William Holt, whose father was frequently out of work, 'and glad to have margarine and bread'.[35] The price of flour was no longer of quite the critical importance it had been in the early decades of the nineteenth century, but the range of meals set out on the table of a family possessed of an income of less than twenty shillings a week would have seemed very familiar to a working-class household two or three generations earlier. Equally the tendency to rely on repairing and remaking, rather than buying ready-made shoes and clothes kept alive skills which were now less often practised in more prosperous working-class homes.

Secondly, the less money the wife had, the more often she went shopping. 'The poor', wrote J.A. Hobson, 'partly of necessity, partly by habit, make their purchases in minute quantities'.[36] Only if she could be absolutely certain that the week's money would last seven days, could the household manager make all her purchases as soon as she received it. Without such security, and without cool, dry, vermin-free storage space,[37] food and sundries were bought in tiny amounts. This level of society still operated a penny economy. As soon as they could walk, children knew the value of any small coin they could bring into the house. These could be exchanged at the local corner shop for a range of pre-packed penny or halfpenny goods, or bulk items such as margarine or tea which could be broken down into the smallest volume.[38] In turn meals were planned in the same currency. 'She kept us clean and tidy and well-fed', recalled the laundry-maid's daughter, Jean Rennie, 'A penny bone, or pennyworth of carrot, turnip, leek, and parsley made a pot of soup that lasted for two days.'[39] It meant last-minute shopping for meals during the week, and on Saturdays late evening visits to the butcher's to buy bargain cuts of left-over meat which would go off by Monday morning.

Thirdly, the more care a wife had to take in managing her finances, the less efficient was much of her expenditure. As Mrs Pember Reeves observed, 'You pay, relatively speaking, more for less if you are poor.'[40] It was undoubtedly cheaper to buy larger amounts of food in bigger shops. Coal was more expensive by the hundredweight than by the ton. The absence of proper ranges and the fuel to keep them going made difficult the slow cooking of the nourishing broths and stews beloved of the middle-class compilers of recipes for the poor. The smaller the rent, the more was paid for each square foot of living space, and higher was the expense of keeping it warm and dry. Then there was the cost of credit, which was a separate issue in its own right.

Going into debt was at once the most rational means of coping with the savage fluctuations in the family economy, and the greatest obstacle to achieving financial security. The system of credit in poor neighbourhoods was based on a shared knowledge of the pressures on the budgets of so many households. Whatever might be the view of charity workers, it was accepted by lenders and borrowers alike that a purse could be empty before the end of the week for many reasons other than wanton extravagance or mismanagement. Equally there was always a chance of the family economy being at least temporarily re-floated. Employment having been lost might once more be found, a child having fallen sick might recover, or die and generate payment from an insurance policy. There was an enforced logic to the decision to buy food from a corner shop which could not be paid for until the following week, or to obtain clothing from a scotch tailor for which the family possessed only a fraction of the purchase price. Short-term credit could make the essential difference between hunger and starvation, long-term borrowing could be the only alternative to reliance on charity and hand-me-downs, and introduced a desirable element of predictability to the pattern of expenditure over a period of time.

The drawback was that families unable to balance their books at the end of the week paid yet more for everything they consumed, and whilst borrowing did something to even out the troughs of absolute poverty, it also flattened the miniature peaks of prosperity. An accumulation on the slate at the grocer's, a commitment to numerous instalments on a new coat, an acquisition of a doctor's bill which could easily run into several guineas, meant that the occasional weeks of relative plenty disappeared altogether. 'Debt', commented Rowntree, 'acts as a leveller of the dietary throughout the year.'[41] A further difficulty was that if sums mounted at the most accessible prospect of credit, the corner shop to which visits were made several times a day, there came a point when it was no longer possible to buy food there at all. Shopkeepers were obvious but extremely unstable sources of borrowing. It was in their interest to tide over regular customers, but their lack of capital and a systematic means of recovering arrears (unlike doctors who often employed their own collectors), rendered them all too likely to join the ranks of their impoverished debtors. Robert Roberts watched from behind the shop-counter as his mother considered yet another request for credit, 'only enough, perhaps, to ward off hunger in the family until Saturday pay time. Here a difficult choice had to be made: one wanted the trade badly, but knew only too well that a little shopkeeper lax in the selection of tick customers rapidly went "bump".'[42]

In these circumstances, the pawnbroker seemed the perfect answer. Here the lender had the security of pledged goods against the possibility of a client falling from poverty to destitution, whilst the borrower had the certainty that she would not build up cash debts, even if her household eventually ran out of clothing and other moveable possessions. The Edwardian period represented the golden era of the pawnbroking trade. Not before or since were there so many shops in so many neighbourhoods, prepared to issue tickets on so wide a range of goods.[43] Virtually anything could be deposited in return for a few precious shillings or pence. Clothing was the most common item of pawn, starting with the husband's Sunday suit, taken in at the beginning of the week and redeemed on Saturday night, followed by other more necessary parts of the wardrobe, bed-coverings, and by portable objects such as clocks and cutlery. *In extremis*, nothing was sacred. Pat O'Mara vividly recalled the practice of a neighbour in his Liverpool slum: 'Mrs Haggarty, who lived below our entry, for years pawned her false teeth every Monday morning, and when she died, Mr Harris [the pawnbroker] hopefully put them up for sale in his front window.'[44] As with a modern property speculator, goods were acquired not only for use but as a means of raising more credit.[45] One instalment on a suit gave possession of an asset which would raise several times the initial payment when presented at 'uncles's'. Unlike objects bought under the inter-war system of hire-purchase, this was perfectly legal; less so was the common device of pledging washing before it was returned to its owner.[46]

The fewer goods the poor possessed, the more they maximised their value, yet the greater their use, the more expensive they became. After 1872 a pawnbroker could charge a maximum of 25 per cent a year on a loan of less than two pounds, but if an item was continually re-pledged throughout the year, the real rate of interest could range from anything from 100 to 1,000 per cent.[47] A widow shivering inside a threadbare coat might as well have been wearing furs for the money she had laid out over years of redeeming it from the pawnbrokers. Furthermore the cash payments were only one element of the total cost. Taking bundles of clothing through the streets and then arguing with the pawnbroker about their current value involved a profound loss of dignity.[48] It exposed to public gaze both the precise state of personal possessions and the general fact that the household was too poor to subsist on its cash income alone. No member of the working-class community was immune from this sense of shame; the only differences were in the steps which could be taken to avoid it. The comparatively prosperous could hope never to make use of the facility; the absolutely poor had little choice but to engage in the Monday morning ritual in full view of their neighbours; in between were a large group who could afford either to restrict their visits to occasional emergencies, or to employ children, who technically could redeem but not pledge, or elderly women who specialised in the task, to conduct the transactions by proxy, in return for small payments which further added to the expense of the exercise.[49]

Nothing did more to unite and divide the homes of the wealthy and the deprived than the desire for privacy. Families living in over-crowded houses in packed terraces were as preoccupied with social space as those ensconced in detached villas inside fenced gardens. Whilst physical necessity generated an intensity of involvement with the lives of neighbours on a scale that both fascinated and repelled outside observers, the concern to set limits to the exposure of domestic circumstances was as fundamental to the patrons of pawnbrokers in urban slums as it was to the wives of stockbrokers in their suburban retreats. 'Secrecy is strongly developed among the poor', observed Margaret Loane, 'and although often sustained by deceitfulness and even fraud, is closely connected with self-respect and independence. Wages and the expenditure of money are always shrouded in thick darkness.'[50] As with so many aspects of their life, some basic goals had to be sacrificed to preserve others. It was worth experiencing the loss of status caused by translating a husband's suit into enough money to provide several meals, if the alternative was applying for Poor Law relief. Painful though it was to wait while the pawnbroker's assistant turned over an item of clothing before giving you half what you needed, it was far preferable to parading the whole family before the Guardians and pledging every detail of its failings in return for assist-ance which was even less sufficient. The shame of engaging in the widespread and widely understood practice of visiting 'uncle's' could soon be redeemed if the family's fortunes improved, whereas the stig-ma of abandoning independence and applying for public relief would take years to pay off.

For the poor, the preservation of total privacy deprived the family of its last line of defence against destitution, whilst the total destruction of privacy marked the final defeat of all its strategies for survival. At one level, the matter was simple. Women managing poor households created structures of mutual assistance with other women within a short walk of their doorsteps, which supplied by far the most depend-able and effective material and emotional support available to them outside their own family.[51] The exchanges of goods and services were in currencies which had too little value to feature in any of the house-hold budgets extracted by the social investigators, although they all knew what took place. 'There was a marvellous neighbourly spirit in those years', wrote John Langley of his poverty-stricken childhood in

Hove. 'If you were ill the whole street was concerned and wanted to do something about it and they did. They took it in turns to make milk puddings and custards out of their little money. Anything they could do to help.'[52] Small, easily repayable items of food, pennies for the gas meter, errands to the shop, hours looking after small children or invalid adults, were freely given and received. At the best of times there was always gossip, at the worst solace and encouragement.

The transactions were founded on shared knowledge and trust. News of a misfortune quickly spread, and assistance was not dependent on prior investigation into the circumstances which had caused it. It was assumed that help would be requested only if it was needed, and that this week's donor could be next week's recipient. Neither affection nor detailed calculation were invoked by this form of charity. 'These respectable but very poor people', observed Mrs Pember Reeves, 'live over a morass of such intolerable poverty that they unite instinctively to save those known to them from falling into it . . .. It was not mere personal liking which united them; it was a kind of mutual respect in the face of trouble.'[53]

Help from above, whether from private charities or public bodies, was by contrast slow, unreliable, inadequate and based on a profoundly unequal relationship. Neighbourly assistance was not merely an alternative to outside intervention but frequently existed as a defence against it. 'No matter how bad our neighbours seemed', recalled Kathleen Dayus, 'they always tried to help one another in their own kind of way. They would never "snitch" on each other, because they were all doing odd jobs on the side without reporting them to the relief officers. They had to do this; it was the only way to make ends meet.'[54] These barriers were an impediment to benevolent researchers, and often an impenetrable obstacle to those seeking to impose behavioural values on the poor, including the police. Behind the barriers the communal spirit was enhanced, as the inhabitants sought to evade the moral and physical sanctions of polite society. At the same time this solidarity was riven with tensions, and was as threatened from within as from without.

In the first instance, poor families did not all live next door to each other in permanently established enclaves of deprivation. This was most obviously the case in rural areas, where the restricted size of communities and the physical distance between them, severely reduced the possibilities of mutual assistance. But even in the towns, the apparent density of suffering was often misleading. Whilst Rowntree discovered plenty of evidence of neighbourly support in York, those most in need were not always huddled together in given streets.

Members of his 'Class A', the very bottom of the pile were 'found scattered almost all over the working-class parts of the city', as were those grouped into 'Class B'.[55] The factors causing families to fall into difficulty, and houses to decline into the condition where the rent was affordable, were too varied and unpredictable to create neat patterns of poor and less poor neighbourhoods.

The high residential mobility of families in rented accommodation constantly threatened the structures of shared knowledge upon which the communal assistance depended. 'The city poor are a wandering tribe', observed J.A. Hobson. 'But among the low working-classes, "flitting" is a chronic condition.'[56] A housewife tempted to liquidate mounting rent arrears by secretly moving to another address was all too aware that if she escaped the vengeance of her landlord, she might also be beyond the aid of those who were familiar with her troubles. In practice it may well be that the sheer frequency of movement made established networks more receptive of newcomers and more prepared to take their troubles on trust. Such tolerance would be greater where the husband worked nearby with his new neighbours and where his family had only moved a few streets. The absolute contrast between belonging and isolation would not be experienced until the longer distant transfers to the occupationally diverse council estates began between the wars.

Even if the necessary residential stability was present, the limits of the assistance which could be rendered to a family in difficulties were quickly reached. Whilst the total amount of aid the poor gave the poor, if ever it could have been costed, far exceeded the efforts of all outside agencies, in relation to the requirements of any one family, it was stretched perilously thin. From day to day small gifts in cash, or more often in kind, could make all the difference, but over a longer period they were never enough. The pooled surpluses of the marginally less destitute could not make good the loss of the breadwinner's wage; sympathy, advice and hot gruel were rarely sufficient to save a dying child. Indeed some of the most valued support was given after the blow had fallen, when collections were made for a bereaved household. Such gifts were soon gone. A magistrate calculated that neighbours, together with local sources of credit, could sustain a deserted mother and her children for about two weeks.[57] Fortunate the family whose troubles were over in a fortnight.

Finally, constant close involvement with the lives of so many people generated as much friction as solidarity. Having to share facilities like outside privies did little to enhance neighbourly sympathies. 'There were always rows over whose turn it was to clean the closets', remembered Kathleen Dayus.[58] In most cases the root cause of the conflict was a general condition rather than a particular grievance. In Dayus's Birmingham slum, 'Tempers were always getting frayed because things never seemed to go right for these people. They skimped and saved to make ends meet, but they knew it was hopeless, so they gave up trying, or, worse, caring. Many's the time I've heard and seen them quarrelling with each other and coming to blows on the least little thing.'[59] Whilst the community could offer relentless opposition to outside discipline, it could be equally implacable against those within who broke its moral code. There was another side to the neighbourly spirit recalled by John Langley: 'The concern was the same if you did not behave yourself. People used to come up and down outside your house with dustbin lids, banging them to shame you, if you were living with another man or woman, that sort of thing. You had to behave yourself.'[60] If the transgression did not justify rough music, it could be dealt with in the continuing exchange of gossip, which through a mixture of information and invention, sympathy and malice, endlessly united and divided the neighbourhood.

At the end of the day, a woman managing a poor man's family was on her own. Central to her sense of worth was the appearance of competence and self-sufficiency.[61] Outside the home, neighbours were met as equals, but they entered only by invitation. For as long as possible a wife and mother strove to maintain the pretence that her strategies for survival were under control, and only genuine necessity would force their exposure to outside compassion or censure. An appeal for assistance did not justify an inquisition into the circumstances which caused it to be made. It was a matter of dignity and status, and also of the limitations of the community's resources. Neighbours sympathised with each other's troubles, but did not identify with them. They had neither the time nor the emotional strength nor the physical means to shoulder responsibility for another household's welfare. More might have been expected of kin living in the area, but the principal concern of sisters-in-law or married daughters remained their own husbands and children. The available help was often necessary but never sufficient to keep a distressed family afloat. Within the walls of her home, a woman's knowledge of how much depended on her resilience and judgement was the source of both pride and despair.

The semblance of effective management also had to be maintained before the head of the household. Husbands played little part in the daily strategies of consumption. They expected no questions about their wages, and asked few about their use. The mutual support systems in the neighbourhood were conducted by women who were not anxious to inform their menfolk of the scale of their contributions and benefits. In the poorest home, the nominal breadwinner had least command over resources. Arnold Wain recalled his father:

> One remarkable thing about my father was that he possessed nothing. Absolutely nothing at all. Not even a pocketknife . . . I never once saw him take out of his pocket any money. He must have had a little money sometimes, because he could buy drink, but this could only have been for an hour or so after receiving his pay . . . . The absolute 'possessionlessness' of my father is perhaps, the clearest memory I have of him. I never once heard 'Put that down. That's your father's.' He had nothing to put down.[62]

The women had responsibilities which they could never properly exercise, the men had power which they could not begin to use. Husbands and wives had separate roles in a joint campaign. Each was threatened by the other's shortcomings, but they retained objectives in common. This was most obviously the case in the one area in which duties were interchangeable. Observers were by turns amazed and appalled at the scale of the apparently wasteful expenditure on burial policies, which extended right down through the working class. No matter how inadequate and unbalanced the budgets which Rowntree set down in his surveys of urban and rural poverty, there was almost always at least threepence a week, and often more, set aside to cover the deaths of members of the family. Given the intense pressure on every penny of the household's income, it seemed quite irrational to sacrifice expenditure on food for benefits which might never be needed or realised. Well over half of the policies lapsed with the total loss of the accumulated premiums, and the industrial societies retained for expenses more than 40 per cent of the gross contributions on those that they did pay out.[63]

Who in the family actually paid the premiums depended on the source of the insurance. The principal male wage-earner would be responsible for benefits supplied through trade unions or friendly societies, those at home would hand over the weekly pence to the collectors for the industrial societies. As elsewhere, the poorer the family, the more likely it was to depend on the least efficient system. During the period up to the First World War, the collecting industrial and friendly societies were expanding faster than the organisations based in the workplace or centred on the convivial meetings of the Oddfellows and Foresters, which catered for the more prosperous sections of the working class. By 1914 the door-to-door salesmen were servicing forty-six million policies a year,[64] many paid for at the expense of food on the table or pennies in the gas meter.

There were two reasons why parents were so willing to sanction these payments. The first was the likelihood of death visiting the family before the children grew up. Rowntree and then Bowley used their poverty lines to draw attention to the disproportionate number of children suffering from inadequate diets and consequent high levels of disease and mortality. Family economies were at their most stretched when the consumers outnumbered the contributors. At least 40 per cent of York's schoolchildren were in poverty at any one time, and more still would experience deprivation for some part of their childhood.[65] Using the narrower 'primary' poverty line, Bowley found that in Reading, the worst of the towns he surveyed, no less than 47 per cent of schoolchildren fell below the minimum.[66] In the poorest area of York, a quarter of all children were dead before their first birthday, compared with one in ten of the 'servant-keeping class'. Within the labouring population, mortality rates above and below the age of five doubled between the most and least prosperous sections.[67] If not inevitable, bereavement was at least foreseeable. The more difficult it was to make ends meet, the more sense it made to reduce the family's income still further.

Death was a result of poverty and could be a cause of destitution. With the cost of burying a small child starting at around 30s–£2, the event was a financial as well as an emotional catastrophe. The second reason for taking out burial insurance was the avoidance of the ultimate indignity of a pauper funeral, a fate awaiting one in five in 1900, which would humiliate every surviving member of the family in the eyes of the neighbourhood, and technically pauperise the father. 'Sheer dread of this horrible problem', observed Mrs Pember Reeves, 'drives his wife to pay out 10d, 11d, or 1s a week year after year – money which, as far as the welfare of the children themselves go, might as well be thrown in the sea'.[68] It was a more extreme version of the equation which led her to the pawnbrokers. Whoever took out the insurance, all stood to lose if the payments were allowed to lapse.

Although the ideological construct of the 'breadwinner' persisted right down the social scale, it bore a diminishing relevance to reality.[69] Once the head of the household could no longer obtain permanent employment, or once his dependants could no longer live on his full-time earnings, there was little practical difference in the income-generating activities of any member of the family. Just as wives sought out half jobs for quarter payments, so their husbands and then their growing children hunted through the interstices of the Edwardian economy for opportunities to make money. When the domestic budget was allocated in pennies, it tended to be financed in a similar currency. Despite the century-long evolution towards occupational specialisation, and the increasingly rigorous attempts to keep school-children out of the labour market, there always appeared a chance of finding some means of alleviating the family's troubles, at least for those living in the towns.[70]

The entrepreneurial spirit flourished nowhere more strongly than amongst those who were the principal victims of the free market. It required immense ingenuity, imagination and persistence to use in-stantly acquired skills to multiply virtually non-existent amounts of capital. Obtaining goods on credit for sale in the streets or in a shop opened in the front room was not easy when all you possessed was debts. Stocking a barrow or a counter from home-grown, caught or brewed food and drink, or with manufactured items which had become surplus to requirements elsewhere, placed a great strain on an underfed physique or an over-stretched respect for the law. Theft and receiving stolen goods had always been crimes, but those seeking to engage in private enterprise faced multiplying by-laws affecting street trading, food standards and school attendance, and newly constructed criminal offences such as off-course bookmaking, which became com-pletely illegal in 1906.

Despite the requirement to spend so much of their time cooped up in a classroom, children had the widest opportunites for making a few pence. There were always errands to be run for those whose health or pride prevented them from making their own journeys to the shop or the pawnbrokers or the off-licence. The young George Noakes used to earn a much prized sixpence for buying a bottle of whiskey for an alcoholic doctor's wife.[71] On a more regular basis, delivering milk in the early morning, or newspapers before and after school became a substitute for the full-time jobs which were now forbidden.[72] For children it was a matter of contributing something rather than noth-ing; for their fathers it was something rather than a living wage. Those who deliberately retired from a skilled job to invest a nest-egg in a properly equipped shop or a public house took a chance, but they might make it. Those forced out of employment into street-trading were driven by visions of destitution rather than wealth. They had all of the risks but none of the hopes of the true capitalist.[73]

Almost as soon as they could walk, every member of a poor house-hold had a duty to explore the possibilities of squeezing a few pence or shillings out of the local economy. The more successful their ef-forts, the nearer the family came to surfacing above the poverty line; the further it rose above it, the later and the fewer of its members went out to work. In terms of the flow of cash into the home, supplementary earnings were of far greater significance to the poor than all forms of welfare provision combined. The joint effort bound the parents and children together, the sense of contributing to each other's survival was a source of satisfaction to all. Yet as they grew older, teenage children, and in particular their mother and father, fought on different battlefields. A wife knew little of her husband's struggles to find a regular job, he was largely unaware of her endless small victories and larger defeats as she strove to maintain the family economy. There was little opportunity for emotional or sexual intimacy.[74] The separation of roles, compounded by mental and bodily fatigue, constantly eroded the domestic sympathies which alone made the hardship bearable.[75] Arnold Wain's parents and four siblings had just two beds between them, yet, as he remembered, 'The family itelf was made up of units which scarcely had anything to do with each other.'[76]

A family in poverty sailed in rough seas. Its members sat on different benches in an open boat. Although they could exercise no control over the weather, they had to work constantly to bail out the vessel and keep it into the wind. Each had a separate task, but each was dependent on the other. A rash move by anyone would capsize the craft, and all were constantly threatened by a general inundation. They were at once crammed together and set apart, with little opportunity for sustained emotional support. Individuals reacted in different ways to extreme hardship, and the basic social networks to which they belonged took on diverse characteristics. But running through all the accounts of those who had direct experience of poverty at this time is a litany of resignation and constant effort, of shared dangers and differentiated responsibilities, of mutual trust and reciprocal apprehension, of physical proximity and distant sentiment.

To many observers at the turn of the century, the poor seemed to live outside time. Their failure to plan for the future or learn from their past was both the cause of their troubles and the chief obstacle to their solution. Like children, they lived in an eternal present, cut off from the reflective and calculative mentality of respectable society. The most lasting achievement of Rowntree and his successors was to demonstrate that the real problem was not that the poor did not understand time, but that society did not comprehend how time conditioned every aspect of the experience of deprivation.

The delineation of the life-cycle of poverty undermined the notion that the poor could have no sense of their own history.[77] It was shown that together with old age, childhood was the period of greatest risk, when the efforts of the contributors to the family economy were most in danger of being overwhelmed by the needs of its consumers.

This had implications for policy-making, but also for the families themselves. As medical science was later able to show in increasing detail, it meant that a period of deprivation could never be compensated for by subsequent years of relative prosperity, or, for that matter, by later welfare reforms. The impact on height, and on physical well-being in general, of a descent below the poverty line in early childhood, would last the whole of a probably foreshortened life. If the child itself was only dimly aware of the future it was losing, the parents had before them the visible signs of the hardships the family had previously endured. 'The past struggle left its mark on the physique of my children', wrote one mother, 'one has since died of heart disease, aged ten years; another of phthisis, sixteen years; my youngest has swollen glands, and not at all robust, though not born in poverty, aged fifteen years.'[78]

As the hopes young mothers had for their babies were confounded, so the constant physical and nervous strain of their lives destroyed the expectations they had once held for themselves. For the poor, time constantly deepened rather than healed the wounds they had suffered. It made it increasingly difficult to prevent material deprivation destroying the emotional interdependence which alone made all their labours bearable. Thus was the case with Robert Roberts's mother:

> Without self-pity she spoke of the early days and early hopes and of the slow acceptance of reality – the toil, the grind, the struggle, the poverty of it all, and of the even more barren lives of those about her; of how in time it stifled human qualities – kindliness, sensitivity, intelligence, and left no way out – the 'too much sacrifice' that 'turns the heart to stone'.[79]

Only the most hedonistic of the rich could properly be said to live in 'a world without a past and without a future, or of only short memory and immediate anticipation'.[80] The horizons of a drunken labourer might be so confined, but sympathetic commentators insisted that contrary to popular prejudice, the poor simply lacked the cash to spend much if any time at the public house.[81] It was not just a matter of registering the long-term effects of malnutrition. The intricate strategies which were adopted to achieve the complex material and psychological requirements of every poor family encompassed a series of time frames which stretched from purchasing food for a meal an hour later, to taking out insurance which could not be cashed in the holder's lifetime. Gross irregularity of income obviously forced a more unstable budgetary regime than was practised by the less destitute. In terms of the bulk of expenditure, it simplifies matters only a little to see the poor living by the day, the skilled working class by the week, the professional by the month and landowner by the year. When the poor told those who questioned them that their chief objective was security, all they meant was a shift from daily to weekly living. But the days had a rhythm through the week, and the weeks mounted into years during which, by a combination of immense effort and some good fortune, the worst disasters could be avoided and at least some of the poor could rise out of poverty, if only for a while.

Viewing poverty in time emphasised in ways which Rowntree was not always willing to accept, that the difference between those in and out of poverty was to be measured not in values and objectives but in cycles of the family and the economy. Those above and below the line were separated not so much by their strategies for living, as by their temporally specific ability to accomplish them. The identification of these cycles paved the way for state intervention, but greatly complicated the task of assessing the consequences. Like their tactics for survival, the causes of the poor's troubles could be calculated in days and in decades. Some, like evolutions in family structure, took generations to complete, others, like a downswing in the economy, could happen in months, or in terms of a given job, overnight. Each family had its *longue durée* of the birth, growth and departure of children, and its *histoire événementielle* of illness, accident and unemployment. For its part, the state could have the most immediate impact, for better or worse, on at least some sections of the poor, or could be rendered into almost complete insignificance by long or short-term changes in areas held to be outside its realm.

STATE STRATEGIES

In 1912 Hilaire Belloc looked forward to the world which had been called into being by the poverty legislation of the Liberal Governments:

> The future of industrial society, and in particular of English society, left to its own direction, is a future in which subsistence and security shall be guaranteed for the Proletariat, but shall be guaranteed at the expense of the old political freedom and by the establishment of that Proletariat in a status really, though not nominally, servile.[82]

His fears were at once representative and idiosyncratic. The pre-war

period was one of intense argument about democracy and social reform. Commentators from every part of the political spectrum were
agreed that the participation of the working class in the state, and the
intervention of the state in their material welfare, were mutually dependent issues, whose resolution would have profound implications for
the new century. At the same time the polarities which informed Belloc's polemic, particularly between freedom and servility, and individualism and collectivism, were deeply misleading. Whilst they were
common currency amongst those who, for varying reasons, opposed
the course of reform, they played little part in the strategies of those
who carried it through. Dicey might denounce school meals for sanc-
tioning parental neglect, pensions for discouraging thrift, and national
insurance for mortgaging Liberalism to the 'doctrines of socialism', but
he, like Belloc, was arguing from the sidelines.[83] The series of enactments were founded on a broad acceptance of the role of the democratic state, and an underlying certainty about the limitations and
strengths of individual action.

It was appropriate that the first welfare reforms of the 1906 Liberal
Government were implemented through the education system. Important though they were, the provision of school meals in 1906 and
medical inspection of schoolchildren in 1907 were only marginal additions to the contribution the classroom was already held to be making
to the abolition of poverty. From the early nineteenth century onwards, mass education had been advocated primarily as a means of
reforming the working-class family.[84] As older forms of transmitting
and enforcing values and social habits were overwhelmed by the
growth of towns and of units of production, it became increasingly
urgent to strengthen or rebuild the training and disciplinary functions
of parents. By the final quarter of the century it was accepted that the
state had not only a duty to finance this remedial work, but the right
to impose it. In every sense, the school-teachers were in the front line
of the battle against deprivation. On the one hand they had the greatest opportunity to instil the instincts of rational self-control which
alone could form a permanent bulwark against destitution, on the
other their labours were constantly frustrated by the hunger and ill-
health of the children who were most in need of their instruction.
Cooks and nurses were brought in not to add to the work of the
schools, but merely to make it possible.

The sense of continuity, of more effectively realising established objectives, makes education in some ways a better representative of official strategies towards the poor than the Poor Law itself, where change
was so often presented as a response to crisis and a prelude to revol-

ution. It embodied the fundamental assumption that the state could act on behalf of the community by promoting the moral progress, or preventing the moral collapse, of sections of society. The Liberal Party had never confused individualism with the absence of Government,[85] and the fiercest critic of its social reforms, the Charity Organisation Society, had always assumed it was legitimate to restrict, coerce and where necessary discipline and punish those unwilling or unable to meet standards of behaviour laid down by an enlightened government.[86] This applied to the growing body of regulations designed to prevent the physical environment rendering impossible a decent way of life, as well as to the elaborate and increasingly expensive structures intended to make a more direct impact on the potentially dissolute or improvident. Having by now lost their schools to the education authorities, the workhouses represented a limited and problematic application of a duty which had never been more widely urged nor less seriously questioned. The issue for the new century was not whether but how the principle of interfering in the conduct of the poor could best be attained.

Edwin Chadwick bequeathed the Edwardian reformers the wrong answers to the right problems. It was increasingly evident that his attempt to solve the tasks of classifying and deterring the poor by the single device of the workhouse test was no longer feasible,[87] but there was little doubt that these remained among the proper objectives of welfare legislation. The figure of the loafer and the wastrel haunted bodies as diverse as the COS, the ILP, the Fabians and the trade unions. The more the poor were helped according to their diverse needs, the greater the danger that the state would lose the capacity to reform or punish the ever-present residuum. The Poplar Guardians were as anxious to find ways of regulating and detaining the 'malingerer' as were the civil servants with whom they battled.[88] Whilst Liberal legislation was attacked by the Bosanquets because individual self-improvement was not properly encouraged, and by the Webbs because individual self-destruction was not adequately punished, they were united in their pursuit of those whose conduct threatened the well-being of every respectable member of society.[89] The penal clauses attached to the 1908 Pensions Act, which disqualified from benefit men and women who had acquired a criminal record during their sixties, or who had wilfully failed to maintain themselves or their families, were at once offensive, inoperable and uncontentious.

The central difficulty was one of reconciling two profoundly held but frequently contradictory beliefs. On the one hand was the general view, enunciated in the first official survey of poverty policy in the new century, the report of the 1904 Inter-Departmental Committee on Physical Deterioration, that 'in the last resort the State acting in conjunction with the Local Authority would have for its own sake to take charge of the lives of those who, for whatever cause, are incapable of independent existence up to the standard of decency which it imposes',[90] on the other was the acceptance that Britain was becoming a fully democratic society, in which every citizen had or would soon have an equal right to control both the local authority and the state. For as long as a whole section of the community was ruled unfit to vote, disenfranchising applicants for relief was an unproblematic form of deterrence. But once those who asked for assistance were otherwise able to participate in the political system which provided it, and were capable of forming organisations to enforce their wishes, the loss of civic rights which the pauper had suffered since the Poor Law Act of 1834 seemed a growing anachronism. More than any other consideration, it excluded the Poor Law from participation in the new remedies for poverty, beginning with school meals in 1906 which could not be supplied by the Guardians in case the children's parents were pauperised, yet the same concern for democratic freedom also caused the rejection of what appeared to be the logical alternative to pauperisation, the package of compulsory labour exchanges, enforced remedial training and penal repression set out in the Minority Report of the 1909 Royal Commission on the Poor Laws.[91]

In the event the 1834 Poor Law was both imprisoned and kept alive by the Liberals' growing sensitivity to the requirements of managing a democratic society. Poverty was not an issue in the 1906 Election, and the party leadership resisted pressure from its radical wing to redefine Liberalism in terms of a coherent attack on inequality and injustice. But it did come to accept that the increased participation by the mass of the population in the affairs of state demanded a more active intervention by the state in their material welfare. In its relations with its clients, the Poor Law belonged to an era which a self-consciously progressive party needed to leave behind. However in its system of control, it was in some ways in advance of national politics. Since 1894, any ratepayer could vote or stand for election, and Poplar was only one of a number of urban unions to demonstrate the possibilities of democratic practice.[92] More optimistic members of the Social Democratic Federation even began to see the Board of Guardians as a potential vanguard of the revolution.[93] If the Government was unwilling to allow the authority of Parliament to be subverted, it was also reluctant to associate Liberalism with the total abolition of a form of popular democracy. The responsibilities of the Guardians could not be extended, but neither could their role be replaced, as the Minority Report demanded, by an unelected registrar of public assistance.

The second main reason for resisting the Minority Report's demand that the existing structure of relief be broken up was that the centre of the crisis lay elsewhere. Although rising costs, particularly from 1901, unwieldy bureaucracy and unacceptable sanctions were real difficulties, the major problem was not the Poor Law itself, but the system of which it was a part. The strategy adopted in 1834 envisaged a tripartite coalition of workhouse, charity and self-help. The principal objective of the legislation was to create the conditions which would enable private initiative, through philanthropy and more permanently through personal thrift and responsibility, to eradicate not only deprivation, but the forms of behaviour which caused it. By the early twentieth century it was evident not just that a lasting solution had yet to be found, but that so far from relieving central and local government of their burden, the mounting shortcomings of the private sector were placing strains on the official machinery with which it could no longer be expected to cope. It was individualism, not the state, which was failing.

The volume of charitable endeavour had never been higher nor less adequate than in the early years of the twentieth century. Although it is impossible to calculate the precise value of voluntary endeavour, in London the many foundations, committees, gifts and bequests were transferring over eight million pounds a year to those in need, the equivalent of the total cost of the Poor Law throughout England and Wales in 1900.[94] Yet the spirit of enterprise which had characterised giving as much as making money during the industrial revolution, was beginning to falter. New charities were not being formed, and existing ones had for some time been struggling to meet their objectives. As one commentator noted, 'in the course of the last two generations the State has been forced again and again to take over tasks for which private philanthropy had found its resources insufficient.'[95] Its shortcomings were most pressingly revealed by an upsurge in unemployment in the years following the Boer War, which neither the established charities nor *ad hoc* efforts such as a new Mansion House appeal could cope with. Caught between inadequate private giving and unacceptable Poor Law relief, the Conservative Government was forced in 1905 to pass the Unemployed Workmen Act, which sanctioned the use of the rates for work creation schemes, and the establishment of machinery to co-ordinate the patchy efforts of Guardians, borough councils and charity organisations.[96] The Act did little for the jobless, but much for the learning process upon which the state had now embarked. In particular it proved that the elaborate system of classification by casework which the Charity Organisation Society had been developing since the 1870s was incapable of responding to the problem of mass distress.

The COS and other voluntary bodies were also demonstrably not achieving their larger objective of complementing the Poor Law's efforts to instil a sense of foresight into the strategies of the poor sufficient to carry them through all the vicissitudes of life.[97] The greatest predictable disaster of all, old age, was, as Asquith was eventually forced to recognise, 'the contingency against which thrift and prudence, however well organised by voluntary effort, are least able to make any adequate provision'.[98] Three generations of working men and women had faced the prospect of ending their lives dependent upon the Poor Law unless they saved or insured, yet 40 per cent of those dying over the age of sixty-five still had to apply to the parish in the last year of their lives. Around a third of all recipients of outdoor relief were aged seventy and over.[99] Whilst the threat of premature death made a burial policy a sensible investment, it discouraged the diversion of income over many years for a pension which might never be required. The average trade union member lived to barely more than fifty years of age.[100] This fact encouraged unions and friendly societies to offer sickness benefits which for older members became *de facto* pensions, but by the early 1900s marginal advances in life expectancy were undermining the crude actuarial calculations upon which such schemes were based. Those too poor to join mutual aid associations could not afford to make their own arrangements, whilst the associations themselves were increasingly too poor to meet the demands of those capable of paying their weekly subscriptions. Self-help, structured or otherwise, was providing insufficient protection for men, and virtually none at all for women who formed the greater proportion of the elderly.

The consequence was the 1908 Pensions Act, which provided non-contributory, non-pauperising benefits of between 1s and 5s a week for the 2.5 per cent of men and 3.4 per cent of women aged seventy and above, providing their income did not exceed £31 10s a year.[101] They were removed from the punitive care of the Poor Law because they were no longer expected to care for themselves.

The minority who opposed the introduction of old age pensions argued that individual initiative should be both the means and the end of the attack on poverty. The distinguishing characteristic of the more radical members of the Liberal Governments was their confidence that it would be possible to introduce greater elements of state provision without curtailing, in the words of Hobhouse, 'the unimpeded development of human faculty'.[102] The state should not exist merely to relieve and punish those on the margins, but rather should use its resources to encourage the moral and physical development of all its members. *The Nation* welcomed pensions as 'a right conferred by citizenship, rather than a boon conferred on poverty alone'.[103] The New Liberals sought to achieve a progressive relationship between hitherto distinct categories of endeavour. 'No view of society', the young Winston Churchill told a Glasgow audience in 1906, 'can possibly be complete which does not comprise within its scope both collective action and individual incentive.'[104] His optimism that the former need not vitiate the latter was derived from a profound sense that history was on his side. It was not so much that he and Lloyd George had a clear-sighted vision of the future, rather that they were unafraid of the direction in which the past was propelling their Party.

Rowntree's *Poverty* ended with an appeal to its readership: 'That in this land of abounding wealth, during a time of perhaps unexampled prosperity, probably more than one-fourth of the population are living in poverty, is a fact which may well cause great searchings of heart.'[105] This most generalised of conclusions was aimed directly at those seeking to redefine Liberalism for the early twentieth century. If they felt a need to react to fears about the military and occupational fitness of the working class, it was from a position of undoubted economic strength, and if they faced a challenge from socialist critics, they responded with a reassertion of the continuing moral vigour of their ideology. The debate on Rowntree's findings took place in the context of a post mortem into the problems of recruitment for the Boer War, and a deepening economic depression which was still causing concern when the Liberals took office at the end of 1905. The ever more apparent strength of Germany was bringing into focus long-standing fears about the eclipse of Britain as the dominant European power. Yet the war had been won, and however underfed and undersized the workforce, there was no shortage of men looking for employment. The argument over the appropriate form of old-age pensions, which had been going on for more than two decades, was finally resolved in favour of a non-contributory system, albeit set at as late an age and as low a level as possible, precisely because it was felt that the state was more able to raise more money from a more prosperous population than ever before. The Liberals' willingness to sanction increased expenditure on both pensions and dreadnoughts, which cost about the same over the period, was derived from their conviction that the land of abounding wealth could bear the strain, and that its citizens, liberated from the constraints and fears which only collective action could deal with, would be more than capable of sustaining the unexampled prosperity through their individual energy.

Liberalism was both flattered and compromised by Rowntree's appeal to its conscience. In the face of the critique mounted with increasing force by left-wing intellectuals and by organised labour, it was more important than ever that its identity as the party of spiritual purpose was preserved, but this task seemed more difficult than ever in the face of the exposure of the Victorian economy's failure to abolish poverty. In the event, however, the principal consequence of the challenge was to make its resolution seem more glorious and decisive than in fact it was. The pressure from outside the party, and from a small group of 'New Liberals' within it, was persistent enough to frustrate the hopes of some in the leadership that social reform could be kept off the political agenda, but was never of sufficient strength to determine the content of the legislation passed. Throughout the period, the Liberal leadership was more concerned with controlling public spending than public order.

Despite the high ambition of their rhetoric, the movements which espoused the cause of the poor were capable of uniting around only the lowest common denominators of theory and practice. It was agreed that the sufferings of the old, the young and the unemployed should be kept constantly before the attention of the public and Parliament, and that neither private philanthropy nor the market economy could alone meet their needs. There was a longstanding and widespread commitment to state pensions. Otherwise the divisions between them reflected and in turn contributed to their lack of political leverage. From 1902 onwards, the ILP and especially the SDF enjoyed considerable local success in getting the unemployed onto the streets. The marches and occasional acts of public disorder attracted press attention and were a factor in persuading the Conservative Government to pass the pioneering, if ineffective, Unemployed Workmen Act.[106] Yet the TUC was reluctant to become involved, as were later to be the first Labour MPs, their mistrust of direct action foreshadowing the conflicts with the National Unemployed Workers' Movement and the Communist Party between the wars. The National Committee of Organised Labour for Promoting Old Age Pensions and the National Unemployed Committee brought together trade unionists and middle-class writers, but the effectiveness of the pressure they attempted to exert was undermined by the absence of mass support, particularly amongst those on whose behalf they were agitating.[107] Whilst all were against deprivation, many, including the trade unions, were deeply suspicious of the deprived, and sympathetic to the persistent government attempts to find new ways of punishing or reforming them.

At the root of their difficulties was a deep uncertainty about the role of the state and their position in it. On the one hand they were attracted by the prospect of using the machinery of government to rectify social injustice, and excited by the possibility of gaining greater control over it. On the other they were alarmed by the threat to democratic bodies which had taken so long to establish or penetrate, and pessimistic about the short-term prospects of influencing government policy.[108] Some wanted to employ the state to overthrow a capitalist system which would always create poverty, others to use it to enhance their capacity to abolish the fundamental cause of poverty, low wages, through traditional collective bargaining. The various positions coalesced in the Right to Work movement, which could mean anything from small-scale public works to full-scale public ownership. The annual Bill was instinctively supported by all Labour MPs, and automatically rejected by the Liberal Governments.[109]

The emergent Labour Party could be used by progressive Liberals to shake the Whig element of their party out of its complacency, but it never gained the level of ideological or electoral authority which would enable it to dictate the treatment of poverty. The last Liberal Governments were engaged in a process of negotiation from a position of strength, rather than a retreat in the face of defeat. Their case for reform rested on the hope of moral regeneration rather than the fear of physical revolution.[110] They disliked the Labour Party's emphasis on class, but were prepared to seek its assistance for legislation which would emphasise the common citizenship of rich and poor alike. In small matters, such as school meals or medical inspection, the handful of Labour MPs could be allowed the luxury of initiating policy. Elsewhere the Liberals' confidence in the moral strength and appeal of their platform enabled them to establish their own agenda, to which Labour could only offer reluctant support or acquiescent dissent.

Despite their landslide defeat in the election of January 1906, the Conservatives always appeared the greater threat, precisely because they were fellow members of the ruling class. The Boer War and then tariff reform had so deflected them from the path of social reform that they were unable to offer any principled opposition to the Liberal legislation. At best they could do no more than fish in troubled waters as one major innovation after another entered the Statute Book, yet it was the prospect of the return to power of a Conservative Government, free to use increased tariff revenues for domestic initiatives, which more than any other consideration impelled Liberals to ensure that their name was attached to the innovations which seemed increasingly inevitable.[111]

The reformers in the Liberal Party preached to the many unconverted in their ranks a higher form of pragmatism. The moral challenge of poverty imposed the duty of action; the moral certainty of individual freedom guaranteed the outcome. The ends were so imperative yet so familiar that it was safe for the Liberals, as for no other party, to experiment with the means. In his 1906 speech on social reform Winston Churchill captured the combination of vision and improvisation which characterised the attempts to deal with poverty before the First World War:

> I look forward to the universal establishment of minimum standards of life and labour, and their progressive elevation as the increasing energies of production may permit. I do not think that Liberalism in any circumstances can cut itself off from this field of social effort, and I would recommend you not to be scared in discussing these proposals, just because some old woman comes along and tells you they are Socialistic. If you take my advice, you will judge each case on its merits.[112]

The prospects of a favourable verdict were greatly increased by the ease with which the new legislation circumvented the central findings of Rowntree's original survey. In the field of social reform, the depth of Liberal confidence was achieved by the breadth of their evasion. Half the primary poverty in York was caused by low wages, and a further quarter by 'largeness of family'.[113] School meals, which were still being provided by only 40 per cent of education authorities by 1911, were a gesture towards the demands of children on the family economy, and the limited introduction in 1909 of wages boards in a handful of sweated trades made a minor contribution to the problem of low pay, but otherwise the Liberal Governments successfully avoided a direct response to the inability of the market economy to provide a minimum level of subsistence to all households whose heads were in full-time employment. To many observers, the basic dimensions of the problem were now inescapable: 'This is no place to give a picture of poverty', wrote Arthur Ponsonby in *The Camel and the Needle's Eye* in 1910. 'It has been done often enough of late years and with faithful accuracy, so that society has no excuse for ignoring the real state of affairs.'[114] In practice, however, the implications of the accumulated body of research seemed more ambiguous.

The capacity of so many well-intentioned, well-informed people to look straight at, yet straight past, the fundamental causes of poverty reflected unresolved difficulties about the way in which the problem was conceived. In the first instance, participants in the contemporary debate were united and divided by their commitment to a 'scientific' approach to the subject. The ever-increasing number of social investigators were capable of reaching diametrically opposed conclusions from a shared commitment to the nascent discipline of sociology. What attracted the young Beatrice Webb to the Charity Organisation Society was the modernity of its techniques: 'the COS appeared to me as an honest though short-lived attempt to apply the scientific method of observation and experiment, reasoning and verification, to the task of delivering the poor from their miseries'.[115] Precisely the same qualities were claimed for Rowntree's work, with its parade of nutritional research, its display of tables and graphs, its conclusions, as Masterman observed, 'estimated statistically and dispassionately, from which there seem no methods of escape'.[116] The new social science disqualified the views of the well-meaning amateur and the tradition-bound bureaucrat. It sought to align the treatment of poverty with the dramatic advances in manufacture, communication and armaments which characterised the new century. Technological progress highlighted both the anomalous condition of the poor, and the obsolete state of the private and public welfare systems. In response the investigators offered methods of enquiry and proposals for reform of equivalent rigour and sophistication.

The scientific study of poverty held out the prospect of placing the issue beyond the reach of argument. Both the COS device of intricate case-histories of individual families, and the full-scale urban studies pioneered by Booth and developed by Rowntree and Bowley, were designed to create bodies of knowledge which would stand above the controversies which had raged around the subject for centuries. The growing consensus that changes had to be made to the nineteenth-century structure of private and public provision was a measure of their success; the continuing division about the substance of reform indicated their failure. Rather than resolving the arguments, the scientific approach recast them in a new form. The issues of individual and collective obligation were subsumed into a fresh dispute about how to understand individual and collective behaviour. In a debate which has yet to be resolved, the quantifiers claimed that concentration on the intricate stories of isolated families obscured the underlying dynamics of poverty and impeded the formulation of effective remedies. Their critics accused them of de-humanising and de-historicising the complex lives of the poor. 'It is not possible', stated C.S. Loch, 'logically to connect large generalisations as to wage with minute investments of the generalised wage in a large number of cases.'[117] This was perhaps the last occasion on which the opponents of state intervention could out-argue the proponents from the position of a more detailed knowledge of the conditions of the poor. They contended that a concentration on aggregate wage data and typical budgets grossly over-simplified the behaviour of families over time. The only legitimate sphere of generalisation was the structure of values and attitudes binding together parents and children in the struggle for existence, which took more patience to unravel than the large-scale investigators could afford to take.[118] 'The true issue', concluded Loch, 'is not income as against expenditure, but social habit.'[119]

Thus it remained possible for the district nurse, Margaret Loane, to write a series of studies of poor families in this period which combined a wide-ranging, sympathetic and deeply informed account of their lives with a flat rejection of low wages as a cause of their difficulties and a persistent hostility to virtually all the contemporary legislation.[120] At every point she rested her argument on her greater familiarity with the problem. On the matter of school meals, for instance, she began with the observation that 'the causes of the insufficient or unsuitable feeding of many children in the poorest classes are numerous and complex, therefore no panacea is possible', concluding 'on strict and close enquiry, it would be found that many of the worst nourished children had parents with ample means to feed them properly'.[121] Her professional expertise became a means of reinforcing rather than undermining the traditional emphasis on the primacy of will over circumstances. What changed was a shift in emphasis from how income was gained to how it was spent. 'To speak of a "living wage"', wrote Loane, 'has always seemed to me an absurdity. It is not so much a question of what a man earns, as of what his wife can do with the money.'[122]

There was a long tradition of middle-class women calling upon the homes of their less fortunate sisters to proffer advice on how to make a little go further. However, the interventions now proposed went far beyond improving tracts and recipes for nourishing broth. The widening preoccupation with motherhood embraced every aspect of the cultural and material responsibilities of working-class wives. The expansion of elementary education in the nineteenth century had rested on the expectation that teachers would be able to act in *loco parentis* to their pupils, rebuilding the family unit from inside the classroom.[123] The dawning realisation that no school could adequately fulfil this function coincided with renewed fears about the physical and moral decline of the race, as the middle-class birth-rate fell, and military and commercial rivalry exposed shortcomings in the youth of Britain. Poverty was seen as a threat not just to the individual but to the society to which he or she belonged. Attempts to reverse the trend now centred on the mother as the key figure in the reproduction of workers and soldiers and in the training of their future wives whose skills would be so crucial to the comfort of their homes.[124] Reforms, which continued throughout the First World War, as the slaughter in the trenches made the task of replacement yet more urgent, sought to combine the established commitment to state education with the growing effort to professionalise health care and social work. The Midwives Act of 1902,[125] the Children's Act of 1908, and the introduction of paid health visitors by local authorities and private charities, were all designed to define a mother's responsibilities and subordinate her performance of them to trained outsiders.

It was not difficult for the new class of visitors to make a case for their intrusion on the privacy of the working-class home. Advances in paediatric practices meant that they had fresh assistance to offer on techniques of child care. They were right to draw attention to the scope and the significance of the housewife's responsibilities for maximising the resources of the domestic economy. As every family in poverty had continually to choose which basic necessity was to be sacrificed to another, and which temporary expedient was to be adopted to avoid immediate disaster, it was all too easy to point to shortcomings in the provision of diet or clothing or in the use of credit and insurance. And whilst so much of the advice emphasised subordination to husbands, to educated superiors, and to market forces, there were points at which the discussion of duties could merge into an assertion of rights, particularly if the discussion took place not in the home but on the neutral territory of the health centres which voluntary organisations began to establish just before the war.[126] This was especially the case in the issue of contraception, which was at last becoming a legitimate topic of medical knowledge. The possibility of exercising some control over the number and frequency of pregnancies offered for the first time a real prospect of escaping the vicious circle of increasing toil and diminishing expectations which had always enclosed the lives of poor women.

For this reason, bodies such as the Women's Co-operative Guild became actively involved in the movement for better motherhood. Yet they remained deeply critical of the double evasion upon which so much of the legislation was based. The regulations and the advice saw women only as mothers, and mothers only as dependants. There was no interest in the unmarried, and little sense that once they became wives, their bodily and mental well-being was of importance in its own right, irrespective of their capacity to bear and raise children.[127] They were not expected to become part of the labour market, nor to question its frequent failure to supply an income adequate to the family's requirements. Those who did raise their voices in opposition made small headway before the war. Organised labour was at best ambivalent about the issue. The unions and their political representatives had little enthusiasm for a programme designed to avoid the basic issue of low wages, but at the same time the promotion of a domestic ideology based on the supremacy of the male bread-winner evoked limited hostility. Ministers were in the main equally unconcerned about wider issues of women's rights, and were relieved to endorse the conclusion that the state's principal responsibility lay in an extension of its established commitment to education rather than in an unprecedented intervention in the operation of the market economy.

The lineaments of the Government response to the debate between structual and behavioural explanations of poverty were set out in the 1904 *Inter-Departmental Committee on Physical Deterioration*. The appointment of this body owed much to Major-General Frederick Maurice, who in two influential articles in the *Contemporary Review* had drawn attention to the problem of recruiting soldiers fit to fight in the Boer War, and demanded a public inquiry to identify remedies. In his bluff, soldierly way he admitted to being perplexed by the conflicting research. His instincts directed him towards the COS emphasis on the moral failings of the poor, but Rowntree's findings pointed in the opposite direction. If York was indeed typical, 'then the impediment to the rearing of healthy children is not the ignorance of the mothers so much or nearly so much as that the conditions of modern life do not enable them to supply their children with sufficient sustenance'.[128] The Committee considered the evidence, interviewed both Booth and Rowntree in person, and reached what was to be the definitive official verdict on the issue. The central problem was 'ignorance and neglect on the part of parents', and the general solution was 'some great scheme of social education, to which many agencies must contribute, legislative, administrative and philanthropic, and by which the people themselves must be induced to cast off the paralysing traditions of helplessness and despair'.[129] School meals and medical inspection were recommended less as a remedy, and more as a precondition for the work of the educational agencies. Their implementation reflected the analysis upon which they were based. In 1913 Sir George Newman, the head of the medical department of the Board of Education, was still claiming that in the field of poverty, 'The principal operating influence is the ignorance of the mother and the remedy is the education of the mother.'[130] The long-term significance of the 1904 Report lay not in the intervention it demanded, but in the legislation it rendered unnecessary.

Rowntree himself bore some responsibility for his failure. His persistent inconsistency over the meaning of 'secondary poverty', which on this occasion he defined as poverty over which families 'have control',[131] and his enthusiasm for various educational endeavours, which had included the distribution of 10,000 handbills in York containing dietary information, gave his critics plenty of opportunity to disregard his findings on the significance of low wages. More important, however, was the attraction of the behavioural explanation of poverty to those seeking to redefine the responsibilities of the state in a democratic society. Not only the Conservative Government which commissioned the Report, but also the Liberal Government which inherited its findings, were sharply aware of the boundaries of their field of action. The ambitions of the reformers in the Campbell-Bannerman and Asquith administrations were contained within a set of widely held conventions. They could propose experimenting with collectivist means of achieving individualist ends only because their conception of the problem of poverty did not call into question basic assumptions about the process of legislating in a pluralist economy. The logical response to Rowntree's research, as its author came to realise, was some form of minimum wage. But the pursuit of this remedy would involve a level of conflict with both the traditions of the Party and the interests of its principal supporters which no responsible minister could contemplate. Better to accept ignorance as a central cause of deprivation, and concentrate on action which would not interfere with the employer's freedom to pay his employees whatever the labour market would bear.

It was in this context that the National Insurance Acts of 1911 were conceived and argued through Parliament. The unexpected cost of pensions ruled out the extension of universal provision to the other forms of personal hardship which self-help and the Poor Law seemed increasingly incapable of dealing with. General taxation was no longer seen as an appropriate vehicle for delivering the degree of income support which the electorate was beginning to demand. An alternative solution was proffered by the friendly societies to which about half the adult males in the population already belonged. Through these institutions the working class had established a structure of contributions and benefits which avoided the patronising inefficiency of private charity and the punitive thoroughness of the Boards of Guardians. The proposal to extend and underwrite the existing system of insurance held a number of advantages. The scrutiny of German provision, which commenced with Lloyd George's visit in August 1908, indicated that reliance upon the societies would avoid excessive bureaucratisation and at the same time permit more prosperous workers to enhance modest flat-rate benefits with additional arrangements of their own.[132] By this means insurance would be less of a burden on the state, and the state would be less of a burden on the people. It was an innovation built upon tradition, a major departure which endorsed a familiar practice.

Above all it dramatised the concern of the state whilst avoiding a direct commitment to either redistribution or interference in the labour market. As left-wing critics pointed out, the legislation represented a tax on working men to cover risks for which they were not responsible. 'Our main objection to it', stated George Lansbury, 'is that you are levying it on people who cannot afford to pay it, and we are strengthened in that not by the opinion of mere Socialists like myself, but of men like Mr Seebohm Rowntree and Mr Charles Booth, and others, who have investigated the lives of the poor'.[133] The element of compulsion was required to make sure that the healthier, more secure workers contributed to the benefits paid to their less fortunate brothers. In common with so many subsequent reforms, the principal transfer of resources took place within the working class. Employers were as free to pass on to their customers their contributions of 3d for health and 2d for unemployment insurance as they were to pay the low or irregular wages which gave rise to so much of the ill-health. The state contributed 2d and 1⅔d a week, but withheld a commitment to tackle the underlying causes of poverty and disease, or even directly to cope with the symptoms. The sick and the unemployed paid 4d and 2d for their benefits, which they received not through their common membership of society, but through their individual contributions to what was, at least in theory, an actuarially sound system.

Lloyd George claimed that his legislation was 'setting up a scheme which will be woven into the social fabric of this country'.[134] It was a large ambition which he sought to realise by accommodating the conflicting interests of the extended political nation. Outside this nation, whether or not they had the vote, were the poor themselves, who in this period were frequently investigated but never consulted. Inside it, when the legislation was first formulated, were the friendly societies, which Lloyd George, in conformity with half a century of government policy, wished to play a larger role in the working-class community. However, he also had to take account both of the doctors, who had long resented their subordination to the societies which contracted about half their profession, and the vast industrial insurance companies, who feared the competition of a state-backed system, even though they themselves offered neither unemployment nor health cover. Eventually the doctors gained a measure of independence from their patients' representatives, and the companies, with an army of 70,000 collectors lobbying on their behalf, forced the Government to abandon plans for widows' and orphans' benefits, and to deprive the friendly societies of any participation in the local administration of the scheme.[135]

The reduction in the scope of the legislation, and the destruction of the substantial element of democratic control which the friendly societies had embodied, was a high price to pay for entry into the social fabric. The Liberals had begun by rejecting the bureaucratic centralism of the Bismarckian system, and ended by imposing a scheme with even less self-government than the German model. For Lloyd George, the prolonged negotiations with all the vested interests was 'almost like interfering with religious denominations. It is really just as if you were starting a new religion, co-ordinating all existing denominations, grouping the small ones and establishing new ones.'[136] At the end of the day, the perceived constraints of the democratic process justified the series of evasions and compromises which the scheme embodied. The bolder the aspiration, the greater the concessions which had to be made to attain it. If the Liberal reformers were to succeed in their enterprise of effecting a permanent transformation in both the identity of their Party and the responsibilities of the state towards the poor, they had to avoid open conflict with powerful institutions just as they had to turn away from irreconcilable controversies over the true causes of poverty. The danger was that the legislation would become so consensual that their opponents could with ease claim it as their own when they came to power, and so modified that it would lose what little chance it had of achieving its practical objectives. The Acts of 1911 did nothing for those most exposed to poverty, the casually employed, or for the wives and children of under-paid workers.

Ambiguity was written into the innovations of the period. It was a matter of design rather than accident that most Labour MPs saw them as a stepping-stone towards something much better, and many Liberals regarded them as a bulwark against something much worse. The constant attempts by government ministers to present the series of enactments between 1906 and 1911 as part of a coherently planned policy of social reform were undermined by the combination of confusion and expediency which characterised each instalment. The radical wing of the Liberal Party had pressed its argument that a minimum level of subsistence was central to the achievement of full citizenship,[137] but in the practice of politics, some members of the community had more status and louder voices than others. If the imminence of full parliamentary democracy had concentrated attention on the rights of citizens,[138] the limitations of the parliamentary process had limited the prospects of their achievement.

IMPACT

During the debate on National Insurance, the Prime Minister stated that the House was 'conferring upon millions of our fellow countrymen by the joint operation of self-help and State help, the greatest alleviation of the risks and sufferings of life that Parliament had ever conferred upon any people'.[139] Those who struggled daily with the risks and sufferings of life had good reason to doubt whether either this legislation, or any other reform of the period, measured up to such a claim. Only 310,000 children were receiving free school meals by 1913,[140] most working men and women died before they reached the qualifying age for pensions, and unemployment insurance applied to only about a quarter of the occupied workforce. Despite all the research, all the argument, all the planning and plotting by ministers and their civil servants, all the rhetoric which accompanied each Act onto the Statute Book, the incidence of poverty, and the basic features of the strategies the poor adopted to cope with their problems, changed very little between the end of the Boer War and the outbreak of the Great War. Bowley and Burnett-Hurst's survey, conducted in the last year of peace, confirmed Rowntree's findings, just as Rowntree had confirmed Booth's.[141] It proved as difficult to find healthy recruits to fight in Europe as it had for the conflict in South Africa.[142] The neighbourhood remained for the poor as essential and as inadequate a means of support as it had done in the latter part of the nineteenth century.[143] Pawnbroking, the pivot of the complex system of credit and debt which diminished the fear of destitution but extinguished the hope of prosperity, reached its peak as the Edwardian period came to an end.[144]

Yet the proportion of the Gross National Product devoted to the social services had doubled between 1890 and 1914. The consequences of this increased expenditure are obscured not only by the shadow of future developments which lay across the Liberal initiatives, but also by the smokescreen of political rhetoric which surrounded them. Winston

Churchill might claim that 'the cause of the Liberal Party is the cause of the left-out millions',[145] but these millions remained outside the consensus he and his colleagues sought to achieve for the legislation. The Government remained more interested in managing their aspirations than in listening to them, and the short-term effects of the reforms have to be sought as much in the outlook of the deprived as in their material conditions.

The one area in which the state had an undoubted impact on the perspective of the poor was also the scene of the most complete failure of its attempt to reform their morals. The behavioural clauses in the 1908 Old Age Pensions Act proved unworkable and were quietly repealed in 1919. Once those who had been receiving Poor Law relief had served out a two-year period of disqualification, the only test of eligibility apart from their poverty was the very substantial hurdle of living long enough. For the small minority who survived to celebrate their seventieth birthday, the new benefit made a significant difference not only to their immediate well-being but also to the burden of anxiety which weighed down their declining years. Five shillings a week was at least double the outdoor relief available from the Board of Guardians. Providing they remained physically capable of looking after themselves, elderly members of the working-class community could for the first time since 1834 look to a future free of the pauperising embrace of the Poor Law. Between 1910 and 1911, the number of men and women of seventy and over who required outdoor relief fell from 132,235 to just 8,420.[146] The Guardians were left with about 50,000 in this age group who needed institutional care, together with a further 50,000 aged sixty and over who were forced to seek outdoor assistance as they waited for their seventieth birthday.

Payment of the pensions through the Post Offices, which since 1861 had been charged with receiving such savings as the working class made, emphasised the division between pensioners and paupers. In the same way, the impact of Unemployment Insurance was coloured more by the decision to distribute benefits through the Labour Exchanges, than by attempts to associate the scheme with devices for retraining or punishing the work-shy. No enquiry was made of the finances or the moral character of those in receipt of benefit. The shipbuilders, engineers and building workers claimed what they had paid for, and their use of the system revealed deficiencies not in their behaviour but in the operation of the economy. In the brief period of peace which remained, the new bureaucracy had time to set in motion what was to be one of its major achievements, the provision of reliable statistics on the state of the labour market. Two-thirds of the insured workers were skilled, the trade-cycle was at its peak, yet it could be shown that in such optimum conditions a quarter of the men were liable to periods of unemployment of four weeks or more in a year.[147] Circumstances which workers had always known but could never adequately describe, could now be communicated to a wider audience in terms which it could accept and understand.

In the penny economy in which the poor lived, 5s for a pension, 7s for unemployment and 10s for health insurance, unencumbered by pauperisation, were solid sums of money which placed real meals on actual tables, and made a discernible impact on the morale, if not the morals, of those eligible to receive them. Yet by 1914 the most striking consequence of the welfare legislation was not how much but how little had changed in the struggle to avoid destitution. A pension would just about feed and clothe a parsimonious couple, but would not stretch to meet any housing costs. Unless they were amongst the tiny number of working-class home-owners, or were living with a grown-up son or daughter, they faced the accustomed difficulty of sacrificing one basic need to attain another. Insurance was payable only to the individual contributor, and even in the case of the larger health benefits, was less than half of the amount required to raise an average family above Rowntree's or Bowley's poverty lines. The justification for these shortfalls became familiar in years to come. The state was to be the partner of the poor, not their sole provider. Pensions and benefits could be topped up by private insurance; the old could consume savings, the sick and the unemployed, in their temporary distress, could anticipate future income. What was given made it easier for the poor to arrange their income over time; what was withheld forced them to do so.

In other areas, the impact of reforms was qualified by their uneven, unplanned development. This was most strikingly the case in respect of one of the earliest initiatives, the provision of school medical inspection. Parents were now told in some detail what the early years of malnutrition had done to their children's health – in the last year of peace, 1.9 million inspections revealed 650,000 cases of disease requiring treatment[148] – and after the Children's Act of 1908, could be prosecuted for failing to seek proper assistance, yet they were not supplied with the means to act upon the often alarming knowledge.[149] Apart from the patchy provision of school meals, nothing was done for the over-stretched family economy which, as the reports of the school medical officers so often confirmed,[150] was at the root of so much of the trouble. The sickness benefits available from 1913 were designed solely for getting the bread-winner back to work, not for raising a future generation of healthier workers. The only additional gain was the maternity benefit of 30s, payable directly to the mother from 1913, which made an appreciable difference to the heavy medical expenses often incurred during pregnancy and childbirth. Otherwise, parents searching for remedies for newly named conditions or diseases could afford neither the visits nor the prescriptions of qualified doctors or opticians, and were forced back to traditional remedies or mass-marketed patent medicines, and to the services of the still flourishing race of unofficial practitioners, whose business boomed at precisely the moment when the British Medical Association was launching a determined campaign to drive them out of existence.[151]

Inside the family the legislation did little to alter the hierarchy of authority and deprivation. In exchange for the critical advice of school medical visitors and, towards the end of the period, home health visitors, women received few material concessions. They were disproportionate beneficiaries of old age pensions in consequence of their greater life expectancy. The fact that nearly three-fifths of the eligible population were female had been an argument against funding the pension through insurance paid by male workers. They also gained more than men from the Trades Board Act of 1909, which covered sweated industries employing almost 100,000 mostly non-unionised, low-paid women, although the absence of adequate inspection enabled their employers to evade the provisions of the Act without much difficulty. Valuable though they were, the maternity benefits were small compensation for the loss of widows' benefits which the industrial insurance companies had removed from Lloyd George's original proposal, and the insurance scheme in common with social policy as a whole in this period enshrined the role of the male bread-winner without enabling him better to relieve the pressures on his dependants.[152] Just as women had been granted no personality independent of their husbands under the Poor Law,[153] so the 1911 Act effectively excluded married women. For them the legislative consequences of the earlier investigations of poverty were yet more inspection and almost as much poverty. As before, a poor man's wife struggling to reconcile the conflicting demands of her family economy looked not to the state but to the sources of assistance and credit in the neighbourhood.

Within the Edwardian period, too much cannot be expected of reforms which had scarcely begun to operate before war broke out. The men found unfit for military service were displaying the consequences of childhood deprivation suffered before the innovations could have any effect.[154] Of greater importance to the labouring population of these years, were the fluctuations in the trade-cycle and the overall movement of wages against prices. The long rise in the standard of living during the second half of the nineteenth century turned into a 3 per cent fall between 1900 and 1909, and the subsequent recovery did no more than restore the position at the end of Victoria's reign.[155] Greater pressure was exerted on the budgets of the less prosperous by a more than average rise in the cost of many staple items of expenditure.[156] The accelerating decline in infant mortality, which fell from 163 per 1,000 live births in 1899 to 105 in 1914 reflected improvements in diet, particularly in the provision of milk,[157] and in housing during the closing decades of the nineteenth century and developments in neonatal and postnatal care in the early years of the twentieth. However, the survival of more mouths to be fed and bodies to be clothed was a mixed blessing for the first generation of mothers to witness the change. The advances were greatest amongst the middle class, and in general this period witnessed what was to become a characteristic phenomenon of the present century, marginal improvements in welfare provision coexisting with a gradual widening of the gap between the resources of the richest and poorest sections of society.[158]

Too much also cannot be expected of reforms which attempted to achieve so little. The problems directly addressed by the legislation of the period – old age, illness and unemployment of the breadwinner – accounted for just 7.42 per cent of the causes of primary poverty identified by Rowntree in 1901 and 13 per cent of the causes in Bowley's 1913 survey.[159] 'It can hardly be too emphatically stated', concluded Bowley, 'that of all the causes of primary poverty which have been brought to our notice, low wages are by far the most important.'[160] The basic structures of economic authority and privilege remained in place, and indeed it may be argued that such efforts as the state made to alleviate their consequences resulted in a further shift in power away from the labouring poor. During the preceding century, the working class had developed its own welfare system in the form of the friendly society movement which, limited though it was in both its membership and its benefits, did constitute a sophisticated bureaucratic response to material insecurity, tuned to the needs of its members and subject to their authority. The Labour MP George Barnes claimed that 'The Insurance Acts marked a great advance in the sense of public responsibility and the contributory system carried with it the right on the part of the contributor to share in the control and therefore it had a democratic value.'[161] In practice, all effective control was lost. The advance of public responsibility caused a retreat in popular participation.

The concept of 'foundations' which is so often deployed in accounts of the poverty legislation before 1914 is in many ways inaccurate. There was no clearing of the ground, no blueprint. Lloyd George's Insurance Acts were as significant for the foundations they demolished as those they laid. The legislation imposed taxes on working men and denied them representation over their disbursement. Hilaire Belloc's analysis was in this respect accurate enough: 'A man has been compelled by law to put aside sums from his wages as insurance against unemployment. But he is no longer the judge of how such sums shall be used. They are not in his possession; they are not even in the hands of some society which he can really control. They are in the hands of a Government official.'[162] The Liberal attempt to bring the treatment of poverty into line with the requirements of a democratic society had succeeded at the expense of important elements of democratic practice within the working-class community.

The reverberations of Rowntree's 'thunder-clap' were selectively absorbed by the political process. Despite the discussion of economic and military efficiency in both his book and the ensuing public debate, poverty was seen as a threat more to the moral than the material well-being of the nation. It was the strength rather than the weakness of the economy which placed reform on the agenda, and it was the fear of the articulate middle class rather than the disaffected working class which set the limits to the changes which could be made. If the metaphor drawn from the building trade is appropriate, it is in the sense that the excavations of the last Liberal Government set the limits to the dimensions of the edifice to be erected by subsequent administrations. Henceforth it was evident that for the most part reform would not extend far into the realm of low wages, nor far beyond the capacity of insurance to deal with the failure of charity and the Poor Law. Increasing national prosperity would be the means rather than the end of legislation. The task was to find a more efficient way of dealing with poverty, not a way of dealing with poverty which would promote a more efficient economy.

In the shorter term, the foundations laid for a generation of Edwardian children were of stunted growth and constitutions permanently undermined by rickets and respiratory ailments. Kirkman Gray in his *Philanthropy and the State* was one of the first to welcome the one small innovation which directed affected their well-being: 'The school dinner is an education in citizenship. Without a word being said, the child gradually absorbs knowledge of its own dependence on and place in the social life. He finds himself a guest at the common table of the nation.'[163] The course of reform in this period ensured that the poor were destined to remain guests at the table of an increasingly prosperous society.

REFERENCES

1. C.F.G. Masterman, 'The Social Abyss', *Contemporary Review,* LXXXI (Jan. 1902), p. 24. Alongside his career as a journalist, Masterman was a Poor Law Guardian for Camberwell between 1901 and 1904, and later M.P. for West Ham (1906–10), Bethnal Green (1910–14), and Rusholme (1923–4).
2. B.S. Rowntree, *Poverty. A Study of Town Life* (London, 1901), p. 117.
3. Rowntree, *Poverty*, p. 301.
4. Masterman, 'Social Abyss', p. 25.
5. J.H. Veit-Wilson, 'Paradigms of Poverty: A Rehabilitation of B.S. Rowntree', *Journal of Social Policy*, **15**, 1 (1986), pp. 71–4.
6. Masterman, 'Social Abyss', p. 26.
7. Rowntree, *Poverty*, p. 115.
8. *The Times*, 23 August, 1902, p. 7. For a spirited and accurate rebuttal of this mis-reading of Rowntree, see *The Clarion*, 5 Sept., 1902, p. 4.
9. Rowntree, *Poverty*, pp. 141–2.
10. *The Times*, 16 September 1902, p. 2.
11. Rowntree, *Poverty*, p. 87.
12. Rowntree, *Poverty*, p. 105.
13. A.L. Bowley and A.R. Burnett-Hurst, *Livelihood and Poverty* (London, 1915), p. 37. For a fuller discussion of the shortcomings of the poverty line by Bowley, see his *Wages and Income since 1860* (Cambridge, 1937), pp. 54–70.
14. H. Bosanquet, 'The Poverty Line', *Charity Organisation Society Occasional Paper, no. 11, 3rd Series* (London, c. 1903), p. 116.
15. Rowntree, *Poverty*, p. 116.
16. For a discussion of the application of the concept see G. Crow, 'The use of the concept of "strategy" in recent sociological literature', *Sociology*, **23**, 1 (1989).
17. In particular P. Townsend, *Poverty* (Harmondsworth, 1979), and J. Mack and S. Lansley, *Poor Britain* (London, 1985).
18. Bowley and Burnett-Hurst, *Livelihood and Poverty*, p. 26.
19. G. Foakes, *My Part of the River* (London, 1974), p. 19.
20. W. Southgate, *That's the Way it Was* (London, 1982), pp. 21–2.
21. Mrs Pember Reeves, *Round About A Pound A Week* (2nd edn, London, 1914), pp. 63–4.
22. E. Ross, '"Fierce Questions and Taunts": Married Life in Working-Class London 1870–1914', *Feminist Studies*, **8** (1982), p. 585.
23. M.L. Davies, *Maternity. Letters from Working Women* (London, 1978), p. 3.

24. B.L. Coombes, *These Poor Hands* (London, 1939), p. 12.
25. Davies, *Maternity*, p. 10.
26. K. Dayus, *Her People* (London, 1982), p. 2.
27. Foakes, *My Part of the River*, p. 22.
28. R. Hoggart, *The Uses of Literacy* (London, 1958), p. 50; J. Lewis, *The Politics of Motherhood* (London, 1980), p. 108.
29. Rowntree, *Poverty*, p. 71.
30. E. Roberts, '"Women's Strategies", 1890–1940' in J. Lewis (ed.), *Labour and Love* (Oxford, 1986), pp. 230–5.
31. A.S. Jasper, *A Hoxton Childhood* (London, 1969), p. 9.
32. M. Loane, 'Husband and Wife among the Poor', *Contemporary Review*, **87** (1905), p. 226.
33. Pember Reeves, *Round About A Pound a Week*, p. 15.
34. J. Burnett, *Plenty and Want* (Harmondsworth, 1968), pp. 206–7.
35. J. Rennie, *Every Other Sunday* (London, 1955), p. 8.
36. J.A. Hobson, *Problems of Poverty* (6th edn, London, 1906), p. 11.
37. On the problems of inadequate or non-existent storage space see Loane, *From Their Point of View*, p. 278.
38. Hobson cited a study of poor families in which on average twenty-seven purchases of tea were made over a seven-week period. Hobson, *Problems of Poverty*, p. 12.
39. W. Holt, *I Haven't Unpacked* (London, 1939), p. 23.
40. Pember Reeves, *Round About A Pound A Week*, pp. 22–3. Also J.A. Hobson, *Problems of Poverty* (6th edn, London, 1906), p. 9.
41. Rowntree and Kendall, *How the Labourer Lives*, p. 41.
42. R. Roberts, *A Ragged Schooling* (London, 1978), p. 22.
43. M. Tebbutt, *Making Ends Meet. Pawnbroking and Working-Class Credit* (London, 1983), p. 137. On the role of the pawnshop in the domestic economies of casual dock labourers, see G. Philips and N. Whiteside, *Casual Labour* (Oxford, 1985), p. 34.
44. P. O'Mara, *The Autobiography of a Liverpool Irish Slummy* (Bath, 1968), p. 64.
45. P. Johnson, 'Credit and thrift and the British working class, 1870–1939', in J. Winter (ed.), *The Working Class in Modern British History* (Cambridge, 1983), p. 157.
46. J. Seabrook, *The Everlasting Feast* (London, 1974), p. 13; Roberts, *Ragged Schooling*, pp. 95–6.
47. Tebbutt, *Making Ends Meet*, pp. 8–9, 117–18, 129–30.
48. For accounts of the fierce bargaining over pawnshop counters, see, W. Greenwood, *There was a Time* (London, 1967), pp. 82–100; T. Callaghan, *A Lang Way to the Pa'nshop* (Newcastle on Tyne, 1979), p. 17; Wain, TS Autobiography, pp. 56–9.
49. A.S. Darby, *A View from the Alley* (Luton, 1974), p. 11; J. Paton, *Proletarian Pilgrimage* (London, 1935), p. 143; Southgate, *That's the way it was*, p. 63.
50. Loane, *From Their Point of View*, pp. 74–5.

51. E. Ross, 'Survival Networks: Women's Neighbourhood Sharing in London', *History Workshop*, 15 (Spring, 1983), pp. 4–6.

52. J. Langley, *Always a Layman* (Brighton, 1976), p. 11.

53. Pember Reeves, *Round About A Pound A Week*, p. 39.

54. Dayus, *Her People*, p. 26.

55. Rowntree, *Poverty*, pp. 43, 48.

56. Hobson, *Problems of Poverty*, p. 13.

57. Cited in Ross, 'Survival Networks', p. 8.

58. Dayus, *Her People*, p. 4.

59. Dayus, *Her People*, p. 29. Also Roberts, *Ragged Schooling*, p. 105.

60. Langley, *Always a Layman*, p. 11. Also Darby, *A View from the Alley* (Luton, 1974), p. xxx.

61. P. Ayers and J. Lambertz, 'Marriage Relations, Money and Domestic Violence in Working-Class Liverpool, 1919–39' in J. Lewis (ed.), *Labour and Love* (Oxford, 1986), p. 20.

62. A.A. Wain, 'One Square Mile', TS Autobiography, (University of Keele, n.d.) p. 42.

63. P. Johnson, *Saving and Spending. The Working-class Economy in Britain 1870–1939* (Oxford, 1985), pp. 27–31.

64. Johnson, *Saving and Spending*, Table 2.1.

65. Rowntree, *Poverty*, p. 382. 'In poverty' referred to 'primary' and 'secondary' poverty combined.

66. Bowley and Burnett-Hurst, *Livelihood and Poverty*, p. 44.

67. Rowntree, *Poverty*, pp. 205–9.

68. Pember Reeves, *Round About A Pound A Week*, p. 69. For a more general discussion of the dread of the Poor Law amongst those facing old age, see Loane, *Queen's Poor*, pp. 15–16.

69. Ross, 'Fierce Taunts', p. 576.

70. J. Benson, *The Penny Capitalists* (Dublin, 1983), pp. 128–30.

71. G. Noakes, *To Be A Farmer's Boy* (Brighton, 1977), p. 23.

72. D. Vincent, *Literacy and Popular Culture. England 1750–1914* (Cambridge, 1989), p. 132.

73. It was estimated that between 40 and 45 per cent of all working-class families were engaged in some form of small-scale entrepreneurial activity in this period. See J. Benson, *The Penny Capitalists* (Dublin, 1983), p. 129.

74. J. Lewis and D. Piachaud, 'Women and Poverty in the Twentieth Century', in C. Glendinning and J. Millar, *Women and Poverty in Britain* (Brighton, 1987), p. 33.

75. Ross, 'Fierce Taunts', p. 577–86.

76. Wain, TS. Autobiography, p. 40.

77. Rowntree, *Poverty*, pp. 136–8.

78. Davies, *Maternity*, p. 37.

79. Roberts, *A Ragged Schooling*, p. 188.

80. R. McKibbin, 'Working-Class Gambling in Britain 1880–1939', *Past and Present*, 82 (1979), p. 162.

81. R.H. Sherard, *The Cry of the Poor* (London, 1901), p. 14; Pember Reeves, *Round About A Pound A Week*, p. 9; Rowntree, *Poverty*, p. 58.

82. H. Belloc, *The Servile State* (London, 1912), p. 183.

83. Introduction to the Second Edition. A.V. Dicey, *Lectures on the Relation between Law and Public Opinion in England During the Nineteenth Century* (2nd edn, London, 1914), pp. xxxv, xxxix, l.

84. Vincent, *Literacy and Popular Culture*, pp. 73–88.

85. H.V. Emy, *Liberals, Radicals and Social Politics 1892–1914* (Cambridge, 1973), pp. 3–8.

86. R. McKibbin, 'Social Class and Social Observation In Edwardian England', *Trans. Royal Hist. Soc.*, 5th Ser., 28 (1978), pp. 194–7.

87. M.A. Crowther, 'The Later Years of the Workhouse 1890–1929' in P. Thane (ed.), *The Origins of British Social Policy* (London, 1978), pp. 43–6; B.B. Gilbert, *The Evolution of National Insurance in Great Britain* (London, 1966), p. 449.

88. P.A. Ryan, '"Poplarism" 1894–1930' in Thane, *Origins of British Social Policy*, pp. 59–60.

89. A.M. McBriar, *An Edwardian Mixed Doubles* (Oxford, 1987), pp. 306–339.

90. *Report of the Inter-Departmental Committee on Physical Deterioration*, PP 1904, XXXII, p. 17.

91. J. Harris, *Unemployment and Politics* (Oxford, 1972), pp. 258–60.

92. On the resulting variations in the practice of different Poor Law Unions see Thane, *Foundations of the Welfare State*, p. 35.

93. Ryan, 'Poplarism', p. 58.

94. D. Owen, *English Philanthropy 1660–1960* (Cambridge, Mass., 1965), p. 478; B.R Mitchell and P. Deane, *Abstract of British Historical Statistics* (London, 1971), p. 416.

95. B. Kirkman Gray, *Philanthropy and the State* (London, 1908), p. 2.

96. Harris, *Unemployment and Politics*, pp. 157–80.

97. F. Prochaska, *The Voluntary Impulse* (London, 1988), p. 70.

98. *Hansard*, 4th ser., CXC (1908), col. 826.

99. McBriar, *Edwardian Mixed Doubles*, p. 45.

100. *Hansard*, 4th ser., CXII (1908), col. 153.

101. Population at 1911 Census.

102. Emy, *Liberals, Radicals and Social Politics*, pp. 104–18.

103. Freeden, *New Liberalism*, p. 203.

104. W.S. Churchill, *Liberalism and the Social Problem* (London, 1909), p. 80. For a more general discussion of the advanced Liberals' perception of the natural harmony between individualism and collectivism, see Clarke, *Liberals and Social Democrats* pp. 116–21; M. Frieden, *The New Liberalism* (Oxford, 1978), pp. 117–69.

105. Rowntree, *Poverty*, p. 304.

106. K.D. Brown, 'Conflict in Early British Welfare Policy: The Case of the Unemployed Workmen's Bill of 1905', *Journal of Modern History*, XLII, 4 (1971), pp. 616–8; McBriar, *Edwardian Mixed Doubles*, pp. 94–101.

107. H. Pelling, 'The Working Class and the Origins of the Welfare State' in *Popular Politics and Society in Late Victorian Britain* (2nd edn, London,

1979), pp. 10–11; K.D. Brown, *Labour and Unemployment 1900–1914* (Newton Abbot, 1971), pp. 18–37.

108. P. Thane, 'The Working Class and State Welfare 1880–1914', *Bulletin of the Society for the Study of Social History*, **31** (1975), pp. 7–9.

109. Brown, *Labour and Unemployment*, pp. 71, 170–1; Gilbert, *Evolution of National Insurance* p. 160; Freeden, *New Liberalism*, p. 212.

110. Freeden, *Liberalism.* 122.

111. Harris, *Unemployment and Politics*, pp. 214–17.

112. Churchill, *Liberalism and the Social Problem*, p. 81.

113. Rowntree, *Poverty*, p. 120.

114. A. Ponsonby, *The Camel and the Needle's Eye* (London, 1910), p. 14.

115. B. Webb, *My Apprenticeship* (Harmondsworth, 1938), I, p. 222. On the enthusiasm of voluntary bodies for scientific methods, see F. Prochaska, *The Voluntary Impulse* (London, 1988), p. 70.

116. Masterman, 'Social Abyss', p. 28. For similar comments, see L.G. Chiozza Money, *Riches and Poverty* (8th edn, London, 1908), p. 5.

117. PP 1904, XXXI, p. 110.

118. McKibbin, 'Social Class and Social Observation', pp. 175–6; MacBriar, *Edwardian Mixed Doubles*, p. 123.

119. PP 1904, XXXI, p. 110.

120. See, *The Queen's Poor* (London 1905); *The Next Street but One* (London, 1907); *From Their Point of View* (London, 1908); *Neighbours and Friends* (London, 1910); *The Common Growth* (London, 1911).

121. Loane, *The Queen's Poor*, pp. 136, 43.

122. Loane, *The Queen's Poor*, pp. 154–5.

123. Vincent, *Literacy and Popular Culture*, pp. 73–92.

124. Lewis, 'Working-Class Wife', pp. 109–11.

125. On the Act, see W.A. Brend, *Health and the State* (London, 1917), p. 106. Despite the legislation, progress to full professionalisation was slow. The Act certified all midwives in *bona fide* practice, and by 1913, half were still untrained.

126. J. Lewis, *The Politics of Motherhood* (London, 1980), pp. 33–4.

127. Davies, *Maternity*, especially pp. 5–9.

128. F. Maurice, 'National Health: A Soldier's Study', *Contemporary Review*, LXXXIII (Jan. 1903), p. 45. See also 'Miles' (F. Maurice), 'Where to Get Men', *Contemporary Review*, LXXXI (Jan. 1902).

129. PP 1904, XXXII, pp. 55, 57.

130. Brend, *Health and the State*, p. 71.

131. PP 1904, XXXII, p. 200.

132. E.P. Hennock, *British Social Reform and German Precedents* (Oxford, 1987), pp. 180–200.

133. *Hansard*, 5th ser., XXXII, col. 1486. Also, A. Deacon, *In Search of the Scrounger* (London, 1976), p. 12.

134. *Hansard*, 5th ser., XXXII, col. 1469.

135. B.B. Gilbert, *David Lloyd George. A Political Life. The Architect of Change 1863–1912* (London, 1987), pp. 431–4.

136. *Hansard*, 5th ser., XXXII, col. 1455.

137. Freeden, *New Liberalism*, p. 214.
138. For an extensive discussion of the new problems of the citizen in a democratic society, see J.E. Hand (ed.) *Good Citizenship* (London 1899).
139. *Hansard*, 5th ser., XXXII, col. 1522.
140. B.B. Gilbert, *The Evolution of National Insurance in Great Britain* (London, 1966), p. 114. Until 1914, the scheme was discretionary. Sixty per cent of Local Authorities failed to make any provision under the 1906 Act.
141. Bowley and Burnett-Hurst, *Livelihood and Poverty*, p. 39.
142. T.R. Gourvish, 'The Standard of Living 1890–1914', in A. O'Day (ed.), *The Edwardian Age* (London, 1979), p. 31.
143. Ross, 'Survival Networks', p. 20.
144. Tebbutt, *Making Ends Meet*, p. 137.
145. Churchill, *Liberalism and the Social Problem*, p. 78.
146. F. Thompson, *Larkrise to Candleford* (Harmondsworth, 1973), pp. 96–7.
147. G. Drage, *The State and the Poor* (London, 1914), p. 82.
148. Harris, *Unemployment and Politics*, p. 361.
149. W.A. Brend, *Health and the State* (London, 1917), p. 120.
150. Gilbert, *The Evolution of National Insurance*, p. 153–5.
151. Oddy, 'A Nutritional Analysis', p. 228.
152. *Report as to the Practice of Medicine and Surgery by Unqualified Persons in the United Kingdom*, PP 1910, XLII, p. 16.
153. J. Lewis, 'The Working-Class Wife and Mother and State Intervention 1870–1914', in J. Lewis (ed.), *Labour and Love* (Oxford, 1986), p. 101.
154. Brend, *Health and the State*, p. 118.
155. Lewis and Piachaud, 'Women and Poverty', pp. 34, 44.
156. Treble, *Urban Poverty*, p. 186.
157. Gourvish, 'Standard of Living', pp. 15–30.
158. M.W. Beaver, 'Population, Infant Mortality and Milk', *Population Studies* **27**, no. 2 (1973), pp. 243–54.
159. On the growing inequality in the distribution of wealth, see, Chiozza Money, *Riches and Poverty*, pp. 310–11; P. Snowden, *The Living Wage* (London, 1912), pp. 71–4.
160. Rowntree, *Poverty*, p. 120; Bowley, *Livelihood and Poverty*, p. 47. Bowley's study was taken too early to reflect the impact of the National Insurance scheme.
161. G.N. Barnes, *From Workshop to War Cabinet* (London, 1923), p. 103.
162. Belloc, *Servile State*, p. 175.
163. B. Kirkman Gray, *Philanthropy and the State* (London, 1908), p. 294.

CHAPTER TWO

Poverty and Power 1914–39

INTRODUCTION

At the General Election of December 1918, Lloyd George and Bonar Law faced up to a new set of political realities:

> The principal concern of every Government is and must be the condition of the great mass of the people who live by manual toil. The steadfast spirit of our workers, displayed on all the wide field of action opened out by the war – in the trenches, on the oceans, in the air, in field, mine and factory – has left an imperishable mark on the heart and conscience of the nation.[1]

The leaders of the Coalition Government looked upon the era of full democracy with a combination of hope and apprehension. The spirit of national unity forged in the war had been contained within the structure of the ruling class, and there was every prospect of the pre-war politicians gaining a sweeping victory at the first contest fought on the extended franchise. At the same time it was evident that if the heart and conscience of the nation were not embodied in effective social reform, there was a real danger of at best a subsequent defeat at the polls, and at worst an overthrow of the entire political system.

Every poor man now had the vote, as did every poor woman over the age of thirty. It could not be supposed, however, that placing a cross on a piece of paper would of itself redeem the debt incurred by their sacrifices during the war, or that voting at intervals in the years to come would constitute a sufficient exercise of the rights of citizenship. Relations between the poor and the state in the inter-war period were determined by the ways in which the newly enfranchised were able to employ their nominal power to extend a real control over their lives and the forces which shaped them. On the one hand, the vulnerability of successive governments to demands for reform reflected the actual or perceived capacity of the poor to mobilise their grievances in effective protest; on the other, the significance of the legislation was most apparent in its impact on the strategies for survival which the poor had developed in the absence of government intervention. There was nothing given about the responsibilities of the state in a democratic society, as the abrupt reversal of social policy during the lifetime of the 1918–22 Coalition Administration demonstrated all too clearly. Equally the channels through which the poor could exercise their citizenship remained to be defined, as was to become apparent in their troubled experiences with organised labour and official bureaucracy between the wars.

DEMOCRACY AND REFORM

The poverty legislation of Britain's first democratically elected government is full of paradox. The programme of reform was preceded by the most coherent planning exercise ever attempted, yet its enactment was dominated by improvisation and curtailed by expediency. The Ministry of Reconstruction which was set up in 1917 lacked nothing in either the ambition of its rhetoric or the detail of its schemes,[2] yet the achievement of the succeeding administration was largely confined to an *ad hoc* extension of the pre-war system. A government which was committed to a vision of regeneration at its outset, and preoccupied with a prospect of bankruptcy at its conclusion, is most remembered now for its conservatism and complacency. Within the space of four years Lloyd George destroyed his reputation as a radical reformer, whilst at the same time engineering the biggest increase in the proportion of the gross national product devoted to the social services ever seen. A three-fold growth in the electorate witnessed a five-fold expansion in the volume of state expenditure on their material needs, but failed to achieve a discernible shift in the balance of political, economic or social power. It remained unclear whether social reform was a result of mass participation in the process of government, or a means of evading the long-awaited consequences of popular sovereignty.

Order may be brought to this confusion by considering the issue of violence. Russia's defeat by Germany was as much at the forefront of the political process in 1918, as Germany's subsequent defeat by the remaining allies. The Coalition Government came back to power at the end of the First World War with one eye on the Edwardian civilisation it had fought to preserve, and the other on the Russian Revolution it now wished to terminate, possibly by force of arms. The danger that servicemen returning to unfit homes and underpaid jobs would follow the example of the Bolsheviks and other European revolutionary movements had two effects on the politicians charged with reconstruction. Firstly it forced some reforms to the head of the agenda and prevented the relegation of others; secondly, and in some respects more seriously, it discouraged the Government from facing up to the latent contradiction between its commitment to a new era of social harmony, and its confidence in the restorative powers of the market economy.

The constructive consequences of actual or potential direct action by the dispossessed were most evident in the field of housing. The Clydeside rent strike of 1915 played a major part in forcing the passage of the Increase of Rent and Mortgage Interest (War Restrictions) Act which represented a significant advance in the state's willingness to intervene in the free market.[3] Its extension in 1919 was ensured by rent strikes at Coventry and Woolwich amidst general concern about the impact on demobilised soldiers of upward pressures on housing costs. The provision of new housing was the most specific undertaking in the Coalition election manifesto. The Ministry of Reconstruction had devoted serious attention to the question, and when its minister, Christopher Addison, took over the newly created Ministry of Health in January 1919, he made this a major priority of the Government. Under the Housing and Town Planning Act, local authorities were to be forced to prepare plans for new estates, and were in return to receive subsidies to bridge the gap between building costs and the rents which the new residents could afford. The programme was seen as the most effective insurance against revolution. The premiums were high, but, at the time, so were the risks. As the houses rose from their foundations, not just the 800,000 anticipated tenants but the working class as a whole would have tangible evidence of the state's gratitude and goodwill.[4]

Beyond housing, the issue was not whether action was required to avoid revolution, but whether revolution would be provoked by a failure to maintain existing commitments. Responsible ministers may not have given much credence to particular warnings of imminent insurrection supplied by Special Branch, but it was all too easy to believe that depriving the labouring poor of the support they had been given as they fought for their country would knock the supports from under the fragile post-war consensus.[5] By far the most substantial and irreversible extension of state expenditure was undertaken because the Government did not dare do otherwise. During the war the working class had been implicitly protected from the degrading embrace of the Poor Law, and the families of servicemen had received the formal assistance of separation allowances, which unlike the insurance system, provided benefits for wives and children.[6] As demobilised soldiers re-turned to their grateful motherland, it seemed impossible to withdraw either concession. The consequent 'out-of-work donation', introduced first for ex-servicemen and then for civilians, enshrined the principles of non-contributory, non-Poor Law support for the unemployed, and of maintenance for their families. The scheme was temporary, but its undertakings were permanent. It had long been anticipated that the experimental unemployment legislation of 1911 would be extended to the remainder of the working class. However, the scheme introduced in 1920, which covered all except agricultural workers and servants, was based on inadequate calculations and its slight prospects of sol-vency were destroyed the following year when the Government was compelled by its earlier commitments firstly to supply 'uncovenanted benefits' to those faced with the Poor Law on the expiry of their fifteen-week entitlement and then to add benefits for dependants.[7]

As a motive for reform, however, the threat of revolution was as insubstantial as it was irresistible. It forced a commitment to a housing programme which the Government did not know it could afford, and to an unemployment assistance scheme which was threatened with im-minent insolvency. Thus a central element of any coherent planning of social policy, a clear articulation of the relationship between the econ-omic development of the nation as a whole and the material well-being of its poorest citizens, was absent from the start. In this vacuum, a revitalised Treasury, which by 1919 had re-established its ascendancy over the machinery of government, was increasingly able to frustrate the ambitious proposals inherited from the Ministry of Reconstruction. Until at least the spring of 1919, the Cabinet was still pursuing what would have been by far the most significant long-term contribution to the alleviation of poverty: the introduction of a minimum wage. For a while it seemed as if a combination of the persistent pressure of Rowntree and his allies and the educational experience of war-time controls had converted not only Lloyd George but his Conservative colleagues to a full-scale statutory intervention in the working of the free market. The Treasury, however, provided a rallying point for the upholders of financial orthodoxy, and gradually its argument that such a departure would threaten both the principle of individual liberty and the practical necessity of reducing wages in a recession, began to erode support. It was unable to prevent a substantial enlargement of the Trade Boards scheme, whose coverage was extended from half a million to three million workers, but the programme of a minimum wage throughout the economy was set aside, never to be revived by any Conservative administration.[8]

The ground for the Coalition Government's retreat from a major extension of the state's engagement with poverty had already been prepared by the time the down-turn in the economy in the autumn of 1920 decisively altered the equation between reform and revolution. As unemployment rose above one million, dragging public expenditure up with it, the argument that costly legislation would do more to erode than promote economic and political stability of society became increasingly difficult to resist. The unemployment insurance system was more necessary than ever, but it was in deficit by July 1921, and instead of constituting the keystone of the arch of welfare provision, it was undermining every other innovation. In particular, Addison's housing scheme now appeared an ill-conceived luxury which the country neither needed nor could afford.[9] The Treasury had already emasculated the building programme and forced Addison from office by the time the Government appointed a committee of businessmen to identify the retrenchment upon which national survival was now seen to depend. The 'Geddes Axe' which fell in February 1922 made a direct impact on the lives of those whose benefits were cut by 10 per cent, but such reductions in the event lasted for no more than two years. More permanent was the renewed faith in the capacity of the market to supply the weapons to ward off Bolshevism.[10]

Such confidence partly reflected the perceived reluctance of the working class to mount a serious challenge to the established order. In the short term this was a matter of the onset of a depression forcing the unions onto the defensive, diverting their attention from wider questions of reform to more pressing issues of jobs and support for those who had lost them. More generally it was a consequence of the embarrassment caused to both the trade union movement and the Labour Party by the threat of direct action. Over the inter-war period as a whole, violence and related forms of civil disobedience caused more difficulty to organised labour than it did to the politicians and bureaucrats against whom it was aimed. Just as the shifting threat of revolution eventually forced the state to choose between social reform and the market economy, so it clarified the ambivalence which the nominal representatives of the oppressed felt about their grievances. During the latter part of the war, the trade union leaders had won a voice in the determination of government welfare legislation which they were anxious not to lose by adventures on the streets.[11] Although the labour movement was in principle in favour of housing reform, the unions had shown a distinct lack of enthusiasm for Addison's campaign, those most directly involved being more interested in advancing their concerns through bargaining with private builders than in risking a dilution of their strength through participation in a crash building programme.[12] The abandonment of the scheme, followed by the imposition of cuts across the whole field of social expenditure, evoked little effective protest from the spokesmen of the organisations which in theory could exercise the most powerful pressure on the Government. Thereafter, the varied incidence of conflict with the law by those directly affected by poverty legislation or its absence, served to confirm the detachment of the labour movement from the immediate interests of the poor, which in turn freed the hands of government in dealing with their problems.

The accounts left by those most directly involved in the struggles of the unemployed, whose numbers remained above a million between late 1920 and the Second World War, are full of physical conflict.[13] They freely employ the language of the military historian in their descriptions of skirmishes and ambushes, running fights and set-piece confrontations, bloody defeats and hard-won victories. The National Unemployed Workers' Movement (NUWM) was founded in the aftermath of the 'Battle of Whitehall' on 18 October 1920, when a demonstration of 20,000 unemployed ex-servicemen clashed with police at the entrance to Downing Street,[14] and its subsequent history was punctuated by scenes of violence outside employment exchanges, inside meetings of Boards of Guardians, or along the routes of demonstrations and hunger marches.[15] The survivors wore their battle honours with pride, as well they might, for it required no little physical courage to face the baton-wielding and sometimes mounted police, whose tactics eventually provoked the formation of the National Council for Civil Liberties in 1934.[16] Yet beneath the heroism and the sacrifice lay insoluble problems of tactics and leadership which severely limited the ultimate effect of what remains by far the most substantial movement of the dispossessed this century has produced.

As with Chartism, the product of the greatest depression of the nineteenth century, the strengths of the NUWM were also its principal weaknesses. Just as O'Connor and his followers derived their identity from their hostility to temporising middle-class radicals but were ultimately rendered powerless by the absence of middle-class support, so Wal Hannington and his Movement were both liberated and imprisoned by their distant and frequently hostile relations with organised labour. The men in fustian jackets generated their momentum through a combination of moral force action and physical force threats, but were halted in their tracks when an obdurate Government forced them to choose between one tactic and the other, and in the same way their cloth-capped successors, who themselves drew up a twelve-point charter in 1929, and collected a million-signature petition in 1932, were eventually faced with the unacceptable choice between full-scale insurrection or capitulation to the status quo.[17] Physical violence was too spontaneous, and in the face of police brutality, too inescapable for the NUWM to walk the paths of legality to which the Labour Party was now anxiously committed, but too unplanned and too limited to force fundamental concessions from governments which became increasingly cynical and sophisticated in their control of public order as the period progressed.

The raw material upon which the NUWM worked was promising enough. Apathy was not a leading characteristic of the men who queued outside the labour exchanges. The ritual of signing-on provided both a forceful reminder of their humiliating circumstances, and a ready-made opportunity for collective action. Discussion turned to complaint, irritation became anger, and if the clerks and the police lacked patience in the face of provocation, the unemployed as often lacked stoicism in the face of aggression.[18] 'It was never the intention of the unemployed to start fights with the police', wrote Hannington, 'but battles frequently occurred when the police resorted to force to prevent the unemployed exercising their rights as citizens to make known their grievances and to agitate for Government action to remove them.'[19] The atmosphere of physical confrontation sharply separated the twenties and thirties from the world later inhabited by the children of the unemployed. 'My generation met violence with violence', recalled Will Paynter in 1972, 'and suffered through courts penalties far harsher than anything meted out today.'[20] Policemen regularly had to be stationed at the exchanges, as one of the Ashton-under-Lyme jobless remembered: 'The Black Maria was always being called out to the Labour Exchange. Men would be fighting because they couldn't get any dole money.'[21] The scale of unrest increased sharply with the introduction of the Means Test. In November 1931, the Metropolitan Police, followed by other provincial forces, found it necessary to issue a temporary ban on demonstrations of unemployed outside labour exchanges.[22] 'The Trenchard ban', recalled Hannington, 'provoked some of the fiercest fighting around London Labour Exchanges that had ever been seen. Day after day bitter conflicts between the unemployed and the police took place and many arrests were made all over London.'[23]

In the following year there were outbreaks of disorder in a number of northern towns, although the violence remained uncoordinated. In spite of a doubling of its membership, the NUWM was still faced with the difficulty of infusing private grievances with a wider perspective, and translating intermittent local antagonism into sustained national protest. After fifteen years of such skirmishing, G.D.H. Cole noted that 'Save for a few, the chronically unemployed, except in the areas in which the trade union tradition is particularly strong, make unreliable Socialists. No effective movement can be built upon them without the stiffening support of the Socialists.'[24] Organised labour was to blame for the isolation of those on the dole:

> Many trade unions have failed to enrol the unemployed, or even to hold their employed members in the ranks; and the movement as a whole has been remiss about taking the lead in organising them and backing up their claims with due appreciation of their natural impatience. It is by no means enough to promise a workless man redress when Socialism comes into its own, or even when a Labour Government is returned to power. He wants redress now, or if not redress at any rate opportunity for vigorous protest.[25]

The NUWM was from the outset capable of providing just such opportunities, but when it looked for the stiffening support which would provide the organisation with funds, structure and leadership, it was repelled by the trade unions and the Labour Party, especially at the national level, precisely because of its engagement in such direct action.[26] Instead it turned to the fledgling Communist Party (CPGB)for activists and eventually for direction, which in turn provided the labour movement with the necessary justification for its institutional and tactical conservatism and its ingrained mistrust of those on the margins of the economy.[27] The street oratory, the brawls, and the arrest and imprisonment at one time or another of virtually all the leading NUWM members, distracted attention from the patient, detailed and frequently effective work on behalf of claimants whilst at the same time confirming the easy assumption of trade unionists and Labour MPs that the organisation was another attempt by Moscow to import red revolution. At the time of the first national hunger march in 1922, both sympathy and material support were readily available from local union branches, and the TUC briefly bestowed formal recognition in the mid-twenties, but the longer the movement had to depend on its own resources, the closer it was forced to the King Street headquarters of the CPGB, and the more implacable became the opposition of Transport House.[28] Eventually the TUC made a largely unsuccessful attempt in 1932 to set up rival associations of the unemployed which were forbidden to associate themselves with the activities of the NUWM.[29]

Until the final major event, the largely atypical Jarrow Crusade of 1936, the hunger marches were symbols more of the disunity of the working class than of its latent power. Even the decision of the Labour Party to put itself at the head of the demonstrations against the new Unemployed Assistance Board (UAB) scales, early in 1935, was based on a desire to contain rather than embrace the militancy of the NUWM and the trades councils.[30] The capacities of the unemployed were thus doubly constrained. The increasing centralisation of the Communist-led NUWM limited their ability to participate actively in the one body directly concerned with their plight, whilst the inertia of the democratic Left excluded them from what remained by far the largest and most powerful agency of opposition to the management of the economy and the organisation of relief.

The initial campaign of the London District Council of the Unemployed, out of which the NUWM grew, was in support of the Poplar Labour Guardians' refusal to apply a work test to the granting of outdoor relief. In turn, the Poplar Labour Party organised the reception of the first national hunger march when it arrived in London in the autumn of 1922.[31] 'Poplarism' had its origins well before the First World War, and its trajectory after 1918 was distinct from that of the NUWM. The campaign was run not by outcast Communists but by the official Labour Party in the borough, whose leader, George Lansbury, was the founder, and, until the end of 1922, editor of the movement's principal journal, the *Daily Herald*. Yet the two forms of protest had much in common. Both founded their case on the contradiction between the admission of the labouring poor to political citizenship and their exclusion from the economic life of the country. In Poplar, as in every Poor Law union, the dispossessed were now able to play a full part in the selection of those to whom they applied for relief.[32] Both represented the view that whilst the abolition of unemployment might have to await the socialist commonwealth, it was essential for the morale of the jobless, for their immediate material well-being, and for the vitality of the labour movement as a whole, that direct action be taken, exploiting, where possible, the political rights gained after the war. Both were prepared to defy the law if the law was being used in defiance of legitimate working-class interests. And both were the cause of acute embarrassment to the Labour leadership, even if it was impossible wholly to disown the activities of the Poplar councillors.

The confrontation which grew out of the rapid growth in unemployment in Poplar in late 1920 and early 1921 owed its form not to Continental insurrectionary tactics, but to a native tradition of political theatre which stretched back to the eighteenth century. In his conduct of the campaign to equalise the rate burden of the London boroughs, the Christian socialist George Lansbury showed himself the true heir of the radical libertine John Wilkes. Every stage of the protest which began with the refusal to pay precepts from the LCC was conducted with the utmost formality and publicity. The councillors entered and left prison in triumphant procession, and during their six-week incarceration did everything possible to distance themselves from the common criminal, even to the extent of holding council meetings behind the walls.[33] Yet to the more cautious members of the London Labour Party, whose permission had not been given for this adventure, the affair was fraught with danger. It was partly that the distinction between civil disobedience and public violence might easily be overridden in the tense atmosphere of the times. Whilst the councillors were bargaining for better conditions inside the prison and trying to unionise the warders, disturbances were taking place elsewhere in London and in other cities. Ten thousand unemployed men besieged the Woolwich Poor Law Union all night in an attempt to force higher scales of benefit.[34] But more generally, the Poplar tactics threatened to undermine everything which the national Labour Party was now hoping to achieve.

Although Herbert Morrison, the young secretary of the London Labour Party, had to acknowledge the propaganda victory of Lansbury, he regarded both the rate equalisation campaign, and the subsequent conflict over the alleged generosity of the Poplar Poor Law payments, as at best a diversion from the long march towards power on the LCC and at Westminster, and at worst a cul-de-sac from which the movement might never escape.[35] The combination of illegality and high expenditure exposed the new party to charges of irresponsibility and incompetence. Such collaboration between militant councillors and embittered claimants called into question Labour's fitness to hold office at the local or national level. It caused administrative dislocation at a time when it was essential to prove managerial capability, it threatened constitutional impropriety when it was crucial to disown the revolutionary Left, and the consequent high rates alienated the more prosperous sections of the working class at just the moment when it was necessary to wean them from the Liberals, traditionally the party of fiscal prudence. Although the Poplar councillors retained the support of their own proletarian borough, elsewhere in the LCC the results of the 1922 elections did not indicate that their campaign was winning converts to the cause.[36]

Furthermore it was feared that the challenge to legality would provoke opponents to adopt similar tactics if Labour came to power, and if it failed to do so, would leave the working class vulnerable to counter-attack from those still in control of making and enforcing the law. In the event the party held office too infrequently between the wars to test the first proposition adequately, but the second was being fulfilled even as Lansbury won his victory over the redistribution of rates. The long-term consequence of direct action against the machinery of relief was a significant accretion of authority both to central government and the agencies charged with enforcing its will.

The Local Authorities (Financial Provisions) Act of 1921, which established the machinery for transferring funds between richer and poorer boroughs, and permitted hard-pressed Guardians to raise loans to tide them over peaks in local poverty, also gave new powers to the Minister of Health to prescribe scales and conditions of relief. This set the scene for a further series of conflicts in Poplar and other boroughs, particularly West Ham, over the supposed extravagance of those elected by the recently enfranchised beneficiaries of the Poor Law. Although Baldwin's Government resisted strong pressure to reintroduce pauper disqualification if only because this would penalise so many ex-servicemen,[37] it embarked on a series of legislative reforms, culminating in the Local Government Act of 1929, which reduced both the autonomy of local democracy and the capacity of the poor to make effective use of the political citizenship they had won in 1918. Auditors were given new powers to inspect and disqualify councillors who responded too generously to appeals from underfed voters or underpaid employees, and the administration of the Poor Law was transferred from the direct control of elected Guardians of the comparatively small Unions to sub-committees of the much larger Counties and County Boroughs. Here the voices of those who received so much from the rates would be drowned by the cries of those who contributed so much to them.[38]

In areas of high regional unemployment in the early 1930s, the new Public Assistance Committees were still capable of exercising sufficient discretion in their dealings with claimants to cause constant irritation to a Government bent on curtailing all forms of public expenditure. The issue was finally settled by the Unemployment Act of 1934, which subjected the support of almost all the jobless to the authority of Whitehall. Tension between the centre and the locality had been implicit in the original Poor Law Act of 1834, with its contentious innovation of Commissioners charged with standardising relief. However, despite a piecemeal extension of national control in the remainder of the century, the Guardians had retained real powers, which after 1894 began to be exercised by working class representatives. What brought matters to a head was the introduction of an almost democratic franchise in 1918, coupled with the removal of pauper disqualification. It then took just a decade-and-a-half of full participation by the poor in their own relief to remove the element of local responsibility which had lasted for more than three centuries.

The last stage in the process of centralisation provoked the final great campaign of resistance by the NUWM. Major demonstrations were held in January 1935 as it became evident that the new Unemployment Assistance Board scales were lower than many prevailing PAC payments. However the retreat of the Government, which suspended the regulations for two years and allowed the unemployed to receive whichever scale was higher, was doubly misleading. The sudden vulnerability of Ministers to direct action owed as much to dissension in their ranks, and to insecurity amongst their backbenchers in what was likely to be an election year, as it did to the scale and vigour of the protest.[39] More generally, the balance of strength between the police and those who took to the streets had been shifting towards the former ever since the first post-war demonstrations, and was to culminate in the Public Order Bill of 1936, introduced to Parliament the day after the last national march.

The founding of the NUWM had led to the reappearance of old traditions of domestic espionage and public disinformation. The Special Branch, originally formed to deal with Irish terrorism, now turned its attention to the threat from below. As the unemployed began to develop a collective voice, their organisations were penetrated by spies and informers on a scale not seen since the demise of Chartism.[40] Although the Government was sceptical about the more lurid reports, it was thought prudent to alarm the public about the danger posed by the initial hunger march of November 1922, and in particular by the men who organised it. There was nothing original about the tactic of undermining opposition by using the press to denigrate its leadership, but the new Conservative Government went about its task with a thoroughness befitting the coming age of mass communication. On the day the march arrived in London, all the national papers save the *Daily Herald* published information supplied from police records and

Special Branch reports on the Communist leanings of the organisers and the existence of a Moscow-inspired plot.[41] The Home Office had already armed itself with extra authority through the Emergency Powers Act of 1920, passed in response to the threatened Triple Alliance strike, and was now taking a more active role in advising provincial police forces on the means of dealing with those who took to the streets. When the Slump came, it was able to build upon the foundations it had laid. A new Commissioner of the Metropolitan Police, Lord Trenchard, was appointed by the incoming National Government to cope with any trouble arising from the cuts in unemployment pay and the imposition of the household Means Test. The Special Branch was able to exploit the increasingly centralised nature of the NUWM, planting an informer on the National Administrative Committee and tapping its members' telephones.[42] Finally the 1936 Public Order Act, ostensibly aimed at the Fascists, whose violence had been more leniently dealt with than the NUWM's, complemented the erosion of local democracy in the realm of poor relief by placing the power of Chief Constables to ban meetings and processions outside the control of the elected police authorities.[43]

The Labour Party approved of the Public Order Act, despite misgivings about the new freedom of the police. Throughout the period, its principal commitment was to parliamentary rather than local democracy. It did not believe that working people were willing or able to seize power by any means other than the ballot box, or that their leaders would ever hold office unless they upheld by word and by deed the constitutional role of Westminster. In the long run, the poor would come to see the inevitability of socialism; in the short term it was necessary to construct the machinery with which to educate them. Amidst the turmoil of the post-war decade the major challenge seemed one of organisation rather than policy. It was essential to turn the party into a mass membership body in order to mount a successful attack on the Liberals whose own constituency associations were falling apart. Equally it was necessary to maintain the growing strength of an increasingly centralised trade union movement, which constituted the best short-term defence against the failings of the market and the most dependable long-term basis for constructing an effective electoral machine. Furthermore, despite the crises just after the First World War, and the disaster of the General Strike, there were real possibilities of institutional co-operation between the leaders of labour and industry which would usher in a new era of influence and stability.[44]

By contrast, the formulation of radical alternatives to the prevailing techniques of managing the economy and helping its victims was at once less important and more difficult. The party's performance in the 1918 Election confirmed that universal suffrage was not going to deliver Parliament into the hands of organised labour overnight. There was no immediate prospect of the kind of freedom of legislative action the Liberals had won for themselves in 1906, and even then there would still be the House of Lords, whose powers had been trimmed rather than abolished. It was too soon to be drawing up blueprints; the party had first to qualify itself for office. At the same time the appearance of mass unemployment in the winter of 1920 suggested that capitalism might indeed be entering its terminal phase, which made it all the more vital to keep Labour's organisation free from infection by strains of socialism committed to exploiting the crisis for extra-parliamentary ends. Whilst for those on the left of a party which since 1918 had been formally committed to the common ownership of the means of production, there seemed little point in expending effort in devising short-term cures for a disintegrating system. It might be desirable to ease the pain by modifying the details of the welfare system which had been botched together in the immediate aftermath of the First World War, but otherwise the ultimate solution to the problems of capitalism would have to await its final collapse.

These considerations were not sufficient to exclude any debate of new means of dealing with the problems of poverty which the pre-1914 reforms had manifestly failed to resolve. However, those with new ideas were faced not just with the indifference of sections of the labour movement, but the latent opposition of its most powerful constituents. This was most notably the case in respect of the campaign for family allowances. Throughout the whole of the inter-war period Eleanor Rathbone and the Family Endowment Society struggled in vain to overcome the ingrained conservatism of the trade unions. The argument that women both deserved and needed payment for raising their families foundered on the rock of the 'living wage'. Union leaders remained committed to solving child poverty by gaining for the male wage earner an income sufficient to support all his dependants without further subventions from the state. Rathbone insisted that the wide variation in family sizes rendered such a goal both wasteful and impractical, and that the unions' resistance was founded on reactionary social values:

> I suggest that the leaders of working men are themselves subconsciously biased by prejudice of sex as well as of class, when they cling persistently to the ideal of a uniform adequate family wage, even when acknowledging that its attainment belongs to a distant and speculative

future. Are they not influenced by a secret reluctance to see their wives and children recognised as separate personalities, 'each to count for one and none for more than one' in the economic structure of society, instead of being fused in the multiple personality of the family with its male head?[45]

The ILP, which enjoyed a greater intellectual freedom than organised labour and was more open to feminist thinking, endorsed both the living wage and family allowances in its *Socialism in Our Time* programme of 1926, but the slow conversion of the rest of the party was finally brought to a halt in 1930 at the behest of the unions who were increasingly concerned that the proposal would intensify the downward pressure on wages.[46]

The absence of a practical critique of the solutions to poverty and unemployment bequeathed by the Coalition Government meant that Labour took office in 1924 and again in 1929 bereft of a coherent programme of economic management or poor relief. The removal by MacDonald's first Administration of the barriers the Conservatives had erected across Downing Street to keep out the unemployed symbolised nothing.[47] The Government's thinking remained fenced in by the legislative framework it inherited, and the poor themselves were kept as far as ever from the making and implementation of policy. Some attempt was made to extend the minor programmes of public works started by the outgoing Conservatives, relief scales which had been cut by the Geddes Axe were increased, the time limit on uncovenanted benefit was abolished together with the three-week 'gap' between insured and uncovenanted benefit, and the Poplar Guardians were relieved of the threat of surcharge and disqualification.[48] However, that symbol of official mistrust, the 1921 Genuinely Seeking Work Test, which exposed to disqualification applicants incapable of proving their intention to find employment, was extended rather than abolished. Only Wheatley's Housing Act, which shifted the focus of government subsidy for new building from the private to the public sector,[49] had any long-term significance for the welfare of the working class, although the impact of council housing on the poorest members of the community was at best indirect.

The preoccupation of the party in the 1920s was with the impetus of its electoral advance rather than the momentum of the attack on poverty. In this sense, the near doubling of parliamentary representation in 1929 justified its strategy. There was, however, still some distance to travel before the attainment of a full majority in the Commons, and in the meantime the second Labour Government had to find a way of responding to the rapid escalation in the number of families in which the chief breadwinner was unable to find work. The crisis had the effect of exposing the order of priorities which the leadership had espoused since 1918. The issue of unemployment was too urgent, and the range of alternative policies put forward outside and inside the party was too great for the subordination of social reform to procedural orthodoxy to remain undisturbed. Of the two positive measures which were adopted, the first was rendered ineffective by the scale of the recession, and the second made the problem worse.

The limited programme of public works sponsored by the Unemployment Grants Committee expected too much of already hard-pressed local authorities which had to meet half the cost, and was consistently undermined by a Chancellor of the Exchequer obsessed with financial stringency. The Unemployment Insurance Act of 1930, by contrast, relieved ratepayers of pressure by passing responsibility for transitional benefits to the Treasury, and threatened to overwhelm the management of government expenditure by abolishing both the Genuinely Seeking Work clause and the twelve-month time limit on transitional benefits, causing an immediate doubling of claims from men hitherto forced to rely on the Poor Law.[50] Every step that was taken confirmed the Chancellor of the Exchequer, Philip Snowden, in his belief that a stable economy and a reduction in poverty were, at least in the short term, mutually exclusive objectives. Before joining the ILP he had enjoyed a career in the Inland Revenue, and as the crisis deepened, his passion for financial orthodoxy became irresistible. He was totally in accord with his Treasury officials, and wholly out of sympathy with the ideas of the Chancellor of the Duchy of Lancaster, Oswald Mosley, who was appointed to develop policy on the unemployed. In Snowden's view, Mosley's proposal to reduce unemployment by expanding social services, particularly pensions, would damage not only Britain's credit-worthiness abroad, but the Labour Party's hard-won reputation for responsible government at home.

The eventual appointment in March 1931 of an advisory committee headed by Sir George May, secretary of the Prudential Assurance Company, was at once consistent with the approach over the previous decade, and destructive of all that had been achieved in that time. Its purpose was not so much the discovery of new devices for retrenchment, which were freely available from the Treasury, but the education of dissident Labour MPs in the responsibilities of statecraft. At the height of the crisis caused by the recommendations of the May Committee, *The Times* observed that Macdonald and Snowden 'have been fighting indeed for nothing less than their party's right to be thought capable of governing'.[51] However strained the argument that the solvency of the economy rested on the level of unemployment relief, there was substance in the claim that it was not MacDonald but his opponents who were abandoning the party's attitude to public office. His mistake was not one of strategy, but of tactics in forcing an open choice between the exercise of power and the defence of the working class, and between the exercise of working-class rights and the defence of the economy. Even so, his dissenting colleagues expected until the very end that it would be possible to fudge the issue and resume the onward march as a united party on the Opposition benches.

In the event, MacDonald, Snowden and Thomas parted company from their Cabinet, joining the Conservatives and most of the Liberals to form a National Government. Snowden remained Chancellor of the Exchequer, and was now free to give full reign to his orthodoxy. In his September budget he cut relief scales by 10 per cent, increased contributions and imposed a household Means Test on transitional benefits. The nation was saved at the expense of the poor, and to the cost of the Labour Party, which was routed in a general election a month later, losing all but 52 of its 288 seats. Denuded of its leadership, and bereft of the sense that history was on its side, the party was forced to adopt a new approach to the formulation of policy. The development of detailed legislative programmes now appeared less a diversion from the task of building an organisation and more a precondition for a recovery in electoral strength. However there was little change in the entrenched hostility to the participation of the victims of capitalism in the making or execution of reform. Dalton and Morrison, who dominated the key Policy Committee of the National Executive, did not believe that new ideas could be found on the streets, or that the dispossessed could be effective instruments of their own salvation.[52] Research into the remedies for unemployment and other forms of deprivation was a matter for experts, as was the construction and administration of the state machinery which alone could bring long-term relief.

The growing enthusiasm for central planning was accompanied by a more disciplinary attitude towards dissent within the party's ranks. Both developments were fiercely resisted by the Left, invigorated by the recent confirmation of the sickness of mature capitalism and the apostasy of the old Labour leadership. The newly formed Socialist League pointed to the trajectory of Mosley's career, and argued that the National Executive was merely hastening the collapse of democracy into Fascism. However its attempt to redefine the stance of socialism towards the liberal state foundered on the rock of the party's commitment to the parliamentary process. Where the League saw Dalton as a proto-Mussolini, the NEC branded Cripps as a would-be Lenin for insisting that the next Labour Government would begin by abolishing the House of Lords and passing an Emergency Powers Act. What settled the issue was the appeal by the League to the militancy of the unemployed following its defeat at the 1934 Scarborough Conference. This confirmed the hierarchy's conviction that its opponents shared the Communists' disregard for law and order, but it also exposed the absence of a mass base for the rebels. In the event the critique of government by experts was being mounted by intellectuals who were themselves part of the elite. The ILP, the focus of imaginative thinking on poverty policy in the twenties, had destroyed itself when it disaffiliated from the party in 1932, and in the same way the League's influence ended when it tried to take on the party from below. So far from eroding the confidence of the socialist planners, its campaign strengthened their commitment to reform for the poor rather than by the poor.[53]

The particular nature of the threat posed by the unemployed does much to explain the combination of conflict and consensus which characterised the growth of the welfare systems between the wars. It was of sufficient strength to force a substantial extension of the volume of government expenditure in the aftermath of 1918, and to prevent any subsequent attempt to permit the Poor Law to resume its pre-war role as the principal source of relief for all those unable to support themselves. It was powerful enough to sustain the largest organisation of the dispossessed since the demise of Chartism, which from the first national hunger march in 1922 through to the Jarrow Crusade and beyond kept the grievances of the victims of the Depression before the eyes of the majority of the population still in employment. It maintained an atmosphere of confrontation, which descended into frequent verbal and sometimes physical conflict inside and outside the labour exchanges. It reflected the pervasive absence of public trust which so sharply distinguished the aftermath of the First World War from that of the Second. Yet in the end the incidence of direct conflict, and the prospect of much greater violence if the state abandoned its responsibilities, rarely had more than a negative effect on the course of events. The influence of the NUWM and less structured forms of protest was too pervasive to be ignored, but too confined to have a constructive impact on either the conception or execution of government policy.

The key factor was the fear the unemployed struck in the hearts, not of the Conservatives, but of their new opponents. The abiding concern of a party which was often uncertain whether its future might be as short as its past, was to place as much distance as possible between itself and forms of action which would blur the distinction between Bolshevism and democratic socialism, and between casual protest and organised labour. The commitment to parliamentary democracy was both a means of obtaining power, and at least until the defeat in 1931, an end in itself. Whilst its electoral progress was dependent on gaining the votes of the newly enfranchised, Labour's campaign sought to marginalise those admitted to the political nation after the First World War. The poor were to remain passive citizens, shunned when they took to the streets, excluded from the policy-making process when the party at last began to lay serious plans for office. For their part, those relegated from the structures founded on employment lacked the capacity to break out of the role which their new representatives had assigned to them.

As a consequence, the Conservatives, who in one guise or another formed all the majority administrations of the period, were at no time faced with a clearly articulated alternative to their own policies. The sequence of reforms was shaped less by opposing ideologies, than by the contradictions created by the initial extension of the insurance and uncovenanted benefit schemes. The forty Insurance Acts passed between 1920 and 1934 were attempts to reconcile benefit generated by membership of a scheme with support justified by membership of society; benefit designed for the breadwinner with support given to all his dependants; benefit guaranteed by contribution with support conditional on behaviour; benefit intended for occasional loss of work with support required for long-term unemployment and benefit funded by actuarial practice with support financed by Treasury subsidy.[54]

The 1920 Insurance Act was insolvent within eight months, and thereafter the high level of structural unemployment not only prevented a return of the scheme to surplus, but obscured a clear view of the problems caused by the hasty response to the threat of revolution after the First World War. In 1925 Chamberlain brought pensions inside the contributory system and extended their coverage to the widows and orphans excluded in 1911. At the same time he tightened the requirement that claimants for unemployment and extended benefit subject themselves to a 'genuinely seeking work' test and soon a fifth of all applications were being disqualified.[55] In 1927 he struggled to resolve difficulties inherited from the first Labour Government by merging standard and extended benefits, and introducing transitional benefits for those who had paid less than thirty weeks' contributions. The incoming National Government reintroduced the twenty-six-week time limit for insurance benefits, consigning those who had exhausted their entitlement to means-tested payments from the Public Assistance Committees. Finally the 1934 Insurance Act imposed as much order on the situation as was possible without a major reconstruction by establishing the Unemployment Insurance Statutory Committee to manage the contributions and benefits on a strict actuarial basis, with equal payments from employers, employees and the state, and the Unemployment Assistance Board to provide central control of means-tested relief for those who could demonstrate need.

The hostility of the unemployed blocked the retreat of the Conservatives, but they were left free to set limits to their own advance. Only three more trade boards were established after 1921, and with the exception of the cosmetic Special Areas Act of 1934, no further attempt was made to interfere with the workings of the market. The criticism of the Labour Party and the aggression of extra-parliamentary forms of protest were safely absorbed in disputes about the relationship between contributory and non-contributory benefits, and about the machinery and conditions of payment.[56] The larger issues, of whether unrestricted capitalism was the most effective agency for the long-term abolition of poverty, and whether in the meantime the working class itself should wherever possible pay for the relief of its casualties, remained largely uncontested.

WELFARE AND FAMILY CAPACITIES

'Compared with what they were at the turn of the century', wrote the economist John Hilton in 1938, 'our social services are a miracle of collective care and collective kindliness. Compared with what they might well be they are in some respects paltry and mean.'[57] It was no easy task to strike a balance between achievement and shortfall in the growth of state expenditure on the poor between the wars. Before 1914, the reforms had been too late and too hesitant to make a discernible difference to the management of most family economies. The subsequent process of expansion and consolidation has to be viewed in terms of both the volume of assistance which was made available, and the means by which it was distributed. Ever since the introduction of the New Poor Law, governments had recognised that the impact of their activities was conditioned as much by the machinery of relief as by the sums of money, if any, which found their way into the homes of the poor. Whilst the value of cash transfers from the state to its citizens grew dramatically between the wars, it remained the case that the impact of the initiatives was a function not only of the scale of assistance, but of the rules and regulations which surrounded it.

There was a five-fold increase in central expenditure on the social services between 1918 and 1938. At the beginning of the inter-war period, £2.4 was spent per head of population, whilst the figure rose to £12.5 at the end. In 1918 2.4 per cent of the Gross National Product was devoted to the social services, compared with 11.3 per cent of a higher GNP in 1938.[58] Although many of the new benefits involved a transfer of responsibility from the Poor Law rates, local authority spending on social services remained at a steady 40 per cent of the state's bill throughout the period. This category of public expenditure includes services such as education, already well established by 1900, or welfare clinics which multiplied after 1918, and understates the scale of the increase in simple cash transfers. Rowntree calculated in 1936 that unemployment insurance and assistance, health insurance, old age, widows' and war pensions were together contributing sixteen times more money, in real terms, to the families of York than had been paid in outdoor relief by the Guardians in 1901.[59] According to the poverty surveys of the 1930s, between 40 and 50 per cent of all working-class families were regularly receiving some contribution to their budgets as a consequence of the reforms which had been set in motion by the last Liberal Government.[60]

Applying for and obtaining financial assistance was no longer an act of last resort. However, it is evident that the changes were neither as consistent nor as effective as the aggregate figures would suggest. The transformation in public expenditure belonged not to the period as a whole, but to the few years of the post-war crisis. Total spending jumped from £114.3 million in 1918 to £490.7 million in 1921, but was still only £498.3 million in 1934. Once the initial commitments had been made, most of the subsequent fluctuations were caused by the changing levels of unemployment. If the emergency cuts in government spending in 1921–22 and again a decade later made little long-term impact, the largely successful attempt to prevent further growth meant that by the 1930s, the rate of increase in the proportion of Gross Domestic Product devoted to the social services was much slower in Britain that in many other parts of Europe.[61]

As might be expected, the less prosperous members of the working class gained a larger share of the expenditure. The social surveys found that between seven and nine in ten families they classed as poor were receiving some kind of cash payment. But if the modern association of poverty with public welfare was now taking form, so was the figure of the middle-class claimant. Although their benefits are not included in the conventional roll-call of social reforms, substantial sums of money were finding their way into the pockets of white-collar workers, either as tax relief on the mortgages they were able to take out for the first time, or as child tax allowances, which were introduced in 1909 and by 1938 were costing the Treasury £87.5 million, twice as much as family allowances when they were introduced in 1945.[62]

Amongst those who were supposed to be the focus of government concern, the impact of the payments was at once substantial and inadequate, widespread and inconsistent. The inquiries which were undertaken well after expenditure had reached its plateau revealed levels of primary poverty ranging from one in ten to nearly one in three of the working class.[63] The figures would certainly have been much worse without the structure of relief – Owen calculated that the withdrawal of all benefits would quadruple the proportion of poor families in Sheffield[64] – but it was clear that the volume of state spending was failing to resolve the problems which had been identified before 1914. In York, Rowntree found that just over a third of all the income of the poor now came from the state, yet this group constituted no less than 31.1 per cent of the town's working-class population.[65]

The relationship between assistance and poverty was complicated by variations in provision, need and eligibility, but a number of general features can be identified. Firstly, whilst all benefits were of value, some contributed much more to the income of a community than others. Health insurance payments, together with associated maternity benefits, were a great help to those who could receive them, but they constituted about 5 per cent or less of the overall payments. Fifteen shillings a week was a great deal better than nothing, but hardly enough to keep a family.[66] Insured and uninsured pensions and unemployment relief dominated the picture, each comprising between a third and a half of total receipts, depending on the local population structure and labour market.

Secondly, whilst all benefits played a part, some forms of deprivation were more affected than others. In York, public relief payments constituted 80 per cent of the income of the unemployed, 66 per cent of the income of the old, but only 1.7 per cent of the income of families forced below the poverty line by some combination of low wages and large families.[67]

Thirdly, whilst most benefits were designed to take account of family circumstances, their capacity to reduce poverty was still deeply affected by the nature of the household. Although slightly more generous in real terms than the original 1908 scheme, pensions were still only adequate if a couple could pool their resources or a single pensioner could move in with married children.[68] Equally, despite intricate differentials between insured and uncovenanted benefit rates, and, until late in the period, amongst locally established Public Assistance scales, there was a common shortfall where there were more than two dependent children, or where there was no additional wage earner still in employment.[69]

Fourthly, whilst wives made great gains through the introduction of dependants' allowances for unemployed workers, they derived no direct benefit from their husband's health insurance. Their status as second-class citizens was confirmed by the Anomalies Act of 1931 which made it extremely difficult for women to retain their entitlement to unemployment benefit once they had married. As part of their husband's household they were expected to be economically inactive.

Finally, whilst successive governments were forced against their better judgement to make non–Poor Law assistance to the unemployed of indefinite duration, its adequacy diminished the longer unemployment lasted. The working class had always been accustomed to coping with periodic crises in which for a week or a month income fell short of minimum expenditure. But when there was nothing left to sell, borrow or recycle, when all that was left was public relief, it was rarely enough.[70]

The pattern of expenditure and requirement foreshadowed the modern welfare state whilst retaining many of the characteristics of the Edwardian era. Receipt of public money was now a commonplace amongst the poor, and far from unknown amongst sections of the working-class community for whom independence of the available systems of relief had once been a fundamental condition of their self-respect. At the same time, few families could expect to subsist adequately on the benefits they were receiving. Whereas the scales of the post-1945 system were supposed to raise claimants to a minimum level, leaving the attainment of higher standards to private initiative, between the wars the poor required both benefits and their own enterprise just to survive.

As in the modern welfare state, cash transfers were supplemented by other social services, but in this period the appearance of a coherent system of support was frequently illusory. School meals, the very first of the Liberal reforms, made little progress. As late as 1938, 15 per cent of education authorities in England and Wales provided no meals at all. During the inter-war period the proportion of children receiving meals fluctuated between 2 and 4 per cent, despite the fact that unemployment never fell into single figures. Although some councils in hard-pressed areas made special efforts, the majority of those children officially categorised as malnourished were still totally dependent on their parents' capacity to feed them.[71] It was not until the 1944 Education Act, nearly four decades after school meals were introduced, that the service became widespread and compulsory. A greater claim for national coverage could be made on behalf of clinics for mothers and children, but those most in need of their assistance made little use of them. On Teeside in 1937 only 36 per cent of successful pregnancies passed through the municipal centres.[72]

A move had been made towards a consistent response to all forms of deprivation, but there remained fundamental lacunae. The combination of large-scale spending on the elderly and the persistent inadequacy of their pensions, which became the dominant problem of the fifties, was already established, although its features were often obscured by the difficulties and demands of the unemployed. The jobless themselves experienced a mixture of unprecedented continuity of non-discriminatory support from public funds and constant uncertainty about the form and extent of relief, and the conditions under which it would be given. Least assisted was the section of the population which had been at the forefront of public concern when the Edwardian debate about poverty was initiated by Rowntree's survey and the problems of recruiting for the Boer War. Growing children were inadequately catered for by the dependants' allowances of unemployment benefits, and largely neglected if their fathers were in full-time but ill-paid work. As a consequence, the new investigations of the 1930s found that between 21 and 43 per cent of all working-class children fell below their poverty lines, and that Rowntree's poverty cycle, with peaks of deprivation in childhood and in young families, was still clearly identifiable.[73] Rickets, the most direct manifestation of early malnutrition was still found in as many as two out of three working-class school children.[74]

In 1913, as the new Labour Exchanges and National Insurance schemes began to get going, Britain achieved for the first time in its history a nominally literate population. Thereafter, the more money the state distributed to the poor, the more use the poor had to make of their schooling. Before the Liberal reforms, the only regular encounter the newly educated would make with forms and official correspondence was in conjunction with the education of their own children. Although Poor Law Guardians were connected to a centralised bureaucracy, their dealings with applicants for relief were conducted on an oral basis. By contrast, claimants for insured or uncovenanted benefit could neither qualify for assistance nor continue to receive it without employing the skills of reading and writing. Whilst historians have taken marriage register signatures as a measure of literacy rates, in practice the great majority of the pre-war population were rarely called upon to write out their names.[75] Now they had to accept that their identity could only be expressed with a pen in their hand.

The daily, or when pressure of demand forced some relaxation of the rules, thrice- or twice-weekly routine of signing on was both a condition of assistance and a symbol of the working man's new subordination to the written word. The influence of the insurance system spread throughout the world of employment. In most areas of the economy, including much of factory production, hiring and firing had always been conducted by word of mouth, but as the 1911 Act was extended, recruits to most occupations outside agriculture had to submit an Unemployment Insurance card for their employer to fill with stamps and collect it when the job ended. The card had then to be handed to the Labour Exchange in return for a receipt, and the claimaint would be given a form upon which to make his own application, and a second for his dependants. Those in doubt could refer to a printed leaflet, or to posters pasted on the walls. If the application was rejected, the insurance officer would issue a further form giving the reasons for his decision.[76]

In theory, the bureaucratisation of relief should have eliminated the element of arbitrary personal judgement which had humiliated generations of paupers.[77] Dissatisfied applicants now had access to a body of rules upon which to challenge a decision, and to a court of referees to make an appeal.[78] In practice, however, there was little sense that the extension of the written word had enhanced either the dignity or the power of those forced to apply for assistance from public funds. This was partly because the separate elements in the post-war system, and the interaction between them, were altered so frequently between 1920, when they first took shape, and 1937, when the Standstill Act came to an end, that even long-term claimants had difficulty mastering their operation.[79] It was partly also because the powers of discrimination possessed by counter staff and investigating officers were greatly increased by the constant attempts to modify the principle of automatic eligibility to take account of assumed shortfalls in behaviour and need which had so attracted Lloyd George to the concept of insurance. The pattern was set in March 1921, when in response to fears of the abuse of uncovenanted benefit, the Coalition Government introduced the 'Genuinely Seeking Work' test, which placed the onus of proof on the applicant, and left him at the mercy of judgements of what constituted a genuine search, and what was appropriate work.[80]

Claimants required both constructive advice and sympathetic assessment, and rarely received either. Overworked and frequently inexperienced clerks had little patience with the complex occupational and domestic histories which were set out before them.[81] The NUWM advised the unemployed to keep their own written record of job applications to convince the insurance officers,[82] who were under constant pressure to disbelieve and disqualify, and to distance themselves from marginally less educated and less respectable applicants. Taught that the jobless were a threat rather than a responsibility, they were easily tempted, as 'One of the Unemployed' Max Cohen discovered, 'to behave arrogantly and unreasonably towards the men who signed-on'.[83] For those unable to find work, the distinction between requesting covenanted and uncovenanted benefit was one of degree rather than kind. 'At the Labour Exchange', recalled Harry Goldthorpe, 'you could beg for what was supposed to be yours, by virtue of insurance, and keep your cap on. But at the relieving office you were expected to grovel even more, and beg with your cap off.'[84]

Rather than extending the traditions of organised self-help pioneered by the more prosperous sections of the nineteenth-century working class, the new structures embodied the spirit of censorious inquisition which the poorest families had always suffered at the hands of Boards of Guardians and charity visitors. Although the friendly societies and trade unions retained a role in the inter-war system, their members no longer had any effective influence over either the levels or the terms of relief. In this sphere, 'self-government', as the first detailed study of the system discovered, 'was a dead letter' by the mid-twenties.[85] Health insurance brought medical assistance to sections of the labouring community which previously could not have afforded to join friendly societies, but the doctors themselves were now free of control by their patients' representatives. The salaried health visitors were of a slightly lower social standing than the Charity Organisation Society volunteers, but they retained the belief that conditions for the poor could be improved if they imitated the behaviour of their betters.[86]

For those who could afford the higher rents and associated travelling costs, council housing offered the prospect of escape from exploitation by landlords, in exchange for subordination to a new set of regulations and to the minor officials charged with enforcing them. 'It is a great achievement to get slum-dwellers into decent houses', observed George Orwell, 'but it is unfortunate that, owing to the peculiar temper of our time, it is considered necessary to rob them of the last vestiges of their liberty.'[87] Tenants were rarely offered direct participation in the design or management of their estates, but were instead expected to conform to standards of conduct set out in rule books, with the threat of eviction or transfer to less desirable property if they failed to do so.[88] For those confined to the private sector, the 1935 Housing Act brought regular visits, often late in the evenings, by inspectors checking on overcrowding.[89]

The housing and sanitary inspectors jostled with older visitors such as truancy and child-welfare officers and the police. As Jerry White observed of an inter-war London slum, 'There was no end to the number of officials whose job it was to tell the people in Campbell Bunk how they should live.'[90] So far from strengthening the resistance of the poor to the pressures of the market economy, the new body of bureaucrats and inspectors had a tendency to merge with the army of private oppressors and redressers to which those on the edge of destitution had always been forced to defer. As Mrs Cecil Chesterton noted:

> 'They' is the generic term for officialdom, benevolent or despotic; officialdom, whose power is far-reaching and ill-defined, fills the poor with fear and enforces a jealous reticence when complaint might rectify flagrant abuses and compel a rack-renting landlord to repair a leaky roof or a broken stair. The ramifications of officialdom apart from duly constituted bodies are enormous. Inspectors of every sort and kind harry the slum dwellers. Welfare workers – with the best intentions – take up their time. Ladies on local pension bodies inquire as to war widows, interviewing them and checking up their various statements by inquiries among neighbours and friends.[91]

Of all the forms faced by the unemployed, of all the visitations by inspecting bureaucrats, by far the most intimidating and humiliating were those generated by the 1931 household Means Test. The claimant who had exhausted the new twenty-six-week entitlement to insurance benefit had to provide written answers to a detailed list of questions covering every aspect of the condition and organisation of his family economy. The submission of the completed form would be followed by a call at his home by an investigating officer seeking to check the accuracy of the replies and assess the value of the household's possessions and resources.[92] The system epitomised the alienation of the poor from both the personnel and the procedures of the machinery for relief. It represented a direct assault on the whole basis of the working-class strategy for survival. Where the maximisation of the earning potential of the subordinate members of the family had always been the most effective defence against hardship, now it was the major threat to the receipt of assistance.[93] Where resistance to periodic misfortune had been increased by the accumulation of savings, or much more frequently, by the purchase of inessential items of furniture which could be sold or pawned in an emergency, now these diminished the value of the claim which the inspector would allow. Where the lines of authority and dependence had been maintained in the most difficult circumstances, now they were reversed as unemployed fathers were forced to rely on the pensions of their resident parents, or the earnings of older children who had yet to leave home.[94] Where families had traditionally huddled together in hard times, pooling resources and taking in lodgers if possible, now they were under pressure to expel all but children below the school-leaving age.[95] And where the last and most valued possession of all had been privacy, now this was the first victim of an application for help.

Initially, the administration of transitional benefit was supervised by Public Assistance Committees of local authorities, and in predominantly working-class areas this enabled the harsher features of the system to be modified by sympathetic councillors.[96] But the basic features of the machinery set up by the National Government could not be altered. In terms of a cost-cutting exercise it was a success. As had been the case in 1834, expenditure was curtailed by less eligibility as potential applicants sought every alternative means of staying alive rather than submit themselves to the destruction of their dignity. Of those who were forced to fill in the form, a sixth were disqualified during the first ten weeks of the Means Test, and a further third had their benefit reduced.[97]

With unemployment rising sharply, and the proportion of the long-term jobless increasing, sections of the working class which had never experienced the shame of appearing before the Poor Law Guardians, nor had ever expected to, now found every aspect of their affairs laid bare before suspicious officials. There were strong elements of continuity in the National Government's concern about indiscriminate payments, but from the perspective of the unemployed, the Means Test threw into reverse the momentum of change which had been set in motion before the First World War. Once more relief was made conditional on the exposure not just of the claimant's poverty, but on the whole structure of relationships and transactions which made up the family economy. The acceptance of a responsibility for the unemployed worker's dependants, which had been a major concession of the Coalition Government, was compromised by the insistence that where possible the claimant should be supported by his co-residing relatives. The Means Test, as Hannington observed, 'was making un-employment a charge upon the family instead of a charge upon the State'.[98] The relief remained more generous than under the Poor Law, and more widely available, but the combination of increasing bureau-cracy and intensifying selectivity introduced new forms of discrimination. The Public Assistance Committees lacked the power to disenfranchise, but unlike the Guardians, they possessed the unpre-cedented right to invade the homes of those who sought relief. Whilst the ladies who went charity visiting had been protected only by their sense of moral and social superiority, the inspecting officers knocked on the door every four weeks throughout the duration of a claim armed with a full set of regulations. Now it was not just well-meaning social investigators like Seebohm Rowntree who were asking neigh-bours about a family's behaviour. If the poor kept their votes, they lost what seemed to them a basic right of citizenship, the freedom to determine who entered their home, and who knew about the life which was lived inside it.[99]

By 1939 there were at least eighteen separate means tests standing between the poor and the relief available from central or local govern-ment.[100] Already these were creating unforeseen conflicts and disin-centives, as the gaining of one benefit caused the forfeit of another, or an increase in prosperity was wiped out by a loss of eligibility. The extension and modification of public welfare which took place over the period diminished the exposure of the labouring poor to the full effects of the shortcomings of the economy but also reduced their capacity to organise their own strategies for survival. The old and the unemployed were less dependent on their own resources than once they had been, but more limited in their ability to make good the shortfalls that remained in the provision of assistance. They faced a host of directions about how they might leave work and find new jobs, how far they might engage in part-time or casual employment, how much they might earn and how they might spend it, whom they should support and who should keep them. Only the working poor and their families remained largely free of the new constraints, and of the new qualifications to citizenship which the bureaucratisation of welfare had introduced. But they had least protection from poverty and the greatest dependency on the traditional forms of individual and collective endeavour in the market place.

THE POOR AND THE MARKET

In 1930, in an article on Mosley's proposals, Keynes summarised the problem of his time:

> For the important question today which we have to face individually and collectively is the question whether those are right who think that the course of prudence and proved wisdom is to trust to time and natural forces to lead us with an invisible hand to the economic harmonies; or those who fear that there is no design but our own, and that the invisible hand is merely our own bleeding feet moving through pain and loss to an uncertain and unprofitable destination.[101]

Ever since the commitment to a minimum wage had been abandoned by the Coalition Government, the ruling answer to Keynes's question was that market forces were the only means of reducing unemployment and spreading prosperity throughout the population. In some respects the faith in the ability of capitalism to cure poverty was even greater than it had been in the heyday of Victorian Liberalism. Whereas it was once believed that substantial government action was required to reform the moral character of the destitute through the workhouse, now the retraining camps to which the long-term unemployed could be sent were peripheral to the main objectives of the welfare system. If pensions and compulsory insurance were a recognition that the old, the sick and the jobless were not wholly responsible for their plight, it was still expected that in the long run the free market would solve its structural weaknesses, and supply the poor with the means of leading a life independent of state assistance. The endless arguments inside and outside Parliament about the terms and conditions of relief deflected attention from the commitment of successive governments to the curative powers of the invisible hand.

The state exposed the poor to the market in two senses. At a general level it relied upon a rise in the level of real wages to resolve the problems of low pay identified before 1914, and upon a recovery in world trade to cure the new phenomenon of mass unemployment. More immediately it left those who had yet to reap the reward of such improvements to make good the shortfalls in the availability of welfare through the devices for getting and spending afforded by the local economy.

A. L. Bowley's *Livelihood and Poverty* had set the seal on the Edwardian rediscovery of poverty. The book was based on research undertaken in 1913 by a professor of statistics rather than a chocolate manufacturer, and employed more rigorous concepts and survey techniques than Rowntree's work, yet its general findings confirmed those of *Poverty*. Ten years later he returned to the six towns of his original survey. To the question of his book's title, *Has Poverty Diminished?*, he was able to give an encouraging reply: 'The improvement since 1913 is very striking . . . the proportion in poverty in 1924 was little more than half that in 1913. If there had been no unemployment the proportion of families in poverty in the towns taken together would have fallen to one third and of persons to a little over a quarter of the proportion in 1913.'[102] Much the most important cause of this transformation was not the welfare legislation of the Coalition Government but the experience of manual workers in the economy. Whereas the cost of living had increased by 70 per cent since the last year of peace, the wages of unskilled labourers had roughly doubled.[103]

For many of the unskilled, the improvements began with the outbreak of war. Although prices rose as sharply as wage rates,[104] the demand for labour and the tendency for wages to level upwards eased the condition of the low paid who had figured so largely in the earlier research. Where the breadwinner was sent to the Front, separation allowances were a more than adequate compensation for what had often been an irregular and inadequate source of income, and the women who were left behind could command much higher rates for their war work than had been available in peacetime. Only where a large family struggled along with a single income-earner did matters seem no better than before. Rent controls and food rationing ensured that the domestic budget was spent more efficiently,[105] and it was the resulting improvement in nutrition, rather than the expanding system of welfare clinics, which made the major contribution to the improving mortality rates of all but the elderly members of the non-combatant population.[106]

The rapid dismantling of most of the war-time regulations, the disappearance of munitions work for women, and the arrival of mass unemployment, threatened a swift return to Edwardian levels of poverty. However the inflation of the war economy came to an end in 1920 and was replaced by a long fall in prices which did not bottom out until the early thirties. This meant that despite periodic attempts to cut wages, the standard of living of those of the working class who kept their jobs continued to improve beyond the point of Bowley's second investigation. Hilton calculated that between 1924 and 1938, real wages of manual workers rose by 12 per cent.[107] Family economies were further strengthened by the isolated survival of rent controls, and the development of new forms of work for wives and daughters in the new generation of light industry. Even for the unemployed, the deflation ensured that it was easier to survive on the dole as the Depression deepened than it had been a decade earlier.[108] The 1932 *New Survey of London Life and Labour* found that poverty had declined to a third of the level in Booth's original study.[109] In 1936, Rowntree followed Bowley's example of a repeat survey and found that in the third of a century which had elapsed since the research for *Poverty*, the standard of living 'available to the workers' in York had risen by about 30 per cent.[110] By this time unemployment was falling, but food prices were beginning to rise again, and it is doubtful whether there was any further improvement before the reappearance of war.[111]

The capacity of the market to reduce the problem of low pay was enhanced by concurrent changes in the size of the working-class family. At around the turn of the century the modification in the traditional pattern of reproduction already visible in the middle class began to spread to the rest of society. Crude fertility rates declined from twenty-eight births per 1,000 in 1900 to fifteen by the early thirties, and as a consequence the proportion of children in the population fell from a third to a quarter. Whereas in the late nineteenth century, 70 per cent of couples had produced at least four children, by the twenties, 70 per cent gave birth to less than four. More of these survived as the infant mortality rates dropped by a half, but even so parents were much less frequently faced with the task of feeding and clothing large numbers of offspring. Although the manual worker's family remained bigger than its middle-class counterpart, it shrank as rapidly. During the first three decades of the century, the average size of a completed working-class family in Britain fell from 3.94 to 2.49.[112] In 1930 Gilbert Slater observed in his *Poverty and the State* that 'the diminution in the number of children annually born is on the whole the most important of all the social changes now taking place'.[113] It was a less visible event than movements in pay and prices, and its consequences were registered more slowly. Bowley estimated in 1924 that demographic factors had contributed only half as much as real wages to the reduction of poverty.[114] However the effects were cumulative, and although the fall in the birth-rate came to an end in 1934, it was in the 1930s that the working-class community began to become accustomed to a more predictable and more affordable family structure.

The general improvement in the standard of living both endorsed and challenged official policy. It could be argued that the Coalition Government's refusal to maintain price controls or to honour its initial commitment to a minimum wage had been justified by events. Despite all the troubles of the post-war economy, the market, acting in conjunction with the free decisions of parents to limit their families, had made a substantial impact on the principal cause of poverty. As one measure of progress, children at the end of the inter-war period were on average three inches taller than their parents at the same age. Yet if the consumption of what the leading expert Boyd Orr termed 'protective foods' had risen by 50 per cent per head of population, a third of families were still subsisting on an inadequate diet in 1939.[115] The continuing incidence of deprivation, particularly amongst children, revealed by the surveys of the thirties, demonstrated how much of an opportunity had been lost by the state's reluctance to take more active steps to reduce unemployment or to cope with the remaining problems of low-wage families. Whilst welfare benefits and special services were sufficient to prevent the Depression reversing the overall decline in infant mortality,[116] they could not prevent increases in maternal mortality or in deaths amongst juveniles from illnesses such as rheumatic heart disease. If the aggregate figures for other forms of child welfare remained largely resistant to the short-term effects of the Depression, there was evidence of deterioration in the most afflicted localities.[117] Across the country, and particularly in the old centres of heavy industry, the loss of jobs put a brake on the growth in prosperity which was now within reach. In all families, and especially those with more than two children, the absence of either statutory basic pay outside the minority of occupations covered by the trade boards, or some form of child allowance, qualified the progress which was being made in levels of physical health, particularly amongst the rising generations.[118] It was in the 1930s that the basic performance indicators of family welfare in Britain began to fall behind the rest of Western Europe.[119]

For those who were victims of capitalism's inability to supply them with a job, or to pay them enough to maintain a family or keep them in their old age, there remained the possibilities of private endeavour in the neighbourhood economy. Public welfare was neither generous enough, nor sufficiently free of stigma, to render collective and individual self-help a luxury rather than a necessity. In the endless battle to stay on the right side of the thin line that separated deprivation from destitution, much still depended on the ingenuity and enterprise with which families could exploit the local resources for maximising their income and minimising their expenditure. Whereas the phenomena of mass unemployment, National Insurance and means tests made the inter-war period very much part of the modern world, the basic techniques for survival adopted by the poor still belonged largely to the nineteenth century. This was most obviously the case in respect of the informal structures of mutual assistance created by those most vulnerable to the shortcomings of the labour market.

May Hobbs was born into a part of East London where for generations those in trouble had learned to depend on each other:

> There were so many ways in which a community would stick together. Neighbours would lend things to take down to the pawn shop so that a family could get some dinner or some grub. Then, if a mum had to go into hospital or the nick, the kids would be looked after by someone or other, or someone would go in to help the old man look after them . . . If you were in hospital or the nick, there was always someone who could come and visit you. You also knew that if you were made homeless you would not have to go a night without having a roof over your head. Even if someone could only offer you their floor to sleep on, you would not be turned away.[120]

Such assistance was given out of sympathy and self-interest. When everyone in the street was exposed to the threat of bereavement, homelessness or trouble with authority, it was a matter of both instinct and prudence to respond to a call for help.[121] If a motherless child had to be taken in without notice, so might your own children need care in an emergency. Casual mutual aid was one of the more dependable resources in an uncertain world, 'a stalwart bulwark against adversity' as Edward Ezard recalled.[122] It was the larger disasters of life which called forth this generosity. When the young C.W. Whitely's father suddenly died in 1935, 'the neighbours, as usual, rallied round and helped the family to get back to normality as soon as possible'.[123]

Between the wars the changing pattern of poverty and state intervention enhanced both the strengths and the weaknesses of this form of resistance to the vagaries of the market. Although dispersal to outlying council estates was beginning to disrupt some urban communities, many others which had only begun to take form in the latter years of the nineteenth century were more tightly bound together than ever before by complex ties of kinship and association, and by lengthening shared experience of hardship and struggle.[124] The increasingly frequent visits of a host of officials bent on altering or disciplining the lives of the poor united the neighbourhood in a common rejection of all forms of outside intervention. The queues outside the Labour Exchanges and, finally and most powerfully, the inquisition of the Means Test, provided a focus of opposition to the new regime of regulation and inspection.

Much of this solidarity remained informal, but as the administration of relief became more bureaucratised, so the response to it became more organised. The principal reason why the National Unemployed

Workers Movement enjoyed so much more success in recruiting the dispossessed than the Communist Party with which it was increasingly associated, was that it was able to provide such practical and effective help for its members. It set up clubs for the unemployed and published cheap guides to the system which were revised with every new change in the regulations.[125] In the twopenny pamphlet *How to Get Unemployment Benefit,* produced in response to the Act of 1927, the authors 'endeavoured, as far as the Act itself will allow, to avoid the legal jargon that is so confusing to the ordinary mind, and to outline the principal features of the Act in a manner that will be understood by every unemployed worker'.[126] From 1930, the work of district committees was co-ordinated by the national Legal Department, which won for the NUWM the right to act as a trade union in representing claimants. During the first full year of the Means Test, the NUWM conducted nearly half the appeals to the National Insurance Umpire, with more than twice the success rate of the others.[127] The advocacy was difficult and time-consuming for the self-taught amateurs who had to become as proficient in the manipulation of forms and regulations as the officials with whom they argued, but it constituted the cornerstone of the NUWM's existence.[128] As the Communist Party frequently pointed out, it would not bring about the revolution, but there was enough scope in the appeal system, and sufficient discretion in the local administration, at least until the Act of 1934, to permit the patient assistance and argument, reinforced on occasions by more direct forms of protest, to make a measurable difference to the well-being of the section of the community the NUWM sought to protect.

The escalation in the complexity of the welfare system, and in the volume of unemployment, endowed the traditional neighbourhood defence systems with a new depth and sophistication. Yet if the investigating officer calling once a month on homes up and down the street epitomised the depth of mistrust and hostility which existed between the givers and receivers of public welfare, his work also exacerbated the long-standing tensions amongst those who depended so much on each other's generosity. As we have seen, the close physical proximity, the inescapable friction over access to shared facilities, the endless opportunities for conflict over the behaviour of over-stretched adults and under-controlled children, were as integral to the life of the neighbourhood as the equally common gestures of solidarity and support. 'There was one toilet and one washhouse in a yard shared between 4 houses', recalled one eye-witness. 'There were constant quarrels over this. Shouting, cursing, quarrelling, were a part of each day.'[129] Whilst disasters evoked compassion, and sudden good fortune general celebration, minor gains and losses could readily generate envy and resentment. Conversation on the doorstep as easily turned to censure as to praise. According to Peter Donnelly, 'There was meaness and pride of family, family troubles and joy in any small success of children or neighbour's children; there was jealousy that sometimes became an obsession.'[130] Those suspected of transgressing communal codes of domestic, sexual or economic morality had more to fear from their neighbours than from outside agencies of discipline. The man who wilfully failed to keep his family, the woman who began to use her body as well as her wits to keep herself, faced persistent verbal and sometimes physical abuse.[131]

The arrival of the Depression and the introduction of new controls over the distribution of relief both increased the pressure on personal relationships and offered a new opportunity of giving vent to jealousies and antagonism. The Means Test placed a monetary penalty on a whole range of domestic behaviour. Questions which had always formed the substance of rumour and gossip, such as who was sharing whose bed or table, who was living off whose money, who had an illicit source of income or a hidden cache of savings, who had bought what luxury or sold what necessity, now had a larger resonance. The greatest source of information on alleged transgressions of the new regulations was not the inspecting officers, whose public enquiries were generally met with silence, but private and frequently anonymous depositions from those who lived and worked alongside the claimant.[132] As Orwell discovered, 'there is much spying and tale-bearing'.[133] The Public Assistance Committees (PACs) were willing enough to believe what they were told, whether or not it was true, and the large numbers of unemployed whose applications were rejected in whole or in part, could never be certain whether it was their enemies or their friends who were responsible for their plight.

The collective defences of the neighbourhood were also threatened in ways which were superficially more benign. The establishment of mass unemployment as a permanent feature of the inter-war economy gave a new lease of life to the tradition of middle-class charity which had been running into crisis in the Edwardian period.[134] In real terms, the receipts of charities were roughly constant in the three decades following the Liberal welfare reforms, but the rapid growth of public welfare, which by the mid-thirties was worth about ten times the value of private benefaction, meant that the donations and legacies could be used in a more concentrated fashion.[135] The main focus of activity was the provision and management of hospitals and other medical services, but now that they no longer had to supply the jobless with all their income, the churches and other voluntary agencies were free to devote their time and resources to various ancillary endeavours, ranging from the provision of free meals, boots and second-hand clothing, to the organisation of recreational clubs for adults and holidays for their children. In Liverpool for instance, the amount of charitable income paid out as direct assistance to the poor actually fell between 1923 and 1933, whilst the proportion spent on forms of social activity doubled.[136] In 1932, as a token compensation for their refusal to tackle the causes of unemployment, the Government gave a small grant to the National Council of Social Services for co-ordinating existing initiatives and establishing a more extensive network of centres for those in need of reforming or retraining.[137]

It was an attempt to placate the still rising number of unemployed, partly by supplying small but significant material additions to means-tested benefits, partly by providing more wholesome social environments than the street corner and dole queue, and partly by re-establishing a gift relationship between those in society whose real income was rising in spite of the dislocation of the economy, and those whose sacrifices were necessary for its long-term stability. Rather than retreating into their neighbourhoods and its organisations, the victims of the Depression were to be encouraged to see themselves as dependent but valued members of a benevolent national community. For its part, the middle class could find a new role within the modern state. As Constance Braithwaite wrote:

> The excellence of the work of a democratic State depends largely upon the quality of its citizens. Individuals do not become intelligent and public-spirited citizens merely by keeping the law, paying rates and taxes, and recording their votes at elections. They require opportunities of insight into the lives of their fellows and into the practical work of group administration. This kind of insight is given by active participation in the work of voluntary associations and of public bodies alike: it is all an expression of voluntary citizenship.[138]

The impact of voluntary action upon unemployed citizens is difficult to judge. Certainly the poorer members of the labouring population made more widespread contact with middle-class giving than for many years. From the groups of destitute workers noisily singing hymns to passers-by[139] to the laid-off skilled labourer quietly accepting clothing for his children to maintain the appearance of respectability, charity invaded the traditional structures of self-help.[140] In the towns, the churches and other voluntary bodies felt that they were opening up roads into the working-class community which had long been closed to them and that they were providing genuine competition for politically motivated initiatives mounted by the NUWM or the ILP, or by Labour-controlled local authorities. The forms of need were mostly familiar, what was new was the occasional presence of official subsidy, and the appearance of theories of 'new philanthropy' which envisaged a coherent partnership with the state, in place of principled opposition.[141] Yet the old problems remained. Despite the efforts of the National Council for Social Services (NCSS), the help was still patchy, with givers competing for the bodies of beneficiaries in some places, and completely absent in others.[142] A few forms of charity, such as the widespread free boot schemes, became so commonplace as to evoke little reaction from the recipients,[143] others were bitterly resented, particularly where the free shoes and clothing were stamped to prevent pawning.[144] Those who in their employment had prided themselves on their independence could only feel degradation at the receipt of such charity;[145] to ask and to receive was a symbol of their exclusion rather than their membership of a civilised community.

Sympathetic councils in areas of high unemployment played some part in sponsoring relief projects, but their principal impact on the neighbourhood support networks was through the construction of new housing on the periphery of the older urban centres. The ambiguities of the traditional structures of mutual assistance, with the warmth and generosity generated by deprivation and defeat and compromised by jealousy and conflict, make the consequences of the municipal estates particularly hard to assess. On the one hand those who were moved out of the inner-city terraces suffered almost as great a sense of dislocation as the nineteenth-century emigrants to the New World. When John Blake left his street in Poplar for a two-bedroomed council house at Dagenham, 'it meant the breaking of all our ties, with both our families, and the neighbours of many years'.[146] Councils searching for cheap land were forced to build away from existing areas of employment and recreation, and were unable or unwilling to provide adequate social facilities in their new developments.[147] The early tenants of the low-density estates had no history of relationships with their new neighbours, and lacked the opportunity to build up the body of shared knowledge about each other's lives and circumstances which formed the basis of any informal exchange of services.[148] Blake's wife felt so isolated in her new house that soon the couple were back in Poplar.

At the same time to move from an over-crowded, damp, vermin-infested terrace into a soundly built semi-detached house fitted with gas, electricity and hot and cold running water, and equipped with an enclosed garden, was to travel in a day from one century to another. The lack of basic amenities in the slums had been both a consequence of poverty and a cause of a whole range of physical and psychological deprivation. 'If poverty did not mean wretched housing', Mrs Pember Reeves had observed, 'it would be shorn of half of its damages.'[149] As with so much else in this period, the transition accentuated the divisions between the winners and the losers in the struggle for a livelihood. Those who found that they could afford the higher rents on the estates and the greater travelling costs, were able to enjoy standards of comfort beyond the dreams of the generations who had formed the defensive communities in the inner-city slums. Those who were too poor to contemplate applying for a house, or who moved but then were driven back by the loss of a job, were more sharply aware than ever before of their deprivation. In the council housing, families were more than ever dependent on their own resources. If they ran into trouble, they could expect little help from other newcomers, and there were few corner shops to give credit, and still fewer pawnbrokers.[150] In a famous survey, M'Gonigle and Kirby found that the death rate was actually higher in some council estates than in the slums which had been left behind, owing to the impact of high rents on poor diets.[151] Except in the rare instances where tenants were allowed a say in the management of the estates, they could do little to create new forms of mutual resistance to the hardships of life.[152]

A family which decided to pull up its roots and move to a council house was taking a risk, but the resources of the neighbourhood it was leaving had never been sufficient to guarantee the minimum levels of material security which parents had always sought for themselves and their children. The principal responsibility for bridging the gap between the shortcomings of the labour market and the inadequacies of the welfare system still lay with the individual and collective endeavours of the family unit. Outside assistance would only be sought in an emergency. The day-to-day struggle for survival was conducted by every adult and child who was capable of exercising any influence over the pattern of domestic income and expenditure.

The first response of families threatened with destitution was to send out their members to find whatever means were available of earning some sort of a living. The deepening Depression brought to the surface the world of casual employment which Henry Mayhew had first depicted. It was as possible as it ever had been, and as difficult and dispiriting, to squeeze a few shillings or pence out of the demand for goods and services in the local economy. With luck and determination, money could be made cleaning windows, gardening, portering luggage, carrying sandwich-boards, delivering parcels, collecting and selling firewood, second-hand clothing or old furniture, taking bets for bookkeepers, if not opening a shop then running a stall or selling goods from door to door, canvassing for newspaper subscriptions, or acting as an agent for insurance companies or hire-purchase firms.[153] In areas hit by large-scale unemployment, signs of such endeavour were everywhere apparent. Jack Shaw recalled the scene outside the Labour Exchange: 'It were like something out of a play – a queue of blokes down each side of the road with trays and they'd got razor blades on and french letters, all kinds of things. Anything to make a bit of money.'[154] Women continued their time-honoured practices of taking in washing, mending or lodgers, making small items of food, drink or clothing for sale, or keeping their own homes by cleaning those of their more fortunate sisters.[155] Their children worked before, after, instead of and beyond school, delivering messages, groceries, parcels and newspapers, serving as assistants in shops, lathering chins for barbers, and supplying cheap, disposable labour to a whole range of small enterprises.[156]

The makeshift economy existed both in spite and because of the developments in manufacture and distribution, and in the provision of unemployment relief. The growth of larger units of production, of mass-advertising, and of chain stores, placed increasing obstacles in the way of the penny capitalists who had flourished before the war. But the transition was far from complete, and the losses were balanced by the greater purchasing power of those in work, and by the additional forms of employment introduced by the new marketing techniques. Prosperous middle-class families could still not acquire sufficient appliances to dispense altogether with the labour of lower-class women in their homes or their husbands in the gardens, although increasingly such work was temporary and non-residential. Street-selling had always been the last rung on the descent to destitution and the first step on the ladder towards prosperity, and if legislation such as the 1927 licensing of market stalls now curtailed older practices, the respectable poor were offered openings as canvassers which promised a small fortune to the successful and nothing to the failures.

The conditions for receiving the dole imposed a distinction between work and idleness which was alien to the established strategies for coping with the loss of a wage. The unemployed had to learn how to do nothing while they waited for a full-time job to become available. Their instinct was to put together a temporary livelihood from whatever means were available, combining relief, which never in the past had been adequate to keep a home, with whatever means of generating scraps of income they and the other members of the family could find. Increasingly such practices were seen not as the embodiment of the entrepreneurial spirit but as the essence of anti-social activity. Casual employment now attracted formal sanctions, but in spite of the army of inspectors and informers, the new regulations failed to bring to an end the informal economy. In East London, the army of street traders had actually grown since the late nineteenth century, as it recruited first amongst ex-servicemen and then the unemployed.[157] If the cautious were deterred, the enterprising merely became more wary. 'Like most men in the neighbourhood', recalled Thomas Callaghan of Newcastle, 'my father was unemployed; but he would not hang around street corners; and with eight of us to feed he could not afford to do so. Therefore from Monday to Friday, he went tatting, for rags and woollens, and lumber. Of course he had to be secretive about it, for if the labour exchange were to learn of his expeditions he would have his dole suspended.'[158] Eventually his father's efforts were exposed, and the small sums they were bringing in suddenly became the family's sole source of income.

For the unemployed, the Labour Exchange was hostile to part-time work and irrelevant to most full-time employment.[159] It was accepted that once a job was lost, the workless man's principal resource was his own feet. As Ifan Edwards wrote: 'It was no use going to the Exchange; nobody ever dreamed of getting a job through them, and in any case the only people to whom the little cards mutely called were specialist tradesmen. No, it was the same heart-breaking tramp all over again, round the works and building contractors until something should turn up.'[160] Instead of queueing for the occasional officially listed vacancy, the unemployed worker walked, from factory gate to factory gate, from foreman to foreman, back and forth across the town and beyond to outlying districts.[161] The tramping artisan was reborn, sometimes in the form of long-distance migrants moving south from the coalfields and the decaying centres of heavy industry, more often as patient, weary pedestrians, setting out for a day's journey to a series of barren destinations.

There were strong elements of continuity in the strategies of spending as well as getting money in this period. Although the standard of living of the working class as a whole rose between the wars, Hilton calculated in 1938 that a third of the population still possessed 'no part whatever in the ownership of the aggregate wealth of the nation'. Another third owned less than £100.[162] There is no evidence that the extension of state welfare undermined habits of thrift, but those able to put aside some of their marginal improvements in prosperity rarely managed to accumulate more than a few pounds in the Post Office savings accounts.[163] The four million families which constituted the true proletariat had no material reserves to draw upon when employment was lost, and indeed many were already in debt. County Court plaints for debt, which mostly involved small tradesmen suing working men for small sums, fell from a pre-war level of 1.2 million a year to half a million in 1921, but then rose throughout the twenties, and were never below a million in the thirties.[164]

All the long-established devices for coping with such an emergency still survived. 'The pawnshops was thriving', recalled a factory worker from Lancaster. 'Queues a mile long on a Monday morning pledging. Queues a mile long on a Friday evening redeeming them out again. A watch. Or a wedding ring. Just to buy food.'[165] The tallyman called from door to door, selling household items on instalment.[166] At best this was a means of spreading expenditure over time, an alternative to the widespread clothing clubs which supplied the goods only after a period of contributions.[167] At worst it was another means of raising cash, as the newly acquired blankets were taken straight down to the pawnbrokers.

Money could also be had more directly. 'Every street had its resident money-lender', remembered a Southampton docker's daughter. In her case, as so often, it was a woman, who charged 'outrageous rates of interest' and took as collateral wedding rings, boots, suits, and occasionally – and illegally – pension books.[168] Then there were debts to the landlord, the corner-shop and the doctor.[169] The poorer the household, the more sophisticated the financial wheeling and dealing. Each day required new plans and calculations, and if destitution was postponed so was long-term recovery, as in the family economy of the miner's son George Hitchin: 'Everything except food was bought on the instalment plan, and on pay-day a stream of tallymen, club agents, money-lenders and insurance men passed through the house, and if they were lucky – for not all got paid – swept away money that might have been spent on food.'[170]

An essential consequence of the growth of mass unemployment was that families who had long based their self-respect on their avoidance of all forms of credit, were eventually forced to adopt some temporary expedient. Much was lost if the wife joined those in the neighbourhood who made surreptitious use of the pawnbroker, paying an old woman to transact the business, or slipping to the side entrance after dark, and everything was gone if the goods were taken and collected in full view.[171] 'You knew everyone was in the same boat', recalled a Liverpool housewife, 'but it didn't make no difference, and it meant that they knew your business.'[172] However, amidst the individual disasters, it is possible to detect some overall movements in the pattern of credit and debt, brought about by both the success of the economy, and the relief now paid in response to its failings. In general, the business of raising and repaying money became less local and personal. The unreliability of the dole, especially after the introduction of the Means Test, meant that sudden crises still occurred, and the longer the period of unemployment, the more likely the recourse to borrowing, but on the whole, the wider availability of welfare made recourse to moneylenders less common. Pawnbrokers were still heavily used in poorer areas, but their numbers fell by almost a half between the wars.[173]

The use of credit was transformed by the development of new devices for obtaining the increasing range of mass-produced consumer goods. Neighbourhood tallymen and shopkeepers lacked the capital to carry debts on the larger sales, which were instead underwritten by finance houses through the system of hire purchase. There was a twenty-fold growth in this business between the wars, and by the end of the period, 50 per cent of furniture, 60 per cent of gramophones, 70 per cent of radios, 85 per cent of sewing machines and 90 per cent of bicycles were being paid for in weekly instalments.[174] Until the industry was brought under statutory control in 1938, its operations were subject to widespread abuse. Families were pressured into agreements without full knowledge of the conditions, and left cruelly exposed to the consequences of sudden reverses in their prosperity. Cases abounded of court-enforced repossessions of goods upon which newly unemployed purchasers had made all but a handful of the total payments.[175] It was small comfort to them that the canvassers who had led them into such trouble were themselves frequently the victims of the Depression, desperately trying to maintain their respectability on the rarely-fulfilled promise of commissions. The new race of canvassers and collectors jostled on the doorstep with the agents for the industrial insurance companies, which were able to exploit the continuing absence of death benefits in the state welfare system.

The interaction between rising expectations, uneven welfare provision and traditional defence mechanisms is best exemplified in the field of health. Compulsory insurance for most working men, together with maternity benefits and free clinics for mothers and babies, resulted in much greater access to much better medical care than had been possible in Edwardian England. At the same time the failure of the insurance system to cover dependants outside the period of childbirth, meant that illness was still a major cause of debt. It took very few home visits from the doctor, 'impressive in shining top hat and morning coat' as Edward Ezard recalled, and charging at least two shillings, or one shilling for a surgery consultation, to capsize a family economy.[176] And whilst more remedies were available, patients lost all control over their treatment through the disappearance of the Friendly Society doctors.[177] Instead poorer families turned back to their own devices, either through purchasing the still widely advertised cure-all patent medicines, or seeking the advice of older members of the community about traditional cures. 'As every street had its resident money lender', recalled Rose Gamble, 'so it had also a wise-woman, who was severally midwife, general practitioner without qualifications, and layer-out of the dead. (You only went to the doctor if you were dying.)'[178]

Within the family, it was the wife who made the least use of the doctor. Once she had given birth, the state had no further concern for her health. Years of feeding herself last and least weakened her ability to cope with bearing children; in the 1930s it was estimated that one pregnant woman in ten was disabled by the experience of childbirth.[179] As the children grew up, their mother's mounting health problems had a low priority in the allocation of the domestic budget.[180]

Despite the pressures on resident elder children and grandparents caused by the Means Test, the most striking feature of the family in the slump was not its collapse, but the resilience of both its structure and the pattern of roles and relationships within it.[181] Illegitimate births remained low, and after the wedding, the new wife assumed her traditional position as the key strategist in the struggle against destitution.[182] Her skills at mending and making do, her vigilance against all waste, and her knowledge of where and when in the neighbourhood bargains in food and clothing were to be had were crucial to the survival of the family. As in her mother's generation, the essence of her task was constantly deciding what basic requirement had to be sacrificed for the attainment of another. 'Families whose budgets cannot be made to show an unexpended balance after purchase of "necessities"', wrote M'Gonigle and Kirby, 'can only pay more for one "necessity" or group of "necessities" by decreeing the amounts spent on other essentials.'[183] As before, the smaller the income, the more effort was made in spending it, with the traditional devices of frequent penny purchases, and expeditions to markets and butchers as they cleared their stocks on Saturday evenings still widely practised.[184] The poorer housewife shopped by the day, the poorest by the hour.[185] Unless she was one of the minority to move to a council estate, the tactics employed to put food on the table, and the labour involved in keeping rooms clean, dry, warm and vermin-free were little changed.

The loss of the head of the household's wage dramatically increased the burden of managing the domestic economy, without the compensation of extra help around the house. Unemployed husbands often saw more of their children, but only rarely more of the stove or the washtub. As before the members of the family were united in the interdependence of their struggle, and divided by their separate responsibilities. They were brought together by occasional times of relative prosperity, and set against each other by prolonged deprivation. 'If we had a full week's work we were in clover', remembered a miner's son. 'The atmosphere of the home was brought to life. It oozed out of the whole household that he'd come home with a good packet. We were able to buy things. You could sense my parents were happy. There wasn't the friction.'[186]

It remained possible to relieve the tensions of an over-crowded, over-stretched family through some form of recreation, and here it could be said that market forces had their most direct and most benign impact. Rowntree claimed that in the period between his first two York surveys, commercialised leisure, together with some forms of public provision such as libraries and swimming pools, 'have had a profound effect on the lives of the workers and on all those with limited means, far more profound than on the wealthier classes who have never lacked means of recreation'.[187] The classic example of this development was the cinema. Between the wars, a combination of large business investment and local enterprise successfully responded to an immense increase in demand for first the silent and then the talking movies. By the 1930s, up to four-fifths of urban populations were regularly patronising adapted or specially designed buildings which catered for a wide range of taste and incomes.[188] Rich and poor found escape in front of the screens, and for the mothers of hard-pressed families the ticket purchased the only opportunity for total relaxation they could ever find. With their children cowed into some degree of silence by the commissionaire, the dark of the cinema represented not so much an alternative to as the one secure refuge from the real world outside. As M.L. Eyles observed, 'The women certainly go to the picture palace to "lose themselves" for an hour; if only they lose themselves in dozing it rests their nerves; if they are sufficiently interested to keep awake, the new train of thought roused by the picture rests their minds, or rather wakens them.'[189]

Yet although the films, and other innovations such as football pools which became a mass industry in the second half of the period, reached deep into the working-class community, the overall impact of commercialised leisure was more limited and divisive than at first appears. Even the cinema, where the flea pits could charge as little as a penny or a halfpenny to the children who crowded into the Saturday matinées, represented a luxury for those on the dole. With standard prices ranging from 3d to 9d, a family outing could only take place at the expense of foregone necessities. As the *New Survey of London Life* discovered, 'A large number of working-class families, when the chief breadwinner is at work, attend the local cinema about once a week. When the head of the family falls out of work these visits become less frequent.'[190]

Elsewhere, the loss of employment meant increasing exclusion from forms of leisure which made a profit out of their customers. In particular, men with no other wealth but the dole could not afford to visit the local pub as freely and as often as once was possible.[191] There was simply not enough cash in their pockets to keep up with the consumption of those still in work, and it was humiliating to be seen to be drinking more slowly or to be waiting on the generosity of others. This is not to say that the unemployed were to a man teetotal, and there were still cases of husbands who drove their families to destruction by their inability to give up alcohol, but in general the more the family's income came from the state, the less of it was spent over the bar. Convictions for drunkenness halved between 1928 and 1932, and then began to rise slowly as unemployment fell.[192] The one physical indulgence which survived when nothing else could be afforded was smoking, which doubled between the wars. This was a private pleasure, and with Woodbines five for twopence, a cheap one. Men who would not receive free pints or stoop to drinking dregs in glasses, would accept the gift of a cigarette, or drag a little more out of one half-smoked.[193]

Poverty meant at least a partial withdrawal from traditional forms of commercial recreation, and prevented participation in many of the new forms of consumption of the period. If the cinema might be within reach, access to the other developments in mass communication was much more difficult. 'There was no wireless', recalled the son of an unemployed iron moulder. 'If you had a wireless you was a millionaire.'[194] It was sometimes possible for an enterprising worker to use his enforced leisure to construct a primitive receiver out of scrap materials,[195] but no amount of ingenuity could supply the family with the other domestic status symbol of the era, the gramophone. A household which had acquired a machine on hire purchase whilst its head was still in work could keep playing the increasingly worn records until the means test inspector called, when such compensations for going on the dole could become the cause of losing it altogether. The same was true of a piano, again an affordable luxury for the fortunate working-class family, and an illegitimate indulgence for the unemployed. Older hobbies, such as pigeon-fancying, which required regular expenditure, were now more difficult, as were newer ones such as photography. Those forced out of the labour market were also unable to share in the belated appearance of paid holidays for manual workers, which grew from 1.5 million in 1931 to 11 million in 1939. Whilst their children might be given an occasional outing by a local charity, they were not likely to feature amongst the 20 million who were able to take annual breaks away from home on the eve of the Second World War.

Instead, the victims of the Depression turned to older and cheaper means of keeping their spirits up. If the scale and duration of mass unemployment was without precedent, the problem of finding amusement when the family had more time and less money than usual was familiar enough. Children would see no more new toys until their father went back to work, but that did not prevent vigorous participation in the complex calendar of street games.[196] Older boys and younger men played team sports on waste ground, and in some of the worst-hit towns, the unemployed formed their own football leagues. Those who preferred quieter pleasures could still go fishing, or tend their gardens. One of the more effective initiatives of the NCSS was to encourage the provision of allotments. Here, as with the channelling of redundant manual skills into hobbies such as carpentry, it was possible to use leisure activities to enhance rather than undermine the family economy. When all else failed, the poor still had use of their feet, particularly as boots were generally available from local charities. 'There was no way of entertainment if you hadn't got any money', recalled one of the Ashton-under-Lyme unemployed. 'It was a matter of going for a walk. We used to go for a walk on moors. Or go visiting relatives. You used to see bags of people, whole families, all walking along. They'd think nothing of walking three or four or five miles to the next town. Seeing Auntie. It was just a matter of passing the day on.'[197]

Men without work were rarely bored. 'My impression from reading the diaries of the unemployed', concluded F.W. Bakke, 'is that they were not idling their time away. Their time is fully occupied, for the most part at useful tasks.'[198] If observers were concerned about the numbers of people merely standing in the streets talking to each other, this was because they had never before realised that conversation was a pleasure, and given cramped housing conditions, it was more likely to take place outside than inside. Rather than transforming the function of recreation, the combination of commercial development and economic dislocation accentuated long-standing strengths and weaknesses. It exposed the natural resilience and enterprise of the labouring poor, and their willingness to make their own pleasure if they could not buy it. It encouraged reliance on collective self-help, as in the clubs run by the NUWM,[199] or on public provision, particularly libraries which were more widely used than ever before.[200] It reinforced the preference for kinds of expenditure, such as betting or the pools, which combined recreation with a form of saving.[201]

At the same time the developments of the period widened the gap between the haves and the have-nots in the working-class community, as they also accentuated the divisions by age and by gender within the family. It was the young rather than the old who went to the cinema, and who were more ready to exploit the other innovations. Those whose schooling had been completed well before 1914 were often unable to enjoy the greater opportunities for reading.[202] And as the wives and mothers fed themselves last when food was short,[203] so they were the least likely to permit themselves the indulgence of a cheap luxury, and would have the most difficulty participating in the various forms of organised social activity. Dozing in the cinema on an occasional afternoon scarcely represented a revolution in their consumption of leisure.

DEMORALISATION

Whether out of alarm or compassion, observers of the Depression were much concerned with the state of mind of its victims. There was a constant apprehension that either the poor would do irreversible damage to the established order, or that the experience of poverty would cause permanent harm to the morale of the workforce and their families.[204] The Pilgrim Trust's study of the 'psychoneurosis' of the unemployed man concluded that after a brief sense of release, 'gradually anxiety and depression set in with a loss of mental equilibrium; finally after several years, adaptation takes place to a new and debased level of life, lacking hope as well as fear of the future.'[205] From a longer perspective of time, however, the most remarkable feature of the period is not the erosion but the survival of the mental equilibrium of those most vulnerable to the failings of the economy. Despite the tragedies highlighted by the NUWM, the suicide rate rose only slightly during the Depression, despite a sharp rise in juvenile offences and the widespread verbal and physical abuse surrounding the development and administration of the welfare system, there was no consistent correlation between crime and unemployment,[206] and despite the constant pressure on domestic relations caused by the struggle to make ends meet and the imposition of the Means Test, family life survived, and with it much of the traditional culture of working-class communities.

Some of the credit for this achievement has to be attributed to the decisions taken by or imposed upon the Coalition Government in the critical early years of peace. The extension of non-pauperising relief to the great majority of the unemployed and their dependants was an important element in the process of containing the damage caused by prolonged large-scale unemployment. Furthermore the faith vested in the market economy to make an impact on the central problem of low wages bore fruit in the rise in real income enjoyed by those of the working class who kept their jobs during this period. However, the benefits were not generous or dependable enough to guarantee the maintenance of a minimum standard of living, particularly where the family economy contained a number of non-contributory members, and the rise in real wages was not sufficient to redraw Rowntree's original graph of the poverty cycle, despite the fall in the size of families. As had always been the case, the poor looked to their own devices to provide them with a last line of defence.

One of the major problems in coming to terms with the history of poverty between the wars is that the drama of mass unemployment obscures the essential elements of continuity in both the incidence of poverty and in the devices adopted by the poor to cope with their difficulties. In many areas of the economy, long-term permanent employment was more of an innovation in the period than its long-term absence. For much of the workforce for most of the nineteenth and early twentieth centuries, a full week's pay for a full week's labour was a hope rather than an expectation. Skilled and unskilled alike were long accustomed to substantial variations in the prosperity of their family economies and had developed strategies of varying complexity and efficacy for keeping going. When the blow fell, the natural tendency was to turn back to older techniques of piecing together a living. As commentators frequently noted, it was the communities where per-

sonal disasters were a commonplace, and the families where deprivation was a constant threat, which could most effectively summon the
necessary reserves of ingenuity and resilience.

At the centre of the newly invented concept of demoralisation, was
the apprehension that the long-term jobless would lose their work
ethic. In practice, as Max Cohen discovered, the difficulty when an
extended spell of unemployment came to an end was re-learning how
to spend rather than earn money.[207] Yet if commentators attached the
wrong label to the wrong problem, there was a sense in which the
developments of the period were presenting particular difficulties to
those unable to afford what were now seen as basic necessities. The
progress and dislocation of the economy, the extension and restriction
of the welfare system and the advance and accommodation of organised labour,[208] together had the effect of making the position of
the poor more marginal than it ever had been. Whereas the almost
simultaneous granting of rights to the vote and to non-discriminatory
relief offered the dispossessed the clothing of full citizenship, in the
event, they were less rather than more able to participate effectively in
the life of the national community.

Partly as a policy of successive governments, and partly as a consequence of shortfalls in the provision of assistance, market forces were a
powerful factor in shaping the relationship of the poor to the rest of
society. The profoundly unequal distribution of both the rewards of
the economy's success, and the penalties of its failure had the effect of
widening the distance between the winners and the losers. New forms
of conspicuous consumption within the working class exposed the
condition of those with nothing to spend on possessions or leisure
activities once they had bought the week's food and paid off the
week's most pressing debts. Between the wars the proportion of the
population with assets of less than £100 fell from seven-eighths to
six-eighths,[209] but the principal beneficiary of this change was the salaried middle class, whose jobs were more secure, whose income was
rising faster, and who were for the first time able to buy their own
homes and fill them with labour-saving devices. Basic inequalities in
areas such as infant mortality and child development were only marginally reduced by the overall improvement in standards.[210] The unbalanced regional and sector growth, and the extreme variations in the
incidence of unemployment divided rather than united the country in
its struggle against the problems of world trade. Within the communities hit by recession, the decay of some older forms of collective
self-help, and the displacement of some local means of raising and
spending money, meant that families were more likely than before to

find themselves operating as separate units in an impersonal market place.

The endless sequence of reform and revision, of debate and inquiry, of *ad hoc* innovations and emergency cuts which characterised welfare legislation in this period were a reflection of the absence of strategic planning on the part of the state, and the intensity of the economic problems which it had to face. Yet there was a clear momentum amidst the confusion. Where possible, the old, the unemployed and the sick were to be relieved of the stark choice between the work-house and destitution, but where feasible forced to contribute to their own assistance and deprived of any control over its disbursement. The young and the dependent were to be given every sort of advice, but were to be deprived of the material assistance which would make such advice either effective or unnecessary. The principles embodied in the Victorian Poor Law, that the propertied should support the property-less, and that the locality should have a direct influence over the scales and administration of relief, became untenable once the extension of the local and national franchise, and the abolition of pauper disqualifi-cation, put real power in the hands of the poor. Instead work began on the construction of a new system based on the principles that redis-tribution should take place horizontally within the working class, and that relief should be administered by central government, with only token parliamentary supervision. The terms of exclusion of the poor from society were redefined to meet the conventions of the modern state. In place of disenfranchisement and the workhouse, there was the Means Test and the inspecting officer policing the management of the family economy. In theory, the bureaucratisation of welfare promoted access and justice, in practice it engendered alienation and fear. Only the old made real gains in dignity and self-respect, but even here the inadequacy of their pensions pushed them back towards the labour market, or towards older forms of dependency on their children or the Poor Law.

The failure of the poor to make greater use of the nominal power they gained in 1918 was a consequence as much of their anger as their resignation. Such progress as they made in exploiting the new possi-bilities of democratic practice encouraged organised labour to keep its distance and permitted the state to set its own limits to the develop-ment of the welfare system and to the arguments about its shortcom-ings. Voters only became active citizens when they could develop structures through which to give effect to their wishes. Whilst the NUWM and a number of local councils represented a more direct expression of the interests of the dispossessed than had been seen since

Chartism and a more substantial threat to the authority of Parliament than was ever to be mounted again, they could not find a means of enforcing their demands on the national Labour Party or on the bulk of the trade union movement, and thus were unable to prevent a successful counter-attack by the state against such forms of participatory democracy. The central problem was not that the Depression demoralised the poor, but that their resentment demoralised those organisations capable of translating their grievances into a full-scale challenge to the assumptions upon which the inter-war economy was run.

REFERENCES

1.   'Manifesto of Mr Lloyd George and Mr Bonar Law', reprinted in F.W.S. Craig, *British General Election Manifestos 1918–1966* (Chichester 1970), p. 3.

2.   K.O. Morgan, *Consensus and Disunity* (Oxford, 1979), pp. 23–4; R. Lowe, 'The Erosion of State Intervention in Britain, 1917–24', *Economic History Review*, XXXI (May 1978), p. 270.

3.   M.J. Daunton (ed.), *Councillors and Tenants: Local Authority Housing in English Cities, 1919–1939* (Leicester, 1984), pp. 8–10; J. Melling, Introduction, in J. Melling (ed.), *Housing, Social Policy and the State* (London, 1980), p. 23; M. Bowley, *Housing and the State* (London, 1945), pp. 15–23.

4.   M. Swenarton, *Homes Fit For Heroes* (London, 1981), pp. 189–93.

5.   A. Deacon, *In Search of the Scrounger* (London, 1976), p. 15; B.B. Gilbert, *British Social Policy 1914–1939* (London, 1970), pp. 25–32.

6.   T. Wilson, *The Myriad Faces of War* (Cambridge, 1986), pp. 162, 175, 405–6.

7.   J.J. Astor et al., *The Third Winter of Unemployment* (London, 1923), pp. 8–9; G.N. Barnes, *From Workshop to War Cabinet* (London, 1923), pp. 141–6; A. Deacon, 'Labour and the Unemployed: The Administration of Insurance in the Twenties', *Bulletin of the Society for the Study of Labour History*, **31** (1975), p. 10; J. MacNicol, *The Movement for Family Allowances 1918–45* (London, 1980), p. 106.

8.   Lowe, 'Erosion of State Intervention', p. 270.

9.   For a full discussion of the costs of the scheme, see Bowley, *Housing and the State*, pp. 26–35.

10.   P. Abrams, 'The Failure of Social Reform 1918–20', *Past and Present*, **24** (1963), p. 44.

11.   N. Whiteside, 'Welfare Legislation and the Unions during the First World War', *Historical Journal*, **23, 4** (1980), pp. 873–4.

12.　Morgan, *Consensus and Disunity*, pp. 92–3.

13.　See especially J. Halstead, R. Harrison and J. Stevenson, 'The Reminiscences of Sid Elias', *Bulletin of the Society for the Study of Labour History*, **38** (Spring, 1979); W. Hannington, *Never on Our Knees* (London, 1967); W. Hannington, *Ten Lean Years* (London, 1940); W. Paynter, *My Generation* (London, 1972); H. Goldthorpe, *Room at the Bottom* (London, 1959).

14.　R. Croucher, *We Refuse to Starve in Silence* (London, 1987), pp. 28–48. Until 1929, the full title of the organisation was the National Unemployed Workers Committee Movement.

15.　R. Hayburn, 'The Police and the Hunger Marchers', *International Review of Social History*, XVII, pt 3 (1972), p. 627.

16.　J. Morgan, *Conflict and Order* (Oxford, 1987), pp. 229–75.

17.　J. Stevenson, 'The Making of Unemployment Policy 1931–1935', in M. Bentley and J. Stevenson (eds), *High and Low Politics in Modern Britain* (Oxford, 1983), pp. 201–2.

18.　W. Greenwood, *There was a Time* (London, 1967), pp. 217–22; M. Cohen, *I Was One of the Unemployed* (London, 1945), pp. 3, 11, 24–7; E. W. Bakke, *The Unemployed Man*, pp. 61, 84; P. O'Mara, *The Autobiography of a Liverpool Irish Slummy* (Bath, 1968), p. 232; J. Stevenson, 'The Politics of Violence' in G. Peele and C. Cook (eds), *The Politics of Reappraisal 1918–1939* (London, 1975), p. 146.

19.　Hannington, *Never On Our Knees*, p. 103.

20.　N. Gray, *The Worst of Times* (London, 1985), p. 83. Also p. 184.

21.　Paynter, *My Generation*, p. 88.

22.　Morgan, *Conflict and Order*, p. 245.

23.　Hannington, *Ten Lean Years*, p. 36.

24.　G.D.H. Cole, *The Simple Case for Socialism* (London, 1935), p. 185.

25.　Cole, *Simple Case for Socialism*, p. 185. See also T. Callaghan, *A Lang Way to the Pa'nshop* (Newcastle on Tyne, 1979), p. 67; H.L. Beales and R.S. Lambert, (ed.), *Memoirs of the Unemployed* (London, 1934), pp. 69, 76, 87, 151, 177; M. Hobbs, *Born to Struggle* (London, 1973), p. 7.

26.　Stevenson, 'The Politics of Violence', p. 155.

27.　Croucher, *We Refuse to Starve*, especially pp. 202–4.

28.　'Reminiscences of Sid Elias', pp. 38–40.

29.　Hannington, *Never On Our Knees*, p. 246.

30.　K. Middlemas, *Politics in Industrial Society* (London, 1979), pp. 231–4.

31.　Croucher, *We Refuse to Starve*, pp. 23, 54.

32.　A. Deacon and E. Briggs, 'Local Democracy and Central Policy: The Issue of Pauper Votes in the 1920s', *Policy and Politics*, **2**, no. 4 (June, 1974), p. 347.

33.　G. Lansbury, *My Life* (London, 1928), pp. 155–61; N. Branson, *Poplarism, 1919–1925* (London, 1979), pp. 60–101.

34.　B. Keith-Lucas and P.G. Richards, *A History of Local Government in the Twentieth Century* (London, 1978), pp. 71–2.

35.　B. Donoghue and G.W. Jones, *Herbert Morrison. Portrait of a Politician* (London, 1973), p. 47; H. Morrison, *Herbert Morrison. An Autobiography*

(London, 1960), pp. 86–9.

36. Branson, *Poplarism*, pp. 54–7; 161.

37. It was estimated that about a quarter of Poor Law claimants at this time had fought in the First World War. For an account of the attempts to reintroduce disqualification, see Deacon and Briggs, 'Local Democracy and Central Policy', pp. 353–8.

38. Keith-Lucas and Richards, *History of Local Government*, pp. 84–91.

39. Stevenson, 'Making of Unemployment Policy', p. 206.

40. Hayburn, 'Police and the Hunger Marchers', pp. 627–32.

41. Hannington, *Never on Our Knees*, pp. 142–3, 146–7.

42. 'Reminiscences of Sid Elias', p. 45; Croucher, *We Refuse to Starve*, pp. 203–21.

43. Morgan, *Conflict and Order*, pp. 238–21.

44. S. MacIntyre, 'British Labour, Marxism and Working Class Apathy in the Nineteen Twenties', *Historical Journal*, XX, 2 (1977), pp. 481–96; Middlemas, *Politics in Industrial Society*, pp. 16–20.

45. E.F. Rathbone, *The Disinherited Family* (London, 1924), p. 37.

46. MacNicol, *Movement for Family Allowances*, pp. 119–50; J. Lewis, 'Eleanor Rathbone' in P. Barker (ed.), *Founders of the Welfare State* (London, 1984), p. 86; A. Marwick, 'The Labour Party and the Welfare State in Britain 1900–1948', *American Historical Review* (Dec. 1967), p. 393.

47. M. Cowling, *The Impact of Labour* (Cambridge, 1971), p. 378.

48. R.W. Lyman, *The First Labour Government 1924* (London, 1957), pp. 131–56.

49. Bowley, *Housing and the State*, pp. 40–3.

50. Gilbert, *British Social Policy*, pp. 95–7.

51. *The Times*, 24 August 1931. On the crisis, see R. Skidelski, *Politicians and the Slump* (London, 1967), pp. 334–83.

52. For Dalton's conception of planning, see H. Dalton, *Practical Socialism for Britain* (London, 1935), pp. 309–15. Also B. Pimlott, *Hugh Dalton* (London, 1985), p. 108.

53. Pimlott, *Dalton*, pp. 41–56.

54. MacNicol, *Movement for Family Allowances*, pp. 103–8; J. Harris, *William Beveridge* (Oxford, 1977), p. 252.

55. Deacon, 'Labour and the Unemployed', p. 10.

56. F.M. Miller, 'The Unemployment Policy of the National Government, 1931–1936', *Historical Journal*, XIX (1976), pp. 453–76; Stevenson, 'Making of Unemployment Policy', pp. 199–200.

57. J. Hilton, *Rich Man, Poor Man* (London, 1938), p. 40.

58. A.T. Peacock and J.V. Wiseman, *The Growth of Public Expenditure in the United Kingdom* (London, 1967), pp. 183–91.

59. B.S. Rowntree, *Poverty and Progress* (London, 1941), pp. 454–5.

60. A.D.K. Owen, *A Survey of the Standard of Living in Sheffield* (Sheffield, 1933), p. 42.

61. For comparative figures, see P. Flora, *State, Economy and Society in Western Europe 1815–1975* (London, 1983), vol. l, pp. 356, 360, 365, 372, 380, 387, 395, 402, 410, 417, 433, 442.

62. MacNicol, *Movement for Family Allowances*, pp. 92–3.
63. The surveys are tabulated in P. Townsend, 'Poverty, Ten Years After Beveridge', *Planning*, XIX, no. 344 (Aug 1952), p. 24.
64. Owen, *Standard of Living in Sheffield*, pp. 24, 43.
65. Rowntree, *Poverty and Progress*, p. 456.
66. For a vivid account of the virtual impossibility of subsisting on such an income, see I. Edwards, *No Gold on My Shovel* (London, 1947), p. 172.
67. Rowntree, *Poverty and Progress*, pp. 455–6.
68. A.L. Bowley and M. Hogg, *Has Poverty Diminished?* (London, 1925), p. 15; D. Caradog Jones, *The Social Survey of Merseyside* (Liverpool, 1934), vol. iii, p. 262.
69. Save the Children Fund, *Unemployment and the Child* (London, 1933), p. 77; The Pilgrim Trust, *Men Without Work* (Cambridge, 1938), pp. 105–9.
70. H. Llewellyn Smith, *New Survey of London Life and Labour Vol. iii* (London, 1932), p. 157.
71. J. Hurt, 'Feeding the Hungry Schoolchild in the First Half of the Twentieth Century' in D.J. Oddy and D.S. Miller (eds), *Diet and Health in Modern Britain* (London, 1985), p. 193; C. Webster, 'Health and Unemployment during the Depression', *Past and Present*, **109** (1985), p. 214; F. Le G. Clark, *Social History of the School Meals Service* (London, 1948), p. 13.
72. K. Nicholas, *The Social Effects of Unemployment in Teeside* (Manchester, 1986), p. 78; Webster, 'Health and Unemployment', p. 221; M. Brown, *Stop This Starvation of Mother and Child* (London, c.1935), p. 11.
73. H. Tout, *The Standard of Living in Bristol* (Bristol 1938), p. 37; B.S. Rowntree, *Poverty and Progress* (London, 1941), p. 459.
74. G.C.M. M'Gonigle and J. Kirby, *Poverty and Public Health* (London, 1936), pp. 66–70.
75. Vincent, *Literacy and Popular Culture*, pp. 17–18.
76. E.W. Bakke, *The Unemployed Man. A Social Study* (London, 1933), pp. 76–9; M. Cohen, *I Was One of the Unemployed* (London, 1945), pp. 99–100; W. Hannington and E. Llewelyn, *How to Get Unemployment Benefit* (London, c.1928), pp. 1–8; S. Elias, *A Practical Guide to the Unemployment Acts* (London, c.1932), pp. 1–14.
77. The Guardians were still very active in the 1920s. For an account of their capricious and insensitive treatment of paupers see R. Gamble, *Chelsea Child* (London, 1979), p. 47; B.L. Coombes, *These Poor Hands* (London, 1939), p. 142; K. Dayus, *Her People* (London, 1982), p. 192.
78. If they lost their hearing, they could then appeal to the Insurance Umpire. For an account of an ultimately successful appeal see Paynter, *My Generation*, p. 82.
79. Webster, 'Health and Unemployment', pp. 208–9.
80. Philips and Whiteside, *Casual Labour*, p. 185; A. Deacon, *In Search of the Scrounger* (London, 1976), pp. 21–4.
81. For a lively account of a form-based non-communication between claimant and investigating officer see Mass-Observation's 'Joe Wilson,

Aggravation at the Labour Exchange, 2 April 1937', in A. Calder and D. Sheridan (eds), *Speak for Yourself* (London, 1984), pp. 23–8.

82. Hannington and Llewelyn, *Unemployment Benefit*, p. 8.
83. Cohen, *One of the Unemployed* p. 9; Gray, *Worst of Times*, p. 153; R. Hoggart, *The Uses of Literacy* (London, 1958), p. 74; F. Greene (ed.), *Time to Spare, What unemployment means. By eleven unemployed* (London, 1935), p. 71; Bakke, *Unemployed Man*, pp. 79–80; R.I. McKibbin, 'The "Social Psychology" of Unemployment in Interwar Britain', in P.J. Waller (ed.), *Politics and Social Change in Modern Britain* (Brighton, 1987), pp. 177–8.
84. Goldthorpe, *Room at the Bottom*, p. 7.
85. R.W. Harris, *National Health Insurance in Great Britain 1911–1946* (London, 1946), p. 87.
86. J. Lewis, 'The Working-Class Wife and Mother and State Intervention 1870–1918' in J. Lewis (ed.), *Labour and Love* (Oxford, 1986), pp. 104–5.
87. G. Orwell, *The Road to Wigan Pier* (Penguin edn, London, 1989), p. 67.
88. Mrs C. Chesterton, *I Lived in a Slum* (London, 1937), pp. 64, 245–6; Daunton, *Councillors and Tenants*, p. 25.
89. For an account of their labours, and the strategies adopted to deceive them, see Ayers, *Liverpool Dockland*, p. 11.
90. J. White, *The Worst Street in North London* (London, 1986), p. 159.
91. Chesterton, *I Lived in a Slum*, p. 48.
92. Beales and Lambert, *Memoirs of the Unemployed*, pp. 105, 144; W. Greenwood, *How the Other Man Lives* (London, 1939), pp. 144–51.
93. A.F. Brockway, *Hungry England* (London, 1932), p. 106.
94. Beales and Lambert, *Memoirs of the Unemployed*, p. 68.
95. Goldthorpe, *Room at the Bottom*, p. 11; Hannington, *Ten Lean Years*, p. 46; Gray, *Worst of Times*, p. 36; Greene, *Time to Spare*, p. 44.
96. Hannington, *Ten Lean Years*, p. 41; Brockway, *Hungry England*, pp. 92, 115, 223.
97. Hannington, *Ten Lean Years*, p. 48; Elias, *Practical Guide*, pp. 14–16.
98. Hannington, *Ten Lean Years*, p. 38.
99. Brockway, *Hungry England*, p. 29.
100. M.A. Crowther, *Social Policy in Britain 1914–1939* (London, 1988), p. 17.
101. J.M. Keynes, *The Collected Writings of John Maynard Keynes* (London, 1981), Vol. xx, p. 474.
102. Bowley and Hogg, *Has Poverty Diminished?* pp. 16–17.
103. *Ibid.*, p. 3.
104. A.L. Bowley, *Prices and Wages in the United Kingdom, 1914–1920* (Oxford, 1921), pp. 105–10.
105. N. Dearle, *The Cost of Living* (London, 1926), pp. 118–9.
106. Wilson, *Myriad Faces of War*, pp. 150, 763–7; J.M. Winter, 'The Impact of the First World War on Civilian Health in Britain', *Economic History Review*, **30** (1977), pp. 496–9.

107. J. Hilton, *Rich Man, Poor Man* (London, 1938), p. 115.
108. Nicholas, *Social Effects of Unemployment*, pp. 58–9.
109. Llewellyn Smith, *New Survey of London Life*, p. 5.
110. Rowntree, *Poverty and Progress*, p. 453.
111. Webster, 'Health, Welfare and Unemployment', p. 212.
112. A.H. Halsey, *Trends in British Society since 1900* (London, 1972), pp. 34, 51, 56; P.E.H. Hair, 'Children in society 1850–1980', in T. Barker and M. Drake, *Population and Society in Britain 1830–1980* (London, 1982), pp. 38–43. The fertility rates are for England and Wales. The rates and family sizes were slightly higher in Scotland, but were falling as rapidly.
113. Slater, *Poverty and the State*, p. 448.
114. Bowley and Hogg, *Has Poverty Diminished*, p. 3.
115. J. Boyd Orr, 'Nutrition and the Family' in J. Marchant (ed.), *Rebuilding Family Life in the Post-War World* (London, 1945), pp. 43.
116. Winter, 'Unemployment, Nutrition and Infant Mortality', pp. 469–9.
117. Save the Children Fund, *Unemployment and the Child* (London, 1933), p. 76.
118. Webster, 'Health, Welfare and Unemployment', p. 219; Pilgrim Trust, *Men Without Work* (Cambridge, 1938), pp. 107–11, 116.
119. C. Webster, 'Healthy or Hungry Thirties', *History Workshop*, **13** (Spring, 1982), pp. 123–5.
120. M. Hobbs, *Born to Struggle* (London, 1973), p. 4.
121. Nicholas, *Social Effects of Unemployment*, p. 191; White, *The Worst Street in North London*, p. 72; J. Seabrook, *The Unprivileged* (London, 1967), pp. 50–68; J. Hooley, *A Hillgate Childhood* (Stockport, 1981), n.p.; Hoggart, *Uses of Literacy*, p. 82; Gray, *Worst of Times* pp. 65, 120, 153.
122. E. Ezard, *Battersea Boy* (London, 1979), p. 27.
123. C.W. Whiteley, *A Manchester Lad/Salford Man*, TS, p. 28.
124. See for instance the account of the development of community life in Liverpool in Ayers, *Liverpool Dockland*, p. 8.
125. Goldthorpe, *Room at the Bottom*, pp. 6, 22.
126. Hannington and Llewelyn, *Unemployment Benefit*, Introduction. Also National Unemployed Workers Movement, *Guide to Unemployment Insurance* (London, 1939); Elias, *Practical Guide*.
127. F. Coperman, *Reason in Revolt* (London, 1948), pp. 68–70; Goldthorpe, *Room at the Bottom*, p. 24; Paynter, *My Generation*, p. 84.
128. Croucher, *We Refuse to Starve*, pp. 113–17; J. Connolly, *An Easy Guide to the New Unemployment Act* (London, 1935), p. 18; Hayburn, 'Police and the Hunger Marchers', pp. 626–7.
129. P. Ayers, *The Liverpool Docklands* (Liverpool, 1988), p. 19; Gray, *The Worst of Times*, p. 180.
130. P. Donnelly, *The Yellow Rock* (London, 1950), p. 111.
131. White, *Worst Street in North London*, pp. 96–100; J. Seabrook, *The Everlasting Feast* (London, 1974), pp. 160–1.
132. Bakke, *The Unemployed Man*, p. 94; Beales and Lambert, *Memoirs of the Unemployed*, p. 153; Deacon, *In Search of the Scrounger*, p. 59.

133. Orwell, *The Road to Wigan Pier*, p. 72.

134. For a notably enthusiastic account of private charity in the thirties, see C.L. Mowat, *Britain Between the Wars* (London, 1955), pp. 496–8.

135. C. Braithwaite, *The Voluntary Citizen* (London, 1938), pp. 92, 177.

136. Braithwaite, *Voluntary Citizen*, p. 131.

137. Miller, 'Unemployment Policy of the National Government', pp. 460–1; Greene, *Time to Spare*, p. 86.

138. Braithwaite, *Voluntary Citizen*, p. 80.

139. D.M. Bailey, *Children of the Green* (London, 1981), p. 57.

140. Nicholas, *Social Effects of Unemployment,* pp. 174–80.

141. Prochaska, *The Voluntary Impulse*, p. 76.

142. D. Caradog Jones, *The Social Survey of Merseyside III* (London, 1934), vol. iii, p. 507.

143. Greene, *Time to Spare*, p. 78

144. Ayers, *Liverpool Docklands*, p. 22.

145. Greene, *Time to Spare*, p. 89

146. J. Blake, *Memories of Old Poplar* (London, 1977), p. 46. Also Bailey, *Children of the Green*, p. 21.

147. Daunton, *Councillors and Tenants*, p. 28.

148. P. Johnson, 'Working-class Consumption and Working-Class Collectivism in Inter-War Britain', unpublished paper (1988), p. 11.

149. Pember Reeves, *Round About A Pound a Week*, p. 41.

150. Hilton, *Rich Man, Poor Man*, p. 103.

151. M'Gonigle and Kirby, *Poverty and Public Health*, p. 108.

152. Chesterton, *I Lived in a Slum*, p. 234.

153. A.S. Jasper, *A Hoxton Childhood* (London, 1969), p. 13; A. Barton, *Two Lamps in Our Street* (London, 1967), pp. 29–30; J.D. Vose, *Diary of a Tramp* (Zennor, 1981), p. 52.

154. Blake, *Old Poplar*, p. 10; J. Sarsby, *Missuses and Mouldrunners* (Milton Keynes, 1988), p. 34; Gray, *Worst of Times*, p. 85.

155. J. Gibney, *Joe McGarrigle's Daughter* (Kineton, 1977), p. 96; Coombes, *These Poor Hands*, p. 42; N. Sharman, *Nothing to Steal* (London, 1977), p. 55.

156. Callaghan, *Lang Way,* p. 21; Gamble, *Chelsea Childhood* p. 90; Blake, *Old Poplar*, pp. 23–30.

157. Llewellyn Smith, *New Survey of London Life*, pp. 290– 328.

158. Callaghan, *Lang Way*, p. 15.

159. Llewellyn Smith, *New Survey of London Life*, p. 175.

160. Edwards, *No Gold on My Shovel*, p. 67.

161. Bakke, *Unemployed Man*, p. 2; Cohen, *One of the Unemployed*, pp. 86–7.

162. Hilton, *Rich Man, Poor Man*, pp. 25–31.

163. Johnson, *Saving and Spending*, pp. 116, 207–15.

164. Johnson, *Saving and Spending*, p. 164.

165. Gray, *Worst of Times*, p. 176. Also Gibney, *Joe McGarrigle's Daughter*, p. 94; G. Hitchin, *Pit-Yacker* (London, 1962), pp. 40–1; Blake, *Old Poplar*, p. 11; Pilgrim Trust, *Men Without Work*, p. 124.

166. Hobbs, *Born to Struggle*, pp. 7–8; Whiteley, *A Manchester Lad/Salford Man*, p. 11.

167. Beales and Lambert, *Memoirs of the Unemployed*, p. 142; Gray, *Worst of Times*, pp. 66, 118.

168. Sharman, *Nothing to Steal*, p. 36.

169. Gamble, *Chelsea Child*, p. 31; Gray, *Worst of Times*, pp. 22, 101, 125.

170. Hitchin, *Pit-Yacker*, p. 18; Blake, *Old Poplar*, pp. 8–9; Callaghan, *Lang Way*, p. 10.

171. Bailey, *Children of the Green*, p. 40; E. Ezard, *Battersea Boy* (London, 1979), pp. 143–4.

172. Ayers, *Liverpool Docklands*, p. 43.

173. Johnson, *Saving and Spending*, p. 169; Tebbutt, *Making Ends Meet*, pp. 137–67.

174. Hilton, *Rich Man, Poor Man*, pp. 131–5.

175. A. Valance, *Hire Purchase* (London, 1939), pp. 58–86; G.C.M. M'Gonigle and J. Kirby, *Poverty and Public Health* (London, 1936), p. 236.

176. Ezard, *Battersea Boy*, p. 137. Medicine was extra.

177. For an account of the emancipation of the medical profession from the friendly societies and the accompanying rise in their status and income, see N.R. Eder, *National Health Insurance and the Medical Profession in Britain, 1913–1939* (New York and London, 1982), especially pp. 356–60; D.G. Green, *Working-Class Patients and the Medical Establishment* (Aldershot, 1985), p. 114.

178. Gamble, *Chelsea Child*, p. 36. Also Gibney, *Joe McGarigle's Daughter*, pp. 22–4; Blake, *Old Poplar*, p. 14. On the early twentieth-century survival of folk medicine see Ayers, *Liverpool Docklands*, p. 45; Vincent, *Literacy and Popular Culture*, pp. 162–71.

179. J. Lewis and D. Piachaud, 'Women and Poverty in the Twentieth Century' in C. Glendinning and J. Millar (eds), *Women and Poverty in Britain* (Brighton, 1987), p. 31.

180. E.F. Rathbone, *The Disinherited Family* (London, 1924), pp. 72–3; Gray, *Worst of Times*, p. 161; Spring Rice, *Working-Class Wives*, p. 198; J. Lewis, *The Politics of Motherhood* (London, 1980), p. 43.

181. See, for example, Foakes, *My Part of the River*, p. 22; Gray, *Worst of Times*, pp. 66–118.

182. Hoggart, *Uses of Literacy*, p. 50; Hooley, *Hillgate Childhood*, n.p.; Sharman, *Nothing to Steal*, p. 6; Gamble, *Chelsea Child*, p. 33; Gray, *Worst of Times*, p. 180; Blake, *Old Poplar*, p. 8.

183. M'Gonigle and Kirby, *Poverty and Public Health*, p. 213.

184. Barton, *Two Lamps*, p. 28; Foakes, *My Part of the River*, p. 35; Hooley, *Hillgate Childhood*; Callaghan, *Lang Way to the Pa'nshop*, p. 8; Gamble, *Chelsea Child*, pp. 73, 76.

185. Ayers, *Liverpool Docklands*, p. 10.

186. Gray, *Worst of Times*, p. 125. See also Bakke's illuminating study of the pressures on contemporary American families during the Depression: E.W. Bakke, 'The Cycle of Adjustment to Unemployment' in N.W.

Bell and E.F. Vogel, *A Modern Introduction to The Family* (New York, 1960), especially pp. 116–8.

187. Rowntree, *Poverty and Progress*, p. 469.

188. Bakke, *The Unemployed Man*, pp. 182–3; Gray, *Worst of Times*, p. 23; Blake, *Old Poplar*, pp. 35–6; Hitchen, *Pit-Yacker*, p. 47; S.G Jones, *Workers at Play* (London, 1986), p. 119; P. Wild, 'Recreation in Rochdale, 1900–40' in J. Clarke, C. Critcher and R. Johnson (eds), *Working Class Culture* (London, 1979), p. 156.

189. M.L. Eyles, *The Woman in the Little House* (London, 1922), p. 118.

190. Llewellyn Smith, *New Survey of London Life Vol. III*, p. 180.

191. Jones, *Workers at Play*, pp. 120–1.

192. H. Mannheim, *Social Aspects of Crime in England Between the Wars* (London, 1947), p. 165.

193. Coombes, *These Poor Hands*, p. 177; Gray, *Worst of Times*, p. 165; Blake, *Old Poplar*, p. 11.

194. Gray, *Worst of Times*, p. 21.

195. Beales and Lambert, *Memories of the Unemployed*, p. 192.

196. Foakes, *My Part of the River*, pp. 22, 25, 75; Sharman, *Nothing to Steal*, p. 23; Gamble, *Chelsea Child*, p. 145; Hobbs, *Born to Struggle*, pp. 20–1; Hitchen, *Pit-Yacker*, pp. 30–4; Ayers, *Liverpool Docklands*, p. 27.

197. Gray, *Worst of Times*, p. 87.

198. Bakke, *The Unemployed Man*, p. 201.

199. Jones, *Workers at Play*, pp. 124–6; Beales and Lambert, *Memories of the Unemployed*, pp. 111, 145.

200. Coombes, *These Poor Hands*, p. 143; Hooley, *A Hillgate Childhood*, n.p.; Bakke, *The Unemployed Man*, p. 194.

201. R. McKibbin, 'Working-Class Gambling in Britain 1880–1939', *Past and Present*, **82** (1979), pp. 162–5; Hilton, *Rich Man, Poor Man*, p. 106; Bailey, *Children of the Green*, p. 27; W. Greenwood, *How the Other Man Lives*, (London, 1939), pp. 38–9.

202. Vincent, *Literacy and Popular Culture*, pp. 270–1

203. Ayers, *Liverpool Docklands*, pp. 35–6.

204. McKibbin, 'Working-Class Gambling', pp. 169–70.

205. Pilgrim Trust, *Men Without Work*, p. 136.

206. E. Stengel, *Suicide and Attempted Suicide* (Harmondsworth, 1973), p. 26; Mannheim, *Social Aspects of Crime*, pp. 146–7.

207. Cohen, *I Was One of the Unemployed*, p. 236.

208. For a summary of the institutionalisation of organised labour in this period and its consequences for direct action by the unemployed, see K. Middlemas, 'Unemployment: The past and future of a political problem', *The Political Quarterly*, **51**, no. 4 (Oct–Dec 1980), pp. 468–70.

209. Hilton, *Rich Man, Poor Man*, p. 36.

210. Webster, 'Healthy or Hungry Thirties', p. 116.

CHAPTER THREE

Poverty and History 1939–64

INTRODUCTION

The Second World War turned Britain into a nation of historians. Hitler's dramatic early success concentrated minds more on what was to be lost than on what was to be gained from the conflict. Then as the tide began to turn in the winter of 1942, and it became possible once more to envisage an end to hostilities, the future was conceived of largely as a view of the past. During the First World War, there was no memory of the aftermath of Waterloo, but as the bombs fell upon a civilian population which initially suffered more casualties than the armed forces, there were vivid recollections of the world to which those who had survived the trenches had returned. James Griffiths, who was to pilot the welfare legislation onto the statute book in the 1945 Labour Government, spoke for his generation in the House of Commons Debate on the Beveridge Report in February 1943: 'Our people have memories of what happened at the end of the last war, memories of the period of depression, memories of the unemployment, frustration, poverty and distress into which large masses of our people were thrown.' Such memories fuelled the 'deep determination among the mass of the people that we must in the years that are to come build up a Britain in which, if there is want which we can prevent, we shall collectively prevent that want and give our people a real opportunity in life'.[1]

The extent to which the burning desire to settle old scores could form an adequate basis for planning a new society depended on both the accuracy of the view of the past and the skill with which the past could be related to the future. Griffiths spoke with assurance on behalf of 'our people', but as the previous chapter indicated, the constituency which his party claimed to represent was riven with mistrust and disunity. Although poverty seemed a common heritage amidst the collective endeavour of war, in fact its incidence amongst the working class had been very varied, and the poor themselves had for the most part been excluded from the structures of organised labour. It remained to be seen whether the coming government fully grasped the dynamics of power and privilege which had shaped the landscape of deprivation between the wars, and whether it would be capable of forging a new relationship between the state and 'our people'.

The past had to be properly understood if it was not to be repeated, but equally it was necessary to grasp how different the post-war decades would be from the world which Hitler had brought to an end. As Griffiths was speaking, wartime inflation was invalidating the figures upon which the Beveridge Report was based, instigating problems which as Minister of National Insurance he later wrestled with in vain. There was a difference between laying to rest ancient grievances and avoiding the creation of new failings as social and economic conditions continued to evolve. In practice it proved extremely difficult to predict movements in the levels of prices, unemployment, dependency and social expectations, or even to build into the system the flexibility which could cope with the inevitable uncertainties. It was one of the ironies of the period that reformers so sensitised to history found such difficulty in devising a poverty programme which could respond to change.

THE COMMON CAUSE

In July 1940 *The Times* took advantage of the lull in hostilities which followed Dunkirk to consider the kind of society for which Britain was continuing to fight. The dictators could only be defeated, it argued, 'by the creation of common loyalties and by a sense of common values'. It was no longer enough to define freedom in terms of nineteenth-century liberalism: 'The European house cannot be put in order unless we put our own house in order first. The new order cannot be based on the preservation of privilege, whether the privilege be that of a country, or a class, or of an individual.'[2] Total war, it appeared, was causing a total revision of the ruling conception of a just society and a responsible state. The combination of shared danger and collective sacrifice was at last forcing an acceptance of the implications of the democracy which had been nominally created at the end of the First World War.

The subsequent programme of welfare reforms implemented or planned by the Coalition Government suggested that *The Times* was both sincere and representative in its vision. By 1945 the range and the substance of the commitments which had been entered into were sufficient to ensure that there was no possibility of the scale or treatment of poverty returning to their pre-war levels. Yet of all the periods in the war, the aftermath of the catastrophe in France was when the gap between rhetoric and reality was at its widest, and there is every reason to treat such public pronouncements with the utmost caution. There can be no doubt that the domestic dislocation and military defeat together established a new mood in the country and set in motion a series of administrative and legislative changes whose cumulative impact determined the ideological and bureaucratic framework within which the problem of poverty has been treated ever since.[3] The nature of the sea-change though, was more prosaic than at first appeared. It had little to do with a new sense of social rights and obligations, and still less with an assault on inequality and privilege. Instead it was largely a matter of order and integration.

The most immediate challenge of modern war to a liberal state was not one of strategy or purpose but of organisation. As was abundantly clear by the fall of Chamberlain in May 1940, it was wholly impossible to fight Hitler with a government still committed to pluralism and retrenchment. Just as the armed forces demanded discipline and equipment, so the home front required both co-ordination and expenditure if it was to sustain what clearly was to be a long drawn-out struggle. It is perhaps not surprising that these truths were recognised by the readers of *The Times* some time before they were forced upon the bureaucrats and their masters. They were the first to experience the scale of the dislocation war would bring. In the month before the official commencement of hostilities, three and a half million people left the centres of population to avoid the expected arrival of German bombers. Two million of these, usually the more prosperous, made their own arrangements, but the departure of a million and a half poorer children was organised by the Government, mostly during the chaotic first three days of September. Such an exercise needed a certain amount of *ad hoc* planning, but little effort was made to think through its full consequences. The reception and distribution of the tired, hungry and bewildered temporary orphans was left to local initiative, with scant guidance and less material assistance from the central authorities.[4] It was the common experience of the shortcomings of Whitehall rather than the very varied responses to the moral and physical condition of the children which did most to change public attitudes.

The invasion of quiet rural communities by bus-loads from the urban slums may have exposed the depths of mutual ignorance between the classes, but it did not necessarily bridge them. Some middle-class householders forced to accommodate ill-fed, ill-clothed, and in their view, ill-reared evacuees, reacted with tolerance and compassion, others with incomprehension and hostility. A Mass Observation study found that far from seeking reciprocal understanding, 'both sides − visitors and visited − waged a war of "atrocity" stories about each other', which were far more numerous than those then circulating about the Germans.[5] Everyone involved, however, could see the need for much greater support from the Government than initially was forthcoming. They were promised billeting allowances, but these were paid late, at too low a level, and, in accordance with the instincts of pre-war provision, were means-tested. Their local social services were overwhelmed, despite the often heroic efforts of volunteer helpers, but all requests to lift restrictions on expenditure were refused in the name of the traditional commitment to public economy at a time of financial crisis. The only temporary relief was provided by the evacuees themselves, who began to drift home once the early panic had subsided. It was not until the eclipse of the hitherto dominant Treasury after the formation of Churchill's Administration, and a new wave of evacuation following the beginning of the Blitz, that the purse-strings were at last loosened. Money was made available to meet the special welfare needs of the host communities and their one and a quarter million long-term guests. Clubs, canteens, nurseries and maternity homes were opened, and a network of hostels was established for children who could not be fostered.

By early 1941, the Government was beginning to catch up with opinion in the country. The emerging consensus was largely a negative one. It was not so much that a section of the community deserved better treatment than it had hitherto received, rather that no group should be unfairly victimised by the emergency. A central characteristic of the experience of the Depression was that the suffering was spread extremely unevenly across the country and between the classes. Whilst the fortunate were enjoying the fruits of a consumer revolution, others were forced back almost to a nineteenth-century way of life. Now it was recognised that in time of war, civilians, no less than soldiers, should march in step, where possible receiving the same support and protection in return for their collective commitment to the struggle.

Beyond the immediate challenge of evacuation, the overriding concern was to prevent inflation wreaking serious damage on living standards. The rise of twenty-two points in the index in the twelve months from 1 December, 1939,[6] forced a major reassessment of peace-time priorities. Thus for instance the pre-war proposal to provide milk and vitamins for pregnant women and infants was suddenly implemented in June 1940, when the rising price of basic foods began to pose a direct threat to the production of healthy children who were needed to replace the inevitable loss of adults.[7] A month later the school meals scheme, whose first beneficiaries were now nearly old enough to be grandparents, was radically extended. Three and a half decades after the pioneering Liberal reform only 130,000 poor and officially unfit children were being fed; by 1945, 1,650,000 were receiving meals in proper canteens.[8] At the other end of the life-cycle the old were cushioned from the effect of rising prices by the introduction of supplementary pensions payable without discrimination through the Unemployment Assistance Board, which as a result began to lose its associations with the Poor Law. The UAB was able to shed the first word of its title, partly as a consequence of its widening welfare functions, and partly because the unemployed themselves had been conscripted. The disappearance of this most mistrusted and troublesome category of claimants, together with the growing administrative difficulties caused by the multiplication of sources of income and the constant population movement, gave Ernest Bevin, now translated from his union to the Ministry of Labour, the opportunity to force through the abolition of the household means test through the Determination of Needs Act of 1941.[9]

This series of concessions to long-established demands for reform was of benefit to specific groups seen to be at risk from food shortages and rising prices, but the claims of the labouring population as a whole had also to be met. Rationing of key goods began almost immediately, and by early 1941 the resistance of the Treasury to full-scale intervention in the market was overcome. In the crucial April budget the Government formally committed itself to stabilise the cost of living through both subsidies and price controls. Income tax was raised to 10s 6d, and the rich were faced with a surtax of 19s 6d in the pound.[10] There was a small element of redistribution in the combination of restrictions and deductions, and the war period and its immediate aftermath witnessed a rise of nearly a fifth in average real incomes, whilst salaries and returns from property fell by a similar amount.[11]

The real message of the budget, however, was not that the balance of wealth was being tipped towards the common man, but rather that the privileged were being forced to participate in his sufferings. The ration book, with its new system of points, stood as both the symbol and the guarantee of the commitment to equal protection and shared sacrifice which underpinned all the welfare reforms and proposals of the period.

The final reversal of pre-war poverty policy was a result of both the innovations and the omissions of the budgetary strategy. The extension of income tax brought increasing numbers of manual workers into the system for the first time, stoking up pressures for higher pay. However wage controls, a logical component of an anti-inflation package, and widely canvassed in Whitehall at the time, were successfully resisted by Bevin at the Ministry of Labour. He presented his colleagues with a stark choice. If the unions were deprived of their traditional bargaining rights, the consequence would be either the end of any prospect of co-operation between the Government and labour, or the beginning of a campaign to socialise industry to prevent employers exploiting their shackled workforce.[12] Neither prospect was desirable, but ministers remained doubtful whether the unions could be trusted to curtail their demands in view of the continuing pressure on their members' prosperity. The solution had been lying on the table for twenty years, spurned by Conservatives, Labour and the trade unions alike.

By 1939 Eleanor Rathbone's long, patient crusade for family allowances had got almost nowhere. Despite constant lobbying by the Family Endowment Society, opposition from the establishment on both the Left and the Right remained entrenched. The Tories accepted the Treasury's rooted hostility to indiscriminate charity, whilst the representatives of organised labour were as suspicious of the threat to the living wage as they had been since the onset of the Depression. The transformation in attitudes which took place in the next three years had little to do with pressure group activity – although as an MP Eleanor Rathbone herself was able to take part in the debate – and still less with concern for the rights and requirements of either mothers or children.[13] Rather it was a product of the need to steer a course between the Scylla and Charybdis of British pay bargaining: a compulsory minimum wage or compulsory wage settlements.

As in the First World War, the need to pay allowances to the wives and children of servicemen was causing anomalies of treatment between different categories of poor families, particularly as support was also being given on behalf of evacuees, but it was only when family allowances were proffered as a means of non-statutory, non-inflationary pay limitation that their attractions as a universal benefit became apparent. An increasing number of Tories saw the allowances as a substitute for the restraining influence of mass unemployment, whilst the TUC's traditional fears evaporated along with the reserve army of jobless. By late 1941 it felt sufficiently confident of its industrial strength to take the risk of adding its voice to the pressure coming from inside the Coalition. There remained arguments about the precise form the allowances would take. With sections of the workforce now receiving child tax allowances, it was thought inexpedient to transfer money from the Inland Revenue, and there was Conservative support for attempts to curtail the overall cost by making family allowances either contributory or means-tested, rather than, as the Labour Party now urged, free and payable to all children of all parents. The arguments were not resolved in the White Paper of May 1942, but the general principle was firmly endorsed.[14]

By this time, the question was also being considered as part of a wider examination of the future of the welfare system. When the Government acceded to the TUC's request for a review of social insurance in June 1941, it had hoped that the modestly titled Inter-Departmental Committee on Social Insurance and Allied Services would be a means of shunting into an administrative siding the mounting clamour for family allowances and other yet more ambitious proposals.[15] That this failed to happen owed much to the unique combination of personal aggrandisement and consensus politics which characterised the Committee's work. Its chairman, Sir William Beveridge, was at once a long-serving member of the upper-middle-class establishment, having recently reached that final haven of the great and the good, the mastership of an Oxbridge College, and at the same time a highly opinionated and utterly self-confident visionary. Having spent his life a bachelor and a bureaucrat, he was shortly to find himself discovering the delights of public fame and, at the age of sixty-three, of matrimony. The Government had packed the committee with civil servants in the hope of emasculating its political impact, but was then forced to allow Beveridge to turn it into his private instrument as he alone of its members was allowed to put his name to the final report.[16]

Beveridge succeeded in bridging the gap between his personality and his constituency through his intense but selective engagement with the past. As a document, the final report belonged to several eras. There was a seventeenth-century use of language, with the Bunyan-esque presentation of Want, Disease, Ignorance, Squalor and Idleness, the 'five giants on the road of reconstruction',[17] an eighteenth-century enlightenment optimism that through the free play of reason 'the total abolition of want' was attainable once peace was restored, a nine-teenth-century liberal faith in the free market as the ultimate provider of the means of progress and justice, and finally the confidence of the early twentieth-century bureaucrat in the creative benevolence of the state. More particularly, the central edifice rested on an appropriation of the history of the preceding two decades.

Both at the time and later, Beveridge laid great emphasis on the breadth of support he attained for his recommendations. As he wrote in his memoir: 'my Report represents to a very large extent the grea-test measure of common agreement in the views of those who have thought most seriously upon its problems. That is what I tried to make it. I tried to make a Beveridge Report which would really be the British people become articulate about what they want in the way of social security.'[18] He had every reason to make this claim. His pur-chase on the future rested on his capacity to present his findings as an embodiment of national wisdom. That the report has dominated the treatment of poverty for almost half a century is a consequence as much of the way it was compiled and presented as of the substance of its particular proposals. Consensus was both a means and an end of the Committee's work. It sought to represent current opinion, and then to use the breadth of agreement to convince future opinion that there were no legitimate reasons for disputing its recommendations. The do-cument was to be seen as both a product and a generator of the democratic values for which Britain was fighting.

However, such an ambition was more easily stated than achieved. In particular there was the problem of bridging the gap between those 'who have thought most seriously on its problems' and 'the British people become articulate'. In its deliberations, the Committee concen-trated almost exclusively on the former. The 126 extra-governmental witnesses included the TUC and some trade unions, the Association of Municipal Corporations and a few local councils, as well as a handful of bodies representing minority interests such as the deaf, the blind, the elderly and the crippled, but otherwise consisted largely of those already involved in the present system.[19] There was no attempt to speak directly to the poor and the unemployed, although the Nuffield College Social Reconstruction Survey was asked to gather from those in 'public and citizen service', 'indications of the views, experiences and difficulties of the consumers of insurance'.[20] The Fabians were about as far left an organisation as the Committee listened to. That Beveridge found little opposition to his proposals among a wide range of vested interests certainly improved the chances of a favourable re-ception for his labours, but it scarcely gave him the right to speak for the nation as a whole. This claim in the end had to rest on his own reading of the historical evidence.

In the introduction to his Report, Beveridge defended its basic principle:

> . . . benefit in return for contributions, rather than free allowances from the State, is what the people of Britain desire. This desire is shown both by the established popularity of compulsory insurance, and by the phenomenal growth of voluntary insurance against sickness, against death and for endowment, and most recently for hospital treatment. It is also shown in another way by the strength of popular objection to any kind of means test.[21]

Wartime impatience of dislocation and disorder provided the impetus for reform, but its practicality and legitimacy had been proved in the trials of the pre-war decades. The ambitious attempt to integrate the separate elements of the welfare services by the single device of compulsory insurance was a child of the confused sequence of legislation which began with the Coalition Government's panicky attempts to cope with the soldiers returning from the trenches. As Beveridge explained, 'this considerable list of changes does not mean that, in the proposals of the Report, either the experience or the achievements of the past are forgotten. What is proposed today for unified social security springs out of what has been accomplished in building up security piece by piece.'[22]

It was accumulated practice rather than abstract theory which pointed the way forward. Several lessons could be derived from gradual extension and growing acceptability of National Insurance. Firstly, left to themselves, working people were always prepared to lay out at least some money against at least some risks. They had done so before compulsion and had continued to do so in order to make good the shortcomings of the levels and range of benefits which became available. Whereas the Means Test was seen as an onslaught on domestic financial strategies, enforced saving against risks appeared a natural extension. Amidst all the unprecedented demands made of the common man in war-time, Beveridge could reasonably claim to be proposing something entirely familiar.

Secondly, left to itself, capitalism would never render unnecessary substantial remedial work by the state. The economy had recovered from the immediate post-war crisis, and had survived the Depression, but the difficulties which the benefits were supposed to ameliorate showed no signs of disappearing. The combination of long-term growth and large-scale residual poverty had undermined confidence in the new Poor Law at the end of the nineteenth century, and forty years on the continued, if occasionally interrupted, improvement in real wages still had not solved the problem. 'The rise in the general standard of living in Britain in the thirty or forty years that ended with the present war', demonstrated, in Beveridge's view, that 'growing prosperity and rising wages diminished want, but did not reduce want to insignificance. The moral is that new measures to spread prosperity are needed.'[23]

Finally, whereas Lloyd George had once argued that collectivism did not mean socialism, the success of his innovation demonstrated that redistribution did not mean revolution. Any solution of poverty required the transfer of money from one pocket to another, but the apparent capacity and willingness of manual workers to pay regular insurance premiums enabled Beveridge to reach the crucial conclusion that 'Want could have been abolished before the present war by a redistribution of income within the wage-earning classes without touching any of the wealthier classes.'[24] There was no need to take money from the rich to give to the poor, or even to divert it from the public house to more responsible forms of expenditure. The sums now being expended under the existing insurance system, and on other voluntary schemes and medical fees, were together less than the projected premiums of the comprehensive scheme.

The data for these conclusions came partly from a review of the record of legislation and public finances, but more specifically from the fierce debate over policy which had taken place in the thirties. Beveridge at once accepted and inverted the meaning of the writings and protests of the period. Whereas the long sequence of social surveys were written on water as far as the National Governments were concerned, now they were to become the bedrock of official policy. His identification of both the extent of the problem of poverty, and its twin causes – interruption of earnings and family size – was based on the findings of the accumulated body of urban poverty studies. The concept of the national minimum was derived from the series of attempts to extend and refine Rowntree's original 'poverty line', and Rowntree himself, the founding father of the twentieth-century social surveys, was brought in to chair a sub-committee on calculating the new subsistence level. Even the riots and demonstrations by the unemployed which at the time had been met with a combination of repression and disdain, were now taken as a legitimate expression of opinion, and an accurate commentary on the shortcomings of state welfare.

The detailed proposals listed in *Report on Social Insurance and Allied Services* demonstrated both the necessity and the difficulty of re-working history. The great strength of the blueprint was precisely that it was not drawn on a blank sheet of paper. Whereas the debate during and after the First World War was polarised between those who wanted to cling to a vanishing age and those who wanted to ignore it, Beveridge was able to exploit the general inclination to frame arguments about the future in a critical reappraisal of the past. Out of the documented failure of public provision to meet private need came the undertaking to set benefits at subsistence level; out of the endless confusion of the forty or so National Insurance Acts came the commitment to a single administrative device; out of the divisive inconsistencies of cash relief came the desire to incorporate the whole of society in the welfare system; out of the reluctance of former governments to promote social progress came the ambition to slay all five giants on the road of reconstruction; out of the old came a scheme which on all sides was seen to make a fundamental break with a world to which few wished to return.

Yet Beveridge could not enjoy the privileges of the remote professional historian. The events he was reviewing had made him, and during the course of a long career of public service, had in some part been made by him. In his basic conceptual approach to the poor and their problems, he remained a product of his times. If he was capable of pushing back the limits of state action, he was trapped in an older view of society and its members. Although at this stage it was not clear whether he would join the Liberal Party,[25] he was at heart a liberal individualist, whose 'English Revolution' owed a great deal more to Mill than to Marx. It was this combination of the radical devices and orthodox values which enabled him to create so broad a consensus for his plan, but it also confined and compromised its impact on the post-war generations.

At first sight, the inclusion in the welfare system of middle-class families whose previous dependency had been confined to child tax allowances, and the proposal of a range of benefits specifically for women, challenged established relations of class and gender, but in practice, little was to be disturbed. Instead of redistribution between 'land, capital, management and labour', the plan envisaged the enforced transfer of purchasing power 'among wage earners themselves, as between times of earning and not earning, and between times of heavy family responsibilities and of light or no family responsibilities'.[26] The scheme would even out the impact of trade and life-cycles, not the inequalities between the better off and the less fortunate. 'It does not decrease wealth', stressed Beveridge, 'it need have no depressing effect on incentive.'[27] Similarly the apparently innovative, and subsequently unfulfilled promises of a marriage grant and a widowhood benefit were conceived in recognition of the woman's loss of her separate, independent identity when she ceased to be single. The grant was proposed as compensation for her loss of insurance rights and her likely withdrawal from the labour market, the benefit as protection for the women bereft of a husband's support. The structure of the family, and its hierarchy of roles were to be reinforced by the new system. The wife's reduced economic responsibilities were reflected in the lower unemployment benefit she received if she maintained her contributions, her central reproductive duties were recognised by a new maternity benefit, set at twice the level of male unemployment or disability benefit in view of the assumed incompatibility of motherhood and work.[28] Although Beveridge had some concern for the children of unsupported mothers, only divorced wives of proven innocence received benefits. The guilty, together with the unmarried, were left to the Means Test.[29]

Beveridge was a conventional individualist, with a conventional view of individual behaviour. The head of household was expected to behave like the rational economic man of old. This was nowhere more evident than in his conception of the residual device of National Assistance. Help for those who fell through the net would have to be not only means-tested to prevent indiscriminate charity, but also less eligible than National Insurance benefits, otherwise the rational individual would either not bother to work and pay his premiums, or feel cheated if he did. Furthermore, he still envisaged that 'penal treatment' would be visited on those who through 'weakness or badness of character' failed either to meet the conditions of benefit, or left their families 'without resources'.[30]

His outlook was born partly of traditional thinking, and partly of traditional ignorance. Despite his familiarity with the social surveys, he still knew next to nothing about the actual management of the domestic economies of the poor. In this he was not entirely to blame. For all their concern, the social investigators had rarely penetrated the homes of their subjects, and issues as fundamental as the distribution of resources within the family, and the determinants of strategies of expenditure and credit, were shrouded in darkness.[31] Even so, it was his own decision to ignore the limited evidence which was available on working-class budgets, and turn instead to the Ministry of Labour Enquiry of 1937–8, and the nutritional studies of the BMA and the Technical Commission of the League of Nations for his calculations of levels at which to set his subsistence benefits. The consequence was a set of rates at 1938 prices which were only about two-thirds of the poverty lines used by Rowntree in both his 1936 and 1951 York surveys, principally because Beveridge made insufficient allowance for items other than food, clothing and fuel. He then increased his difficulties by using an inadequate cost of living index to measure the impact of war-time inflation, and substituting for the actual rent paid, which had been used by all the social investigators, an average figure set between the wide variations across the country and within neighbourhoods.[32]

This short-fall was critical to the success of his enterprise. If insurance benefits were to fall below the National Assistance payments, where the actual rent would be allowed, then the relationship between contributory and means-tested welfare would be turned upside down, and if the measurement of subsistence was flawed from the outset, the prospect of abolishing real want disappeared for ever. What prevented Beveridge from rescuing himself from this impending disaster was his basic view of the relationship between the state and the claimant, which turned a lack of detailed information about spending patterns from a vice into a virtue. Central to his conception of an autonomous individual in a free society was that the state should not seek to know or to influence how he spent his money. For Beveridge, as for Lloyd George before the First World War, the abiding virtue of insurance was that it tackled deprivation by means of standardised benefits for standardised conditions, thus avoiding the morally offensive and bureaucratically expensive forms of inquisition pioneered by the Charity Organisation Society. In a modern, efficient system it was necessary to classify need, but not to distinguish between the needy within a given category.

Similar considerations underpinned the insistence on flat-rate contributions, which further reduced the prospect of defeating poverty by imposing a regressive tax on the working class, and limiting the overall sum available for distribution. Just as notional rents could be defended on the grounds of administrative simplicity and personal privacy, so could the avoidance of what would be in effect means-tested contributions. In Beveridge's vision, the requirements of the bureaucrat and the wishes of the claimant reinforced each other. The working class had long made plain their deep resentment of the enforced disclosure of their circumstances, and the essence of new machinery was that it would extend coverage but reduce expenses. However, the convergence of interests produced a mode of simplification which was largely illusory; in practice, Beveridge's scheme sought to meet the needs of an imaginary individual by means of a fictional device. There was no such being as the normal claimant whose needs could be accurately assessed and fully met by a distant state, and there was no such entity as an actuarially sound insurance system which could meet unpredictable requirements by means of standardised contributions.

At every point the latent inadequacies and tensions were obscured by Beveridge's restricted view of citizenship. He insisted that poverty was inconsistent with democracy, and constantly invoked the wishes of the people, but in practice never entertained the prospect of altering their subordinate relationship to the centralised state and its staff of experts. Thus proposals to allow claimants direct participation in the administration of their relief were dismissed on the grounds that this would lead to unpredictable variation and the reintroduction of discretion. Equally the suggestion that the distribution of benefits be undertaken by locally controlled social workers who would exercise long-term care over the claimants and instruct them in their rights was rejected on the grounds of cost and personal intrusion.[33] There was no sense in which those exposed to the risk of poverty should extend control over their lives by developing the resources of their community, or by participating in the operation of central government by any means other than an occasional visit to the ballot box.[34] Instead they could exercise their individual freedom in the market place by choosing the form and extent of the private insurance which would be required to bridge the gap between a minimum and a comfortable standard of living.[35] The available evidence suggested, however, that the poor had always regarded commercial provision, particularly in the form of the industrial insurance companies, as a negation of active citizenship. In the most deprived areas, which were reported to be 'riddled with door-to-door insurance touts', the firms with their high overheads and low sales techniques were seen as a threat rather than an adjunct to effective self-help.[36]

Beveridge's fellow professionals were united in their enthusiasm for his Report. 'It is a State document in the grand manner', concluded *The Political Quarterly*, 'clear in conception, acute in analysis, bold in solution, comprehensive in outlook, humane in spirit, distinguished in style.'[37] However in Parliament, the Government's lukewarm response to the inquiry it had commissioned caused the most serious divisions since the fall of Chamberlain. Churchill's attitude was a combination of embarrassment, indifference and extreme caution. He deeply resented Beveridge's success in turning what had been intended as an internal exercise in pressure absorption into a major public relations event. Well before publication, on 1 December 1942, Beveridge was at work raising the expectations of Fleet Street, and the launch of the document, aided initially by the Ministry of Information, turned

Cmnd 6404 into an instant bestseller. Whilst Churchill as a war leader was at last beginning to go on the offensive following the victory at El Alamein a month earlier, as a domestic reformer he was now permanently on the defensive.

The Government initially compromised itself by hurriedly reversing Brendan Bracken's publicity campaign and recalling two Army Bureau Current Affairs bulletins on the Report, and then provoked a major backbench rebellion by its handling of the House of Commons Debate in February.[38] The Conservative Party had made no contribution to the inquiry, and its Coalition Ministers could do no more than praise its findings with faint damns. The Chancellor of the Exchequer, Kingsley Wood, who once had led the opposition to Lloyd George's scheme as spokesman for the Industrial Insurance Companies, rehearsed all the objections of his horrified Treasury officials, burying his endorsement in a forest of double negatives: 'nothing we have decided so far as finances are concerned', he concluded 'can be in any way regarded as unsympathetic or inimical to any of these proposals'.[39] There was to be no binding commitment to all or any part of the Report, and no timetable for its implementation.

The Labour members of the Coalition were also inclined to accept Churchill's view that domestic ventures on this scale could only divert energies from the war effort, but they at least were just about able to remain in touch with their parliamentary colleagues who were pressing for immediate action, whilst the Tory Party was seen to be seriously split. Opinion divided around two issues in particular. The first was the old problem of potential post-war dislocation and violence. Churchill, who with good reason doubted whether a debt-laden peacetime economy could afford so large a scheme, was concerned lest expectations be raised to an unrealistic level, leading to a repeat of the 'homes fit for heroes' fiasco, whilst Quintin Hogg (later Lord Hailsham), a leader of the rebellion within his Party, drew the opposite conclusion: 'if you do not give the people social reform', he warned, 'they are going to give you social revolution'.[40]

The second was the even older dilemma of the relationship between political will and economic reality. Although Beveridge had worked closely with Keynes to produce practical costings, in the midst of so exhausting a military conflict all estimates of future income and expenditure could only be provisional, even supposing that 'social insurance' could be properly self-supporting, which Keynes himself doubted. But for the Report's supporters, the figures were not the main point. By bringing so much together and giving it so clear an identity, Beveridge had created a scheme in which the whole was far more original than its often familiar parts, and had in turn succeeded in appealing more to the imagination than to the pockets of the electorate. It was not just that an endorsement of the Report was important for both military and civilian morale, more fundamentally it was a statement of a determination to subordinate financial management to the deliberate pursuit of social objectives, and thus reverse what Quintin Hogg described as 'the pre-war attitude of mind in this matter'. The reconstruction of Britain, he argued, depended 'not so much upon economic as upon moral decisions and upon our ability to continue the community spirit new in time of peace but not unfamiliar on the battlefield in time of war. As I see it the Government have been guilty of what I can only describe as a major political blunder in not recognising that fact.'[41]

Mistakes on the battlefield cost lives, blunders on the home front lost votes. There was a broad vein of electoral calculation running through the idealism of the Tories who voted against the Government at the end of the debate. A Mass-Observation survey taken in the autumn of 1942 indicated that Beveridge was in most respects preaching to the converted;[42] a poll conducted immediately after publication found 90 per cent in favour of the Report, which, together with a threepenny official summary was eventually to sell nearly two-thirds of a million copies. Amidst all the technical detail, the message had been conveyed that at last a means had been found to 'Abolish Want'.[43] Particularly ominous for the Conservatives was the revelation of the depth of support amongst the party's natural constituency in the middle class, where despite some worries about further increases in taxation, there was a large majority for adoption, whether or not they expected to make personal gains from the new benefits. Some of these relatively prosperous altruists in the month of the Beveridge debate transferred their allegiance to the newly formed Common Wealth Party which in a series of dramatic by-elections registered huge gains against Government candidates on a platform founded on an unqualified endorsement of the Plan.[44]

The Common Wealth Party also benefited from the discomfiture of the Labour leadership, who were increasingly identified as part of the political establishment, and it was by no means certain that parliamentary socialism would be the beneficiary of the enthusiasm for social reform which Beveridge had brought to the surface. Whereas the Report in both its compilation and reception appeared to represent the summit of progressive, responsible Government, in reality it was the product of a far more negative set of attitudes which were only confirmed by the Coalition's mishandling of the subsequent debate. Early in the war, Mass-Observation set out to identify the conscripts' attitude to politics: 'The foremost characteristic of their outlook', it concluded, 'is a cynicism about everything.'[45] This mistrust of authority in all its forms was rooted in the experience of peacetime, when neither those in power nor those seeking it had been able to provide an adequate response to the manifest injustice and suffering. Now that the National Government had proved as incapable of dealing with Hitler as it had with the Depression, there was a pervasive expectation that the defeat of Fascism would only lead to the resurgence of mass unemployment. Social insurance was sought for defensive rather than constructive reasons. It was welcomed in anticipation of the return of the old world rather than the construction of a new one.

The more realistic Labour politicians were well aware of what lay beneath the visionary rhetoric. Opening the Beveridge debate, Arthur Greenwood warned: 'It is unfortunate, but it is undeniably true, that in many quarters of the country, and among members of the Forces, there exists an atmosphere of cynicism tinged with bitterness which may be dangerous for our future.'[46] Subsequent polls indicated that the conduct of the debate had merely deepened the pervasive mistrust of the motives and competence of politicians in general. Amidst the fears of a war which was visiting death and destruction at home as well as at the Front, there had been offered the prospect of relieving the anxieties that had blighted so many existences in peacetime: 'If it should be adopted and prove workable', noted a housewife two days after the Report's publication, 'it will change the whole face of life for working people and remove the main fears of their lives.'[47] With its author now a pariah in Whitehall for breaking the conventions of hidden government,[48] and the Prime Minister scarcely willing to admit to the Report's existence, there was every reason to wonder whether adoption was inevitable.

In the event the sheer weight of public opinion sustained the momentum of the plan. The Parliamentary Labour Party's memories of the Depression were too vivid, and it had been pursuing office for too long to let slip the opportunity for seizing power with which Beveridge had presented them. The National Executive Committee succeeded in curbing the leadership's inclination to follow Churchill not only during the war but into another peacetime coalition, and was able to exploit the Conservatives' evident discomfort with the whole notion of full-scale social reform. Whereas between the wars Labour had twice been burdened with the responsibilities of office but not the power, during the war it enjoyed the authority of government without the discipline.[49] Its members were free to condemn the caution of the Coalition to which they belonged, and present themselves simultaneously as sober patriots and radical reformers. The newer parties were too far from office, and the older ones too compromised by it. Lloyd George was able to cast his last vote in the House of Commons at the end of the Beveridge debate, going into the lobby against his co-founder of the insurance system, but the Liberals could benefit from neither their long record in the field, nor their success in recruiting the hero of the hour. Their organisation had decayed too far and it remained as difficult as it had been two decades earlier to associate them with a major extension in state intervention and expenditure. The party which had been so damaged by the First World War was virtually destroyed by the Second, and they could muster only twelve seats in the new Parliament. To his bitter disappointment, Beveridge himself was treated with even less gratitude than his great predecessor in the field of social reform, Edwin Chadwick. Having been expelled from the ruling elite for courting popular support, he was then rejected by the electorate in his Berwick-on-Tweed constituency in 1945, and was reduced to spectating from the House of Lords as his proposals were translated into legislation.[50]

Labour's landslide victory in 1945, which confirmed the findings of all the opinion polls in the preceding two years, but confounded the predictions of all the political experts,[51] presented them with unprecedented opportunities, and almost impossible difficulties. Ten days after the election results were announced, the Americans dropped the first atomic bomb, and the sudden end to the war with Japan precipitated the unexpected termination of Lease Lend, which threatened the new Government with as large an economic crisis as the Wall Street Crash had caused last time it held office. Keynes staved off disaster by negotiating a new, harsh loan from the Free World's banker, whilst at the same time making it plain to Attlee and his colleagues how bleak were their financial prospects. Thereafter the programme of social reform represented a vivid combination of incontestable innovations and insoluble dilemmas.

In spite of the earlier reservations of the now defeated and demoralised Tories, it was the absence of any serious argument about the principles of the Beveridge Plan within the Labour Party which was most striking.[52] At least at the constituency level, Labour had a long record of opposition to the inter-war process of bureaucratic centralisation which was finally completed by the National Insurance Act of 1946, and the National Assistance Act of 1948. Beveridge's greatest achievement may have been not to convert the Tories to the welfare state, but Labour to state welfare. Few voices were raised from within their ranks against the obliteration of the last vestiges of direct popular control over the relief of poverty. Henceforth local authorities were to confine their efforts and their expenditure to the personal social services whose role was expected to be marginal to the final crusade against want. Only in the construction of the National Health Service was a rearguard action fought against the loss of real local initiative and participation, but eventually Bevan overcame Morrison's defence of the municipal hospitals in the name of consistency and efficiency.

The extensive indifference to the dangers of a system in which every official from whom claimants received money was controlled from Whitehall was, like so much else, a product of both the recent and the more distant past. It was partly that during the war Labour had become more accustomed to viewing the state as a benevolent agent of progress, and partly that in the long peacetime struggle against the use of discretion in welfare, most dramatically and most bitterly in the form of the household Means Test, the movement had become increasingly attracted to the sheer impersonality of the kind of insurance system around which Beveridge had organised his plan.[53] To most of the Labour Party, the indivisible concept of 'the national minimum' policed by disinterested officials seemed infinitely preferable to its apparent alternative, local variation controlled by cost-cutting ratepayers or rule-making inspectors. Little concern was registered either in the Party or amongst its voters at the creation of a huge new bureaucracy answerable to its clients only through the cumbersome mechanism of ministerial responsibility.[54] Few MPs were as aware as Arthur Evans of the scale of the problem which still lay ahead. The new administrators, he warned, 'have a very difficult job if they are to remove the stigma of the Poor Law. They have to humanise the relationship between the poor and authority – a difficult and complicated task, and one which cannot be done merely by passing legislation.'[55] As he watched the growing mountain of paperwork created by his Ministry's dealings with its new customers, the most that James Griffiths could do was instruct his officials to make their letters as free as possible of bureaucratic jargon.[56]

Such doubts as remained were quelled by two central promises of the Beveridge Plan which in the event proved impossible to implement. The first was that the system would provide subsistence-level benefits for all but a small and decreasing minority of claimants, and thus render into insignificance the element of means-tested discretion embodied in the National Assistance Act. There seems little doubt that as they devised the machinery and set the benefit scales, James Griffiths and his fellow ministers genuinely believed that this was exactly what they were doing.[57] They accepted the recommendation of the 1944 White Paper that pensions be paid in full rather than phased in over twenty years, as Beveridge had proposed, if only because they did not wish to force pensioners onto the Means Test, and regarded the basic single and married rates of 26s and 42s as generous by pre-war standards and in line with the original calculations.[58] In practice, the National Insurance scales were, in real terms, below even Beveridge's inadequate formulations, and for an increasing number of claimants less than the means-tested support available from National Assistance.

Although the atmosphere of financial stringency played a part, this was one occasion on which the Treasury was largely free of the blame for frustrating a welfare programme. Its only major success was in ensuring that family allowances, which became law before the fall of the Coalition Government, were set at 5s rather than 7s 6d as first proposed, and were payable only to the second and subsequent children. The specious rationalisation for these savings was that the cash shortfall would be covered by other welfare benefits, and that parents should share with the state the financial responsibility for raising their families.[59] For the most part, the problem was not that ministers asked for more than they were given, rather that they were not aware of how much they needed. The central failing was an inability to resolve the basic contradiction between insurance and subsistence bequeathed to the Labour Government by the plan it was now committed to implementing.

When the moment came to translate illustrative figures into actual payments, the difficulty of making an actuarially sound system of contributions and benefits responsive to variations in need over time and between cases became painfully apparent. Inflation presented a major challenge both in retrospect and prospect. Modifications clearly had to be made to the 1938 prices in the Beveridge Report, but there were substantial technical difficulties in measuring the wartime growth in the cost of living, particularly as the package of price controls and food subsidies had made a variable impact on different sectors of the population. It now seems that the final decision to increase Beveridge's sums by almost a third left the insurance benefits about 10 per cent lower than he had intended.[60] More seriously, there was no natural mechanism for further uprating in response to the continuing pressures of post-war inflation, an entirely unfamiliar dilemma for ministers whose outlook had been formed in an era of long-term deflation. As Griffiths later admitted, maintaining scale rates at their initial level 'was, and has remained, an insoluble problem'.[61] An insurance system is properly funded by past contributions, and its payments cannot logically be determined by changes in the current cost of living. There is no such obstacle to the revision of non-contributory assistance scales, and the consequence was that in the early years of the new structure the latter were adjusted much more frequently than the former.

The inconsistent pattern of uprating exacerbated the imbalance between the National Insurance and National Assistance rates which was inherent in the structure from the outset. The Labour Government did not wish to challenge Beveridge's insistence that in the interests of simplicity the rent component of benefits be standardised, but neither could it abandon his incompatible undertaking to meet the subsistence needs of every claimant. The result was a vague compromise, by which an intention was stated of setting the rates 'broadly in relation to the present cost of living'.[62] The National Assistance scales, however, freed from the Procrustean bed of flat-rate insurance, were set at 40s plus the actual rent, which embodied a more generous assessment of need for all but the minority who had little or no housing costs. With equal vagueness, it was hoped that members of the National Insurance fund would not bother to claim additional sums from an Assistance scheme which was not meant for them. However, for those without savings and living in an expensive housing area, means-tested assistance was significantly closer to their actual requirements, particularly as insurance benefits began to fall behind inflation. In July 1948 there were 842,000 National Assistance claimants, two-thirds of whom were also in receipt of inadequate Insurance benefits, and by the time Labour finally left office in 1951, the figure was rising towards a million and a half.

The second major attraction of the Beveridge Plan was that the abolition of want would only be one element of an assault on the whole structure of pre-war injustice. The concern amongst some on the Left that the emphasis on the insurance principle represented an implicit endorsement of market capitalism was countered by the sheer breadth of the campaign against the 'five giants' which Labour was now equipped to wage. Disease was tackled through the establishment of the National Health Service, funded by the same insurance system and holding out the prospect of at last dealing with so large a cause and consequence of deprivation. Ignorance had already been attacked by the 1944 Butler Education Act which the new Government was pledged to implement. Squalor was the target of the Ministry of Health, whose housing programme was aided by Dalton's policy of cheap money. Finally idleness was countered by the maintenance of war-time controls and the development of new policies of regional development, and although there were inevitable difficulties as a debt-laden economy sought to cope with demobilisation, there was no recurrence of unemployment on the scale which had so disfigured the record of the Lloyd George Coalition.

Yet the impression of an integrated plan of reform was fundamentally misleading. The relation of the parts to the whole had not been thought through, and little compensation was offered for the shortcomings of the poverty legislation. Direct economic intervention was eventually superseded by demand management, and none of the ambitious package of income and price controls which Beveridge had once envisaged was ever implemented.[63] Wages and welfare remained separate spheres, as did taxation and benefits, despite the appearance of the first proposals for a tax credit scheme. Except possibly in the area of industrial health, the nationalisation of basic industries had minimal impact on the welfare state. The Health Service itself did play a complementary role in the reduction in suffering and anxiety, but the ambition of establishing a coherent programme of disease prevention was never realised. The system of grammar and secondary modern schools, introduced under the 1944 Act, perpetuated divisions within education. There was little sense of equipping the whole of the rising generation with the range of tools they would require to participate effectively in the new structures which were being created by concurrent reforms.

Over the period of the Labour Governments, there was only a marginal downward redistribution of wealth, whilst in most spheres, power was shifted towards a new generation of managers, professionals and bureaucrats, working for or protected by the state. Patients had more access to, but even less effective control over their doctors;[64] workers in nationalised industries gained no direct authority over those who ran them; the new generation of claimants had more status and better benefits, but just as little ability to influence the priorities and conduct of either local officials or their distant masters. In many ways the middle class were the more consistent beneficiaries. By 1960 only 4 per cent of the population were failing to receive cash benefits, whether in the form of family allowances, pensions, National Insurance or Assistance, or grants for further education.[65] In 1963 even the wealthiest households were receiving an average of 1.4 per cent of their income as state benefits.[66] The better-educated gained access to a wide range of welfare benefits for the first time and acquired new prospects of privilege and employment in its provision and administration.

LIVING WITH WELFARE

The first verdict on the Labour reforms appeared within three years of the final legislation. In 1951 Seebohm Rowntree, now eighty years old, published his third report on poverty in York. Unlike his two earlier inquiries, which had attempted to recapture the entire texture of working-class life in the town, *Poverty and the Welfare State* was narrowly concerned with the impact of family allowances and the structure of National Insurance and National Assistance, together with the still operational body of war-time subsidies. His conclusion was unequivocal: 'whereas the proportion of the working-class population living in poverty has been reduced since 1936 from 31.1 per cent to 2.77 per cent, it would have been reduced to 22.18 per cent if welfare legislation had remained unaltered'.[67]

His findings set the seal on his own half century of research and propaganda, as they did on the career of his contemporary, Beveridge. Less predictably, they also provided an epitaph for the reforming ambitions of the Labour Party, which lost office immediately after the book's publication, despite purloining its findings during the election campaign.[68] In a double sense it represented the end of an era. The victory over poverty was almost attained, and the long argument about whether and how the state should act was concluded.[69] Rowntree's original *Poverty* had created a political issue by describing the lives of the people of York, now his study of their grandchildren was to remove the subject from the political agenda. Labour had already claimed in its 1950 manifesto that 'Today destitution has been banished',[70] and the incoming Conservatives, reluctant to interfere with a programme to which they had given their nominal support but opposed to further legislation or expenditure, were content to accept this conclusion.[71] They were as anxious as Labour to demonstrate that in the field of poverty, the modern world represented a clear break with the past. Apart from altering the basis of housing subsidies in 1956, and introducing a limited scheme of graduated pensions in 1961, no attempt was made to alter the structure they had inherited. With the death of Eleanor Rathbone in 1946 and the ending of the Family Endowment Society in 1949, there were no vocal extra-parliamentary groups agitating for further reform. The most influential left-wing manifesto of the period, Crosland's *The Future of Socialism*, took as its point of departure the assumption that 'nine-tenths of the poverty which existed in 1936 had disappeared'.[72]

The principal problem now facing government was the persistent pressure of inflation, with the cost of living index almost exactly doubling between 1946 and 1964. Family allowances had suffered the most complete eclipse as a political issue, and accordingly the threat to their value received the least attention. The post-war reversal of the long fall in the birth rate dissipated fears of depopulation, and the steady rise in wages relieved concern about child poverty, which, according to Rowntree, had virtually died out by 1950.[73] The allowances were increased from 5s to 8s in 1952 to take account of the ending of food subsidies, and the rate for three or more children was put up to 10s in 1956, but otherwise they remained unchanged until 1967, by which time their real value had fallen by a third and Britain was spending less on child support than most of Europe.[74] As had been the case before the war, the chief beneficiaries of the state's assistance to parents were those paying income tax. For a two-child family on average earnings, child tax allowances were worth almost three times as much as family allowances in 1950, and nearly five times as much by 1965.[75] These subsidies were still, however, not regarded as part of the programme of public welfare.

The terms of the original insurance and assistance schemes, which envisaged a five-year review of the former but allowed more frequent revision of the latter, could only exacerbate the initial imbalance between them. Between 1948 and 1965 there were ten upratings of the means-tested system, but only six of the contributory, constrained as it was by the increasingly unsuccessful attempts to keep the National Insurance fund solvent. Not until the mid-sixties, when the Government finally abandoned its efforts to maintain a link between contributions and benefits, was it possible to begin moving the two sets of rates in tandem.[76] Before then the relationship between them was consistent only in that a household with an average level of housing expenditure would always have fallen below the Assistance scale if it was solely dependent on Insurance benefits.

Whereas Beveridge had envisaged a reduction in the role of National Assistance once the early anomalies had been resolved, it was evident that the passage of time was having the reverse effect. By the time the Conservatives left office, the number of households in receipt of assistance had reached two million.[77] In the early fifties, with a quarter of National Insurance claimants also applying for means-tested help, Beveridge himself began to complain that his plan was being seriously damaged.[78] However, the concern was confined to problems of just one sector of the population. For most of society there seemed much to celebrate. Unemployment, which had dominated the issue of poverty between the wars, now regularly fell below 2 per cent. The standard account of the post-war social security system was able to conclude in 1968 that, 'Long-term mass unemployment has been eradicated in this country.'[79] The economy grew steadily, albeit more slowly than Britain's main competitors, and as it did so, standards of living rose. And in spite of the difficulties with inflation, the welfare state began to share in the increasing prosperity. National Assistance moved ahead of inflation in 1959, and by the mid-sixties the rates were worth half as much again in real terms as their original value. Between 1949 and 1964 expenditure on social security benefits tripled, increasing their share of GNP from 5.86 per cent to 7.49 per cent.[80] The only group in society whom it was feared were in danger of being left behind by the economy and mistreated by the state were those who had completed their working lives before the new order was established.[81]

The problem of the elderly was partly a function of demography. Their numbers had been growing rapidly between the wars, but the scale of their demands on the contemporary welfare system had been disguised by the crisis over unemployment. Now they stood exposed to the gaze of politicians and social scientists alike. When Rowntree conducted his first survey of York, the proportion of the British population aged sixty-five and over stood at 4.7 per cent; by the time he returned to the town for the last time, it was 11 per cent and still rising. He now found that they dominated his tables, accounting for 68 per cent of the causes of poverty, with sickness the next largest category at 21 per cent, and unemployment failing to register at all.[82] It seemed as if the basic problems of vulnerability and dependency were being concentrated at one end of the life-cycle. With marriage rates at an all-time high, early parental death becoming much less common, and divorce, although more widespread than before the war, still a small danger to working-class families, the threat of deprivation appeared to be reserved principally for the men and women who had outlived their capacity to keep themselves.

It was this group which most dramatically exposed the shortcomings of the new welfare system. Pensioners were more likely than any other category of National Insurance claimant to turn to means-tested relief with around a quarter receiving National Assistance in any year, compared with about one in six of the unemployed and one in eight of the sick, and because of their much larger numbers, they dominated the work of the National Assistance Board throughout the whole of its existence.[83] The doubling of the Board's work did nothing to reduce the proportion of men and women of pensionable age, who accounted for 63 per cent of weekly allowances in December 1948, and 68 per cent in December 1964. Little was achieved by the introduction of an earnings-related pension scheme in 1959, which in practice increased contributions far more than benefits.[84] Only about a fifth of pensioner claimants comprised the cases for which National Assistance had been intended, those who had slipped through the insurance net and were relying on earlier non-contributory benefits, or had failed to gain eligibility for any other public aid at all. The rest found that because of the more generous structure of disregards and extra allowances, particularly housing payments which had increased almost three-fold to an average of 27s 2d by 1964,[85] they could legitimately seek supplementation of their contributory pensions in order to bring them up to the official poverty line.

The unplanned but unstoppable flood of applications from the elderly had an ambiguous impact on the operations of the means-tested relief. On the one hand it made the administration and cost of the system much more onerous than had been expected, on the other it enabled the National Assistance Board to get far closer to the ideal of the welfare state than it ever could have hoped, or indeed than its successors have ever managed. The pensioners were in most respects much easier to deal with than other categories of claimants. They did not enter and leave the system at frequent intervals, or undergo dramatic changes of circumstances. There was always some movement as the balance between National Insurance and National Assistance rates varied, and as increasing age caused new problems, but they were a far more stable group than the unemployed. Unlike those who had lost their jobs, there was little question of concealing employment or cohabitation, and no need to apply the disagreeable device of the wage stop. Of 2,096 prosecutions for benefit fraud in 1960, for instance, just forty-five involved retirement pensioners.[86] Above all they were not inclined to cause trouble. They were too old, too unlikely to belong to self-help organisations, and too aware of how much worse things had once been. Because of differentials in life expectancy, they were also disproportionately female. Only a third of pensioner claimants were men, compared with nine-tenths of the small group of unemployed.

Freed from so much of the mutual mistrust and antagonism which had characterised the work of the pre-war Public Assistance Committees and Unemployed Assistance Board, the newly appointed NAB officials could make a genuine attempt to realise the requirement of the 1948 Act that they should 'exercise their functions in such manner as shall best promote the welfare of the persons affected'. They were trained to see themselves not as warriors against the strategies of the household economy and the moral shortcomings of its members, but rather as pivotal figures in the newly emerging structure of state, local authority and voluntary welfare provision. The NAB 1954 Annual Report explained their function:

> Every person who is receiving regular grants of assistance or a non-contributory old age pension is visited periodically by the Board's local officers, and one of the questions to which special attention is given, especially where the person visited is of advanced age and is living alone, is whether there is a need for any of the services provided for old people by other statutory bodies or by voluntary effort . . . . It is the business of the Board's visiting officers to know what services are available locally, to recognize the need for them where it exists and to effect the necessary contacts.[87]

Special training was given not only in the availability of local services but in interviewing techniques, and, as the 1964 Report put it, 'in the acquisition of the skill and of the insight and understanding of human behaviour called for by their often delicate duties, particularly with people whose personalities are in some way abnormal'.[88]

With eight million home visits a year taking place by the mid-fifties, there was plenty of opportunity to practise such skills. If the task of effectively co-ordinating the proliferating branches of the welfare state was beyond the officers, at least they recognised the problem. There was no overall planning of the relationship between the services now being offered,[89] and no other agency was in a position to ensure that the poor made full use of them. It was partly a matter of encouraging the ageing to overcome a life-time's fear of the cost and condescension of the health professions and partly of making them aware of the increasingly complex body of concessions to which they were entitled, inside and outside the National Assistance scheme. Although the overall number of means tests had been sharply reduced by the postwar move towards universal entitlement,[90] the trend was once more being reversed, not only through the unintended growth of non-contributory benefits, but also through the introduction of optical, dental and prescription charges in 1951 and 1952, and the officers had instructions to ensure that the poor gained the refunds to which they were entitled. However limited their practical effect, the new generation of domestic intruders evoked a generally positive response from the elderly.[91] 'I've told all that to my Assistance man', replied one indignant old lady to a social investigator: 'he looks after me, why do you want to know it all?'[92]

For its part, the NAB was able to paint a rosy portrait of the section of the population which had become its chief responsibility:

> The overriding impression left on the visiting officers by this large group
> of old people is that . . . the overwhelming majority are comparatively
> healthy, independent, reasonably contented, and in frequent touch with
> relatives and neighbours; grumbling a little about the cost of living, their
> rheumatism and the weather, feeling their age and the disappearance of
> most of their own generation, but not neglected and not unfriended.[93]

However, the view from outside was less optimistic. A series of surveys began to question whether the old had greater cause for complaint than they seemed to realise. Despite the reforms, retirement still
sent a substantial proportion of the working class spiralling down towards the subsistence level, and Abel-Smith and Townsend's re-working of the 1953-4. Household Expenditure Survey revealed that
two-thirds of all units below the level had heads who were retired.[94]
Cole and Utting discovered that not only was the National Assistance
scheme placing a ceiling on the income of applicants who would lose
benefit if they found income elsewhere, but amongst the elderly not
applying for means-tested relief, a quarter were living at or below
subsistence level. Half of these were rendered ineligible by inconsistencies in the rules, and half had not bothered to claim. This latter group
of apparently voluntary poor represented one and half times the total
number who had successfully applied for assistance.[95]

These findings suggested that the problems of means testing had not
evaporated as easily as its new administrators wished to believe. It was
partly that the past itself was an obstructive force, maintaining suspicions which in the absence of the household Means Test and the
presence of better-intentioned bureaucrats may not have been fully
justified, and breeding resignation to standards of deprivation which
were more commonplace before the war. But there were also real and
continuing problems with the present arrangements. Despite its re-
packaging, the means test was still an embarrassing intrusion into the
privacy of men and women who had been promised in 1946 that
henceforth they would have subsistence level benefits as of right.[96]
Pride remained a factor, as did ignorance. It had proved impossible to
reconcile the objectives of justice and simplicity in devising the regulations for eligibility. The rules were complex, and although towards the
end of its life the NAB began to respond to criticism and make greater
efforts to publicise them to those too confused or intimidated to apply,
it had little success.[97] The impact of publicity and courses in human
relations for staff was undermined by the persistence of attitudes
formed under the Poor Law and by the continuing pressure to restrict
public expenditure.[98] Those who did claim still faced the problem of
getting the best out of the system. Additional payments were available

for a range of needs including special diets, laundry and heating costs, and there were substantial variations in the exercise of the wide discretionary powers vested in officers despite the training and supervision they now received.[99] For all the sense of a new beginning in state welfare, the physical environment of the new system was much as it had been in the strife-torn days of the thirties. In 1954 less than one in ten of the 408 Area Offices had been built since the war.[100]

Two-thirds of the elderly who had not applied for the assistance for which they were eligible were sharing housekeeping costs with their children or other relatives.[101] Rather than eroding the structures of communal support, the extension of state welfare established a new and more complex relationship between the alternative sources of help for those threatened with destitution. Where once relatives, and to a lesser extent neighbours, had constituted the basis of whatever security was available, frequently more reliable than official relief and often in conflict with it, now the private and the public spheres were more complementary. The sheer volume of cash paid out as contributory or non-contributory pensions dwarfed the small sums which could be spared by those amongst whom the elderly lived, but at the same time the inadequacy of the rates and the shortcomings in their administration meant that those beyond retirement age still made extensive use of informal networks of assistance.

Thus it was that half the elderly were principally dependent upon the state for their livelihood, yet almost as large a proportion regularly received financial help from their families.[102] Only about one in ten received no state benefits of any sort, and as they grew more infirm, few could escape an encounter with the new national and local Health Services, but at least in the established urban communities, they maintained extensive and mutually supportive contact with their relatives, in particular their children. Townsend's sample of old people in Bethnal Green had an average of thirteen relatives living within a mile, and saw three-quarters of all their children at least once a week.[103] These visits were a source not just of company, but of real material benefit, which partly compensated for the limitations of the welfare state, and partly subsidised its operation. Had the public services been more co-ordinated and had the old been more willing to use them, there would have been less need for the small donations of money and much larger gifts of time and effort, particularly in emergencies such as illness; had grown-up children, especially daughters, been less willing to assist their parents, there would have been greater demand on the personal social services, and more complaint about the failings of the pension system.

Amidst this patchwork of effort, the old had lost some of their fears, and gained a little freedom. The workhouse no longer loomed over the horizon and it was not now as necessary to waste precious resources on expensive policies against pauper funerals, though the National Insurance Death Grant was barely adequate when it was introduced in 1948 and became progressively less so.[104] In the late fifties, pensioner households were on average spending just 2d a week on the once essential subscriptions to private and friendly society insurance schemes.[105] If the poorest amongst the retired were often to be found sharing another household, they were not being forced to abandon their independence as often as once was the case. Whilst both the numbers applying for means-tested relief, and the numbers failing to do so in spite of their eligibility, were an indictment of the system set up by Labour, the incidence of absolute destitution amongst the elderly had declined.

Fear had been replaced by constant uncertainty as large numbers of retired men and women were forced to piece together a living from a variety of sources in the absence of an absolute right of access to an adequate basic livelihood. The greater freedom to organise their own pattern of living was constrained by the constant limitations on their budget. Except in a few cases, there was usually enough money for meals. The National Food Survey of 1955 found that the diet of pensioner households was on average above BMA recommendations in almost every category.[106] However, for the 50 per cent of retired householders who lived on or just below the official subsistence levels,[107] it was still a matter of balancing some basic necessities against others. A new pair of shoes, for instance, would undermine a pensioner's domestic economy for weeks on end. With electricity and gas far more widespread, fuel bills were a growing threat, reaching an average of 13s a week by the early sixties and provoking increasing demands for the discretionary additions payable by the National Assistance Board.

The outlook was particularly bleak for the quarter or so who in their old age had no surviving children, and as always, for the women. As long as their marriages lasted, they retained the arduous responsibility for bridging the unbridgeable gaps in the household budget. Although they made relative gains in status as their husbands lost their pay packets on retirement and were reduced to taking pocket money out of the pension, they lost none of their duties. Few working-class men filled in their new free time with planning and preparing meals, or visiting the shops.[108] And as the partner most likely to be widowed, they were more exposed to the greater difficulty of managing a home on a single pension, and more vulnerable to the shortcomings in the local medical and social services.

The welfare state in conjunction with an expanding economy had reduced the troughs in the poverty life-cycle Rowntree had identified half a century earlier, but its basic outline was still clearly visible. Those most threatened by deprivation were either in small households at the end of their lives, or in big ones at the beginning. Although the large and growing body of pensioners dominated the perspective of both the managers and the critics of the early system, there remained a substantial number of children in families either reliant on means-tested relief or living below the official subsistence levels. The National Assistance Board was paying dependency allowances for 300,000 children under sixteen in the early fifties, and for more than 400,000 a decade later.[109] When Abel-Smith and Townsend carried out the first major reassessment of poverty in the welfare state, they found that about 30 per cent of low-income households contained children. In 1960 a quarter of all households of six or more and two-fifths of eight or more were below the poverty line, and two-thirds of a million children were in homes where the income was less than the basic National Assistance scale.[110]

As with the old, the continuing presence of poor children was a consequence of the inability of the Beveridge system to cope with economic and demographic change. Even when they were introduced, family allowances had fallen short of the cost of raising children, and with their value frozen at 1952 prices, they became progessively more incapable of keeping low-income families above the poverty line, or of protecting families without incomes from recourse to means-tested relief. At the same time the post-war baby boom meant that just as there were increasing numbers of elderly in the population, so also larger families were again becoming more common. The rise in real wages ensured that where the head of the household was in full-time employment, it was usually possible to maintain two or three children, but the declining family allowances could not offer an adequate defence against the arrival of more mouths to feed. Neither were they of sufficient help to the small but growing group of single-parent families.

The number of divorces and maintenance orders actually fell in the first post-war decade, but by the end of the fifties they were on the increase, as the consequences of the sharp decline in the average age of marriage began to become apparent. The change was most striking at the bottom of the social scale. The proportion of wives of unskilled labourers who had married in their teens jumped from 20 to 41 per cent between 1947 and 1961, whilst the percentage of teenage brides of employers and managers rose just one point to nine.[111] More ill-supported marriages were at risk, and more failed. In 1955 the NAB was supporting 50,000 separated, deserted or divorced mothers who were responsible for an average of two children each, and by 1964 the figure had almost doubled.[112]

Mothers without husbands, no less than men without jobs, exposed the extent to which the welfare state had inherited rather than abandoned the traditional association of public charity with the official control of the behaviour of its recipients. The post-war legislation had incorporated most of the pre-war methods for discouraging abuse and encouraging a return to jobs or husbands.[113] Whereas it was now accepted that the elderly and the certifiably sick had a right to relief subject only to an examination of their material resources, the unemployed and women unable to register for work because they were the sole support of children had to meet a rigorous set of behavioural standards. Deserted and separated wives came under intense pressure to pursue their husbands through the magistrates' courts, and as a last resort, the National Assistance Board undertook prosecutions on their behalf. Under section 51 of the National Assistance Act, failure to support a family was, as it always had been, an offence punishable by fines or more often, by imprisonment, and these powers were used with increasing vigour throughout the Board's career.[114] In this work the Board was supported by the social work profession, whose prevailing objective in the fifties was to maintain or rebuild the patriarchal family.[115]

The lower unemployment became, the greater the suspicion that fell upon those who seemed incapable of finding work. As an early NAB report delicately put it, 'Much time has been spent, not only by the Board's officers but also by the staff of the Ministry of Labour and by members of the Board's Advisory Committees, in reminding able-bodied persons who appear to have settled down on public funds of their responsibility to make themselves self-supporting.'[116] Those who persistently rejected such advice were eventually threatened with a total withdrawal of their relief unless they attended a 'Re-establishment Centre' where they were subjected to a general moral and physical 'toning up'. Fraud was energetically pursued from the outset, and by the end of the 1950s a special group of officers had been detached from their normal duties to interrogate those suspected of hiding jobs or live-in lovers. Finally the time-honoured belief that the rational working man would abandon work for means-tested relief if the latter offered better rates was enshrined in NAB policy. Allowances were consistently given at a lower rate to those disqualified from insurance benefit on the grounds that they left jobs without good cause or failed to provide adequate explanations for their failure to find new ones.[117] In addition, widespread use was made of the wage stop, under which 11 per cent of all unemployed allowances were being reduced by 1964, mostly because the claimant had the misfortune not only to lose an ill-paid job, but also to be responsible for a large family. By this means the NAB was, on its own admission, consigning 57,000 children to poverty.[118]

The pressure was severe, but it fell on a comparatively small group of individuals. Only one in fifteen recipients of National Assistance in December 1964 belonged to the ancient army of the able-bodied poor, with another one in eight who although fit and of working age was not expected to seek employment because of his or her family circumstances.[119] Except in the case of the wage stop, there was a widespread imbalance between the attention devoted to moral control and the actual numbers involved. When the first Re-establishment Centre was opened in 1951, for instance, it had difficulty in raising its occupation above double figures. Despite the draconian powers vested in the NAB, only nine men in the initial cohort of trainees were there under compulsion, and less than three times as many were being forced to undergo a refurbishment of their work ethic in the early 1960s. In spite of Beveridge's earlier enthusiasm, the state still showed little interest in combining relief with training. Similarly the use of the courts directly affected only between one and two thousand claimants a year although more may have been influenced by the example of fines and imprisonment.

The confinement of punitive action to a fraction of a minority of those dependent on non-contributory relief enabled the early welfare state to sustain a far more benign public image than the pre-war agencies. Yet there was an underlying continuity of approach with the previous era. Most supervisors had been trained before 1948, and the executive officers under their control displayed sharply contrasting attitudes towards the deserving and undeserving amongst their clients. As with pre-war relieving officers they retained extensive latitude in determining eligibility to benefit. Judgements about why a claimant had left a job or a husband were made with little charity and less expectation that they would be successfully challenged. The advisory committees which were set up in 1948 to mediate between the officials and the local community turned out to be wholly ineffective.[120] If anything they were more inflexible than the bureaucrats, who were left to establish their own practices. In interpreting the hundreds of pages of the 'A' Code on discretionary payments, the inspectors were generally responsive to the needs of the elderly and as frequently dismissive of the requirements of those with irregular domestic or occupational histories.[121] If the numbers involved were still limited, the machinery existed in embryo for the coming rapid expansion of the contentious categories of unemployed men and unsupported mothers.

Within their own community, those lacking a sufficient income to supply their families with the basic necessities were also living in both the past and the future. Older strategies of collective survival were under pressure from new forms of state provision and new styles of working-class living, but the impact of both was still limited. Shortcomings in the structure of contributory benefits and family allowances forced their recipients back towards some combination of the means test and traditional modes of self-help, whilst the radical developments in patterns of consumption were still incomplete.

The particular balance between continuity and innovation was exemplified by the responsibilities borne by wives and mothers in post-war households threatened with deprivation. Benefits for children and widows and access to free health care reduced some of the anxieties which had worn down their own mothers and grandmothers, yet the inadequacies of state support renewed many of the more wearisome pressures and practices. In the field of women's employment, as elsewhere, the Beveridge system was based on the past rather than the future. The 1944 White Paper on Social Insurance observed that 'The last census showed that seven married women out of eight were not in gainful occupation. Their primary need is, therefore, support when their husband's earnings are interrupted.'[122] Just as the official record underestimated the volume of economic activity by poor wives between the wars, so the new welfare structure overestimated the protection that would now be provided for those with too many children or too small a contribution from their husbands.

By the mid-sixties, official statistics indicated that after remaining static at about 30 per cent during the century before 1951, the rate of female participation in the economy was beginning to rise sharply. This was especially true of married women, whose rate of employment increased from 13 to 30 per cent between 1931 and 1951.[123] Given the volume of unrecorded labour in earlier decades, it is impossible to gauge the precise level of growth. Although over half of women in their late thirties and nearly two-thirds of those in their late forties were now registered, about half the employment was part-time, of which at least a proportion would have been more formal versions of hitherto hidden domestic or casual labour.[124] It is clear, however, that

the women who, for instance, went out cleaning offices in the evenings or early mornings were making a crucial contribution to the welfare of their families.[125] The more threatened the family economy the
more likely they were to work, and the more they worked, the
greater the likelihood that the home would be kept above the poverty
line. Given the absence of a minimum wage, and the presence of such
obstacles as the wage stop, which particularly affected large families of
low earners, the wife's labour was in fact the only absolute guarantee
of basic subsistence. Beveridge's vision of a partnership between the
state and the citizen had not envisaged that it would rest on the overworked backs of wives and mothers, neither had it been intended that
the structure of benefits should constitute a ceiling rather than a floor
for the enterprise of the poor. In practice, the unexpected use of
means-tested rather than contributory support meant that the regulations constantly prevented subsidiary earners in the family from making
a major contribution to the domestic budget.[126] There were few opportunities for women to find well-enough paid jobs to permit them
to escape the confines of state support altogether.[127]

If more women's work took place away from the home, there is
little evidence that on their return they were relieved of any of the
responsibilities they had inherited from their mothers. They were still
faced not only with all the cooking and washing, and with feeding and
clothing themselves last, but also with the relentless task of conducting
the day-to-day struggle to balance the family economy. The new
structure of benefits had drastically reduced the prospects of absolute
destitution, and family allowances had given mothers of two or more
children their first wholly reliable if still inadequate source of income.
What was lacking was any margin of security. Even when paid in full,
none of the state benefits allowed any surplus for savings.[128] In the
mid-fifties, as between the wars, a third of the population had no
liquid assets at all, for instance in the form of Post Office deposits or
savings certificates, and another third possessed less than £100 as a
defence against the uncertainties of life.[129] Although the spread of
council housing removed the drain on the domestic budget caused by
rooms which could never be kept adequately warm or dry, they imposed increased rents without giving the poor access to home-owner-
ship which had always been the single most important material
resource. The proportion of the population which was virtually
propertyless stood at around 75 per cent both before and after the
Beveridge revolution.[130]

Women managing budgets on or below the National Assistance
scales faced the familiar dilemma of a maximum range of decision-

making and a minimum room for manoeuvre. The lower the family's income, the less there was left over to spend on those necessities which could be postponed from one week to the next. Whereas the richest households in the 1953–54 Expenditure Enquiry devoted a quarter of their outgoings to the inescapable items of food, housing, and fuel, light and power, the poorest spent two-thirds, and the proportions were unchanged a decade later.[131] Pensioners were forced to commit 41 per cent of their slender resources to food alone in the first survey, and the marginal improvements in the real value of National Assistance in the later fifties did little to relieve the pressure.[132] The impact of inflation on these basic items was greater than the official cost of living figures, thus undermining the apparent rise in the real value of the National Assistance scales.[133] As had always been the case, those with the least need to economise found it easiest to do so. Three-quarters of the richest families in the survey now possessed a car with which to make and carry home bulk purchases, and two-fifths owned a refrigerator in which to store what had been bought. The equivalent figures for families attempting to subsist on less than £200 a year were 0.3 per cent and 0.7 per cent.[134] It was still a matter of shopping little and often, with the care invested in spending standing in inverse proportion to the savings that could be achieved.

Where there was more than one child, the payment on Tuesdays of the family allowance was of some help in bridging the yawning gap between the end of the weekend and the next pay-day. But as the benefit was not enough to support one child, let alone the family, the requirement to use debt as an instrument of budget management still remained. Land's study of large families found that of those living below the basic assistance scales, three-quarters owed money in some form.[135] The hierarchy of borrowing followed the priorities of spending. Rent arrears were the largest problem, followed by fuel bills and credit purchases for clothing or furnishing. The pattern of change established between the wars was extended. Pawnbroking continued its decline, and hire-purchase its increase. It was virtually unknown for a household exposed to poverty to buy furniture for cash. Twice as many manual workers as managers used this more expensive means of acquisition.[136] Families which were both large and poor, and which therefore had the most need for expensive items such as new beds and the least ability to pay for them, were on average sacrificing 8 per cent of their income on hire-purchase payments. Those just above the poverty line bought clothing with the aid of Provident checks, those below relied upon the providence of jumble sales.

Time was against the family whose head had left or lost his job. It was no longer as short as the fortnight facing the Edwardian deserted wife,[137] but the longer the household was forced to rely on National Assistance, the more the inadequacies of the scales became apparent, and the greater the difficulty of replacing crucial items of clothing and domestic goods.[138] For mothers as well as grandmothers, the need for assistance from friends, neighbours and relatives was reshaped rather than abolished by the new opportunites of public support and private labour. The timeless tension between the desire for independence and the search for help took on new forms. To avoid the humiliation of seeking aid, increasing numbers of women found some kind of paid employment. Widows with families, for instance, were pushed into the labour market partly by the inadequacy of the new National Insurance benefit, and partly by the urgency of the old desire to maintain their privacy. But as they more often found jobs away from the home and the neighbourhood, so they more frequently required the services in kind if not in cash from those around them. If the children's mother did not work, they might not be properly fed, if she did, they might go without food or supervision unless unpaid help was available. The transactions were always between women, sometimes as friends, more reliably as kin. Whilst the chances of making contact with those a little more prosperous was greater as the patterns of winners and losers became more variegated, the prospect of those able to help living at too great a distance to be of any use also increased.

During this period, the proportion of council tenancies in the housing stock doubled, whilst private rented accommodation halved, leaving them roughly balanced by the early 1960s. On the new estates, the move towards a more fragmented, home-centred culture, which had been visible in the pre-war developments, was continued, but at a slow pace.[139] This was partly because family networks were capable of surviving the uprooting from the centres to the peripheries of the towns and cities, albeit on a more limited scale,[140] and partly because the patterns of recreation associated with rising working-class living standards took some time to establish themselves.

The most symbolic change in the ways of escaping from the endless struggle to make ends meet was the replacement of the trip to the cinema by the evening in front of the television. Film audiences reached an all-time peak immediately after the war, then fell with gathering momentum till they were only a fifth of their former level by 1964. At the same time the proportion of the adult population in possession of a television licence rose from 4 per cent in 1950 to 40 per cent in 1955 and had passed 90 per cent a decade later.[141] The exchange in forms of visual entertainment accelerated the slow domestication of leisure, but the process was extremely uneven. The elderly, who eventually were to make the most significant use of the television, were little affected by the decline of cinema-going. As early as 1951, Rowntree and Lavers found that three old people in five never went to the cinema, and the proportion of regular film-goers in this age-group was lower than amongst those under five.[142] On the other hand the poor in general were least able to exploit the new form of communication. A television was an expensive consumer durable, and until the second-hand and rented markets developed, it was out of reach of those on or near subsistence level. The young still kept up their weekly visits to the cinema, which itself was more expensive, with no tickets less than a shilling, whilst their parents and grandparents waited and saved for the time when they could see moving pictures in their own homes.

In the short term, those unable to afford to travel to entertainments from the new council estates found their greatest compensation not in the development of new luxuries, but in the consolidation of pre-war innovations. The wireless was no longer the possession of just a few homes in the street, and in this period did most to fill the quiet hours of the indigent elderly. Those who had been rehoused now had electricity, which made it possible not only to run a radio, but also to have really adequate lighting, which together with free spectacles and a rapidly expanding public library service made reading an easier and more extensive pastime. If the increasing consumption of books was a direct result of the National Health Service, the other great inheritance of inter-war recreational changes was to be an immense if still unrecognised burden upon it. The per-capita consumption of tobacco increased by nearly a half between 1930 and 1955,[143] by which time it was no longer regarded as a luxury by any section of society. As Zweig noted in his study of poverty in the late forties, 'The expenditure on smoking is like that on food – for most smokers the expenditure is regarded and treated exactly like that for other necessities of life.'[144] Households at the bottom and the top of the income tables both devoted about 3 per cent of their budgets to tobacco.[145] The poor rolled their own rather than bought cigarettes, in 1950 spending 1s 2d a day for half an ounce of tobacco and each week paying back to the Exchequer roughly the equivalent of a newly introduced family allowance.[146]

Only half as many women smoked as men, and in general those in poorer households were still restricted in their recreational activity by their lack of surplus cash. It could be argued that the later development of the television-centred evening at home made possible the first form of capital-intensive leisure which husband and wife could share regularly and on an equal basis. Until then, however, the move out to the estates left mothers shut up in homes which with the higher rents, they frequently could barely afford to furnish and heat, whilst their menfolk had access to the traditional urban pleasures during their working day or by bus in the evening. If council-house gardening provided a relatively cheap pastime in which either sex could participate, other forms of free leisure, in particular gossiping on the doorstep or over the counter, were less available. There were no corner shops, many fewer street traders, and it was much more difficult to generate the old level of neighbourly contact.[147]

The house-building programme was slow, particularly during the Labour Government, and there were many left in pre-war conditions of squalor. Those who gained for the first time the basis of a civilised form of living, exchanged the most extreme forms of deprivation for a more diffuse sense of helplessness. Their homes were no longer so damp that no heating could keep them warm, so infested with vermin that no housework could keep them clean, but at the same time they had little sense of gaining control over their lives. The estates were run by a remote local bureaucracy which gave tenants no direct voice in their management. If their family economies did well, they might eventually become part of the growing minority of working- class families who went abroad for their holidays or the smaller number who could afford their own cars,[148] if not, their sense of exclusion from the growing national prosperity was compounded by the ignominy and inadequacy of means-tested benefits, and by the increasing poverty of communal support systems. Little was forthcoming from neighbours,[149] and whilst there still might be relatives scattered about the estate, they could no longer provide the guarantee of assistance in a crisis which once was available. As one rehoused old lady told Young and Wilmott, 'You notice the difference out here, when you fall on hard times. Up there where you were born, you could always get helped by your family. You didn't even have to ask them – they'd help you out of trouble straight away. Down here you've had it.'[150]

PAST AND FUTURE

In the second reading of the National Assistance Bill in November 1947, Bessie Braddock, one of the handful of Labour MPs who could legitimately speak for the poor of inter-war Britain, stood facing the past.

> I am particularly glad that I have had a part in this Bill, as a Member of the party responsible for it. I am very bitter about what has happened in the past to those people who found themselves in need of assistance. I am bitter because I know what has happened to them. I am bitter because I have been a part of them. I have sat on a committee where public assistance had to be given out, and it has been a horrifying experience to me when people have come in and asked for a pair of boots and have had to stand in a corner and show the soles of their boots before another pair could be given to them. . .. I have been in a committee where the chairman, who was not of my party, persisted – and I protested – in seeing the underclothing of old people before the committee was prepared to give an order that new underclothing should be supplied. These things remain with us. We remember them.[151]

The legislation was justified by a history and would in turn put an end to it. The speech concluded with the hope that it would be possible 'now to forget the horrors of the past in the joy of realising that we are living in a country that is going to produce for the benefit of the citizens as a whole'.[152] A verdict on that future is given by Carolyn Steedman, who was born in the same year as the Commons debate:

> The 1950s was a period when state intervention in childhood was highly visible. The calculated, dictated fairness that the ration book represented went on into the new decade, and when we moved from Hammersmith to Streatham Hill in 1951 there were medicine bottles of orange juice and jars of Virol to pick up from the baby clinic for my sister. This overt intervention in our lives was experienced by me as entirely beneficent, so I find it difficult to match an analysis of the welfare policies of the late forties which calls 'the post-war Labour government . . . the last and most glorious flowering of late Victorian philanthropy', which I know to be correct, with the sense of self that those policies imparted. If it had been only philanthropy, would it have felt like it did? I think I would be a very different person now if orange juice and milk and dinners at school hadn't told me, in a covert way, that I had a right to exist, was worth something.[153]

Especially for those at the beginning and the end of their lives, the breadth of the state's commitment to their well-being and the apparent disconnection of collective caring from public censure did indeed represent a watershed in the history of the century. Such a response was real enough to survive the subsequent decades of compromise and crisis. Yet even at the time other categories of the needy, especially the unemployed and the single parents, were being made sharply aware of underlying continuities in their treatment. As their numbers began to rise, so arguments began to surface about the scale of the changes which had been made.

By the late fifties, the heady excitement which had accompanied the publication and implementation of the Beveridge Report was being replaced by a more negative assessment of its place in history. 'The Welfare State as it exists today', stated Peter Goldman, the Director of the Conservative Political Centre, in 1958, 'is the delayed reaction to Victorian poverty and inter-war unemployment. As standards of living continue to rise, many of the assumptions upon which it is based are seen to have been falsified.'[154] This perception that the legislation of the Labour Government was increasingly incapable of dealing with economic and social change was common to critics of the Right and the Left.[155] Far from making a decisive break with the past, as Beveridge had hoped, both the means and the ends of his scheme seemed trapped in history.

Although their final prescriptions were diametrically opposed to each other, those seeking to re-establish a distinctively Conservative approach to social policy and those seeking to reawaken the passions of reform within the Labour Party started from similar positions. Both were concerned that not enough money was being spent on those who most needed it, and too much on those who did not. There was a shared conviction that the insurance principle at the heart of the Beveridge system was little more than a convenient official myth. A new generation of politically connected social scientists challenged the early optimism about the victory over want, and argued that deprivation amongst children and the elderly in particular was widespread and increasing. Townsend, who had raised doubts about the adequacy of the rates as early as 1952, finally published with Abel-Smith in 1965 *The Poor and the Poorest*, which concluded that seven and a half million people were living below the level of the benefits obtainable under National Assistance, and nearly four million were subsisting below the basic scale.[156] At the same time it was argued that not only were the middle class making disproportionate claims on the welfare state, especially by their use of the NHS and further education, they were also developing their own welfare system through employment privileges such as occupational pension policies, which doubled between the mid-thirties and mid-fifties.[157] In 1954 the Government contributed £70 million to its own National Insurance system, and £100 million by way of tax relief to nominally private superannuation schemes.[158]

Rather than transferring resources from the rich to the poor, the state was in danger of doing the reverse – raising half its revenues from regressive indirect taxes, most notably on alcohol and tobacco, providing an increasing range of tax concessions for high-income earners, and levying a flat rate poll tax to pay for insurance benefits.[159] The proportion of social security payments funded by contributions had risen from just over half in the early 1920s to almost three-quarters by the mid-1950s.[160] In Abel-Smith's view, these post-war developments invalidated the assumption that

> State intervention should only provide a minimum of civilized life – the legacy of mutton-eating Beatrice Webb and the Poor Law. This is just hypocrisy when the employer is intervening to do exactly the opposite for his salaried employees. The subsistence minimum was an excellent target when the State was hardly doing anything at all, but it makes no sense in a community which is getting rich at the rate of the last ten years. With rising standards of life, a belief in a subsistence minimum is a belief in ever increasing inequality and class distinction.[161]

From the standpoint of the Left it seemed that the historical commitment to the national minimum was becoming hostile to equality of condition: to the Right it appeared more and more inimical to equality of opportunity. Whereas to socialists this reappraisal demanded a far more radical attack on the distribution of power and privilege in society, to their opponents it confirmed that the time had come to scale down the intervention of the state. Whilst opinion was divided amongst Conservatives on the political feasibility of a rapid dismantling of the welfare state,[162] all agreed that it should have a diminishing role in a successful economy. Universal benefits had been extravagant in conception, and with growing national prosperity were wasteful in practice. 'We squander public money', argued Goldman, 'providing indiscriminate benefits and subsidies for citizens, many of whom do not need them and some of whom do not want them.'[163] Although reluctant to endorse the larger estimates of residual poverty, the right-wing critics also drew attention to continuing deprivation, which they used to justify the extension of means-tested benefits. In the more ambitious proposals, these were to be integrated with the tax system.[164] National Insurance might have a role in so far as it promoted the virtues of prudence and foresight amongst the spendthrift, but only if it was operated on a strict actuarial basis and confined to those unable to make their own arrangements.[165]

In the midst of this debate, the poor were being rediscovered and redefined in much the same way as a native tribe might be discovered and argued over by visiting anthropologists. They had been told that they existed, that they were worth something irrespective of their place in the market,[166] but they were still not expected to take an active part in the resolution of their problems. *The Socialist Register* could argue that, 'We have to focus attention upon the demands of the working class for social justice and upon an analysis of the political strengths of the working class',[167] but no such dialogue was taking place. Whereas between the wars the cries from below had been heard, even if they had not been listened to, now it was assumed that the victims of the variously defined shortcomings of the welfare state were too old or too young or too few to have a politically effective voice. Only the middle class, unduly privileged or unjustly threatened as they might be, were vocal in defence of their interests. Although the evident failings of the pensions system had featured as an issue in the 1959 General Election, the pensioners themselves remained a marginal presence in the parliamentary process.

In many ways the controversies provoked by the rapid obsolescence of the Beveridge system could not have been more wide-ranging nor more forward-looking. It may be argued that the major rethinking of the Edwardian assumptions began not in the early 1940s but two decades later. The first real attempt was taking place to reconsider the relationship between poverty and inequality, and the outlines of the later full-scale attack on state intervention were clearly visible. At the same time the debate was curiously old-fashioned in its conduct. Academics and political writers attacked each other and the Government in articles and books, whilst their subject matter looked on in silence. The more they criticised Beveridge, the more they endorsed the assumption that permeated his scheme, that those threatened with destitution were to be passive recipients of the goodwill of the state.[168]

REFERENCES

1. *Hansard*, vol. 386, (18 Feb. 1943), col. 1964. On the power of the Labour Party's collective memory of the Means Test, see O. Stevenson, *Claimant or Client* (London, 1973), p. 14.
2. *The Times*, 1 July 1940, p. 5.
3. R.M. Titmuss, 'War and Social Policy' in *Essays on 'The Welfare State'* (3rd edn, London, 1976), pp. 81–7.
4. A. Calder, *The People's War* (London, 1971), pp. 40–58.
5. Mass Observation, *War Begins at Home* (London, 1940), pp. 305, 312.
6. D. Moggeridge (ed.), *The Collected Writings of John Maynard Keynes, vol. XXII* (London, 1978), p. 261.
7. Lewis, *Politics of Motherhood*, p. 187.

8. Hurt, 'Feeding the Hungry Schoolchild', p. 200.

9. A. Deacon and J. Bradshaw, *Reserved for the Poor* (London, 1983), pp. 36–40.

10. G.C. Peden, *British Economic and Social Policy* (Deddington, 1985), pp. 128–34.

11. P. Addison, *The Road to 1945* (London, 1975), p. 130

12. A. Bullock, *The Life and Times of Ernest Bevin, vol. II* (London, 1967), pp. 84–92.

13. MacNicol, *Movement for Family Allowances*, ch. 7; Land, 'Introduction of Family Allowances', pp. 181–6.

14. Thane, *Foundations*, pp. 241–2.

15. J. Harris, 'Some Aspects of Social Policy in Britain in the Second World War', in W.J. Mommsen (ed.), *The Emergence of the Welfare State in Britain and Germany* (London, 1981), pp. 249–50.

16. Harris, *Beveridge*, pp. 82–8.

17. W. Beveridge, *Social Insurance and Allied Services* (London, 1942), p. 6.

18. W. Beveridge, *Power and Influence* (London, 1953), p. 303.

19. Beveridge, *Social Insurance*, Appendix C. For a discussion of this survey see J. Harris, 'Did British Workers want the Welfare State? G.D.H. Cole's Survey of 1942', in J. Winter (ed.), *The Working Class in Modern British History* (Cambridge, 1983).

20. Beveridge, *Social Insurance*, p. 18. See also Harris, 'Some Aspects of Social Policy'.

21. Beveridge, *Social Insurance*, pp. 11–12.

22. *Ibid.*, p. 17.

23. *Ibid.*, p. 166.

24. *Ibid.*, p. 167.

25. He contemplated joining both the Labour and the Liberal Parties, but eventually accepted an offer to stand as Liberal candidate for Berwick-on-Tweed in 1944. Harris, *Beveridge*, p. 443.

26. Beveridge, *Social Insurance*, p. 167.

27. *Ibid.*

28. The benefit was introduced in 1948, and reduced to the level of male unemployment benefit in 1953.

29. E. Wilson, *Women and the Welfare State*, (London, 1977), pp. 149–54.

30. Beveridge, *Social Insurance*, p. 142.

31. The first academic study of this question was Michael Young's 'Distribution of Income within the Family', *British Journal of Social Policy*, III, no. 4 (1952).

32. A.W. Dilnot, J.A. Kay and C.N. Morris, *The Reform of Social Security* (Oxford, 1984), pp. 35–5; P. Townsend, 'Poverty: Ten Years After Beveridge', *Planning*, XIX (1952), pp. 25–33.

33. Harris, *Beveridge*, p. 416.

34. D. Marquand, *The Unprincipled Society* (Fontana, 1988), pp. 29–33.

35. For a discussion of Beveridge's emphasis on voluntary insurance, see K. Judge, 'Beveridge: Past, Present and Future', in C. Sandford, C. Pond and R. Walker, *Taxation and Social Policy* (London, 1980), pp. 173–4.

36.   Harris, 'Did British Workers Want the Welfare State?', pp. 211–13.

37.   W.A. Robson, 'The Beveridge Report: An Evaluation', *Political Quarterly*, XIV, 2 (1943), p. 163.

38.   The best account of the launching of the report is by Beveridge's personal assistant, the then Frank Pakenham (later Lord Longford), in *Born to Believe* (London, 1953), pp. 125–33.

39.   *Hansard*, vol. 386, (17 Feb. 1943), col. 1823.

40.   *Ibid.*, col. 1816.

41.   *Ibid.*, col. 1809.

42.   Mass-Observation, 'Social Security and Parliament', *Political Quarterly*, XIV, 3 (1943), pp. 246–7.

43.   Pakenham, *Born to Believe*, p. 125.

44.   Addison, *Road to 1945*, pp. 225–8; Calder, *People's War*, pp. 608–14.

45.   A. Calder and D. Sheriden (eds), *Speak for Yourself* (London, 1984), p. 114.

46.   *Hansard*, vol. 386, no. 30 (16 Feb. 1943), col. 1126.

47.   Beveridge, *Power and Influence*, pp. 319–33.

48.   Mass-Observation, 'Social Security', p. 247.

49.   Marwick, 'Labour Party and the Welfare State', p. 397.

50.   Harris, *Beveridge*, pp. 443–8. He had won the seat at a by-election the previous autumn.

51.   For an accurate preview of the election, see T. Harrison, 'Who'll Win?', *Political Quarterly* XV, 1 (Jan.–March, 1944); for the election itself, K.O. Morgan, *Labour in Power 1945–1951* (Oxford, 1985), pp. 36–44.

52.   Morgan, *Labour in Power*, p. 171.

53.   Harris, 'Some Aspects of Social Policy', pp. 251, 255.

54.   Harris, 'Did British Workers Want the Welfare State?', pp. 213–14.

55.   Cited in *Hansard*, vol. 444 (24 November, 1947), col. 1675. See also the warning of the Tory MP William Shepherd (col. 1670).

56.   J. Griffiths, *Pages from Memory* (London, 1969), pp. 86–7.

57.   J. Hess, 'The Social Policy of the Attlee Government', in W.J. Mommsen (ed.), *The Emergence of the Welfare State in Britain and Germany 1850–1950* (London, 1981), p. 304.

58.   In fact the major improvement in pensions took place under the Assistance Board, and by 1944 they were at least at the level set in 1948. J. Bradshaw and A. Deacon, 'Social Security' in P. Wilding (ed.), *In Defence of the Welfare State* (Manchester 1986), p. 86.

59.   Land, 'Introduction of Family Allowances', p. 201.

60.   A.W. Dilnot, J.A. Kay and C.N. Morris, *The Reform of Social Security* (Oxford, 1984), pp. 33–7; P. Townsend, 'Poverty: Ten Years After Beveridge', *Planning*, XIX, 334 (1952), pp. 29–33.

61.   Griffiths, *Pages from Memory*, p. 85.

62.   Memorandum by James Griffiths, cited in A. Deacon, 'An End to the Means Test? Social Security and the Attlee Government', *Journal of Social Policy*, **11**, 3 (1982), p. 297.

63.   G.C. Peden, *British Economic and Social Policy* (Deddington, 1985), p. 152.

64. D.G. Green, *Working-Class Patients and the Medical Establishment* (Aldershot, 1985), pp. 136–7.

65. A. Harvey, *Casualties of the Welfare State* (London, 1960), p. 4.

66. Ministry of Labour, *Family Expenditure Survey. Report for 1963* (London, 1965), p. 12.

67. B.S. Rowntree and G.R. Lavers, *Poverty and the Welfare State* (London, 1951), p. 40.

68. Briggs, *Social Thought and Social Action*, p. 322,

69. R. Miliband, 'Politics and Poverty', in D. Wedderburn (ed.), *Poverty, Inequality and Class Structure* (Cambridge, 1974), p. 186.

70. Craig, *British General Election Manifestos*, p. 132.

71. A. Gamble, *The Conservative Nation* (London, 1974), p. 64.

72. A. Crosland, *The Future of Socialism* (London, 1956), p. 43.

73. Rowntree and Lavers, *Poverty and the Welfare State*, p. 34.

74. MacNicol, *Movement for Family Allowances*, pp. 218–19; Land, 'Introduction of Family Allowances', pp. 226–7.

75. D. Piachaud, *Family Incomes Since the War* (London, 1982), p. 6.

76. Dilnot *et al.*, *Reform of Social Security*, p. 21.

77. A.B. Atkinson, *Poverty in Britain and the Reform of Social Security* (Cambridge, 1969), p. 26.

78. Harris, *Beveridge*, p. 463.

79. V. George, *Social Security: Beveridge and After* (London, 1968), p. 99.

80. Social security benefits here refer to National Insurance, National Assistance, non-contributory pensions, family allowances and war pensions. See George, *Social Security*, p. 65.

81. D. Bull, 'The rediscovery of family poverty' in D. Bull (ed.), *Family Poverty* (London, 1971), p. 13.

82. Rowntree and Lavers, *Poverty and the Welfare State*, p. 34.

83. *Report of the National Assistance Board for the Year ended 31st December, 1951*, Cmnd 8632 (London, 1952), pp. 5–12, 31–2; *Report of the National Assistance Board for the Year ended 31st December, 1954*, Cmnd 9539 (London, 1955), pp. 5–6, 41; *Report of the National Assistance Board for the Year ended 31st December, 1959*, Cmnd 1085 (London, 1960), pp. 7–9, 45; *Report of the National Assistance Board for the Year ended 31st December, 1964*, Cmnd 2674 (London, 1965), pp. 15–16, 63.

84. George, *Social Security*, pp. 52–3.

85. *NAB 1964 Report*, p. 24.

86. George, *Social Security*, p. 97.

87. *NAB 1954 Report*, p. 16.

88. *NAB 1964 Report*, p. 58.

89. P. Townsend and D. Wedderburn, *The Aged in the Welfare State* (London, 1965), p. 68.

90. Deacon and Bradshaw, *Reserved for the Poor*, p. 30.

91. P. Townsend, *The Family Life of Old People* (London, 1957), p. 162.

92. Cited in D. Cole and J.E.G. Utting, *The Economic Circumstances of Old People* (London, 1962), p. 97.

93. *NAB 1954 Report*, p. 19.

94. B. Abel-Smith and P. Townsend, *The Poor and the Poorest* (London, 1965), p. 30.

95. Cole and Utting, *Economic Circumstances of Old People*, pp. 53, 65, 101.

96. K. Hood, *Room at the Bottom* (London, 1960), p. 9.

97. In 1964, in addition to distributing posters on entitlement, it caused leaflets to be inserted in National Insurance Pension Books explaining the possibilities of additional relief.

98. T. Lynes, 'Poverty in the Welfare State', *Aspect* (Aug. 1963), p. 10; M. McCarthy, *Campaigning for the Poor* (London, 1986), pp. 30–1.

99. Cole and Utting, *Economic Circumstances of Old People*, pp. 96–7.

100. *NAB 1954 Report*, p. 35.

101. Townsend, *Family Life of Old People*, p. 163.

102. Townsend, *Family Life of Old People*, p. 62; Townsend and Wedderburn, *The Aged in the Welfare State*, p. 124.

103. Townsend, *Family Life of Old People*, p. 205.

104. P. Marris, *Widows and their Families* (London, 1958), p. 105. The only major item of consumer expenditure to show a sharp fall in real terms between 1938 and 1956 was insurance. A.M. Carr-Saunders, D. Caradog Jones and C.A. Moser, *A Survey of Social Conditions in England and Wales* (Oxford, 1958), p. 155.

105. Ministry of Labour, *Family Expenditure Survey. Report for 1957–59* (London, 1961), pp. 11–19.

106. Carr-Saunders *et al.*, *Social Conditions*, p. 215. The exception was the consumption of iron, which stood at 90 per cent of recommended levels.

107. Townsend and Wedderburn, *The Aged in the Welfare State*, p. 125.

108. F. Zweig, *Labour, Life and Poverty* (London, 1948), p. 90; Townsend, *Family Life of Old People*, pp. 68– 71.

109. *NAB 1954 Report*, p. 6; *NAB 1964 Report*, p. 12.

110. Abel-Smith and Townsend, *Poor and the Poorest*, p. 41.

111. *Report of the Committee on One-Parent Families* (Finer Report), Cmnd 5629 (London, 1974), p. 28. The figures are for England and Wales. Equivalent Scottish percentages were 19:39; 5:7.

112. *NAB 1954 Report*, pp. 15–16; *NAB 1964 Report*, p. 15.

113. Hood, *Room at the Bottom*, pp. 44–5.

114. In 1965, 178 men were prosecuted for this offence. George, *Social Security*, p. 232.

115. E. Wilson, *Women and the Welfare State* (London, 1977), p. 90.

116. *NAB 1964 Report*, p. 40.

117. The operation of this policy is discussed in Lynes, 'Poverty in the Welfare State', p. 10.

118. *NAB 1951 Report*, pp. 8–9.

119. *NAB 1964 Report*, p. 63.

120. George, *Social Security*, p. 93–5.

121. M.J. Hill, 'The Exercise of Discretion in the National Assistance Board', *Public Administration*, **47** (Spring, 1969), pp. 77–89; Harvey, *Casualties of the Welfare State*, pp. 28–30.

122. *Social Insurance*, Cmnd 6550 (London, 1944), p. 26.
123. George, *Social Security*, p. 20.
124. *Finer Report*, pp. 35–6.
125. Political and Economic Planning, 'Social Security and Unemployment in Lancashire', *Planning* XIX (Dec., 1952), p. 119; H. Land, *Large Families in London* (London, 1969), pp. 16–29.
126. M. Wynn, *Fatherless Families* (London, 1964), pp. 36–42.
127. See for instance the problems encountered by widows who exhausted their National Insurance benefit and were discouraged by National Assistance wages regulations from earning: Marris, *Widows and their Families*, p. 97
128. Lynes, 'Poverty in the Welfare State', p. 63.
129. Carr-Saunders et al., *Social Conditions*, p. 180.
130. A.H. Halsey, *Change in British Society* (Oxford, 1972), p. 37.
131. Ministry of Labour and National Service, *Report of an Enquiry into Household Expenditure in 1953–54* (London, 1957), pp. 24–9, *1963 Family Expenditure Survey*, pp. 26–33.
132. The proportion had fallen to 37.4 by 1959. *1953–54 Household Expenditure Enquiry*, p. 246; *1957–59 Family Expenditure Survey*, pp. 8–19.
133. Lynes, 'Poverty in the Welfare State', p. 11.
134. Carr-Saunders et al., *Social Conditions*, p. 181.
135. Land, *Large Families*, p. 95.
136. Carr-Saunders et al., *Social Conditions*, p. 156.
137. See above, p. 15.
138. Wynn, *Fatherless Families*, p. 31.
139. M. Stacey, *Tradition and Change* (Oxford, 1960), p. 115.
140. M. Young and P. Willmott, *Family and Kinship in East London* (London, 1957), p. 102.
141. A.H. Halsey (ed.), *Trends in British Society* (London, 1972), pp. 552, 559.
142. B.S. Rowntree and G.R. Lavers, *English Life and Leisure* (London, 1951), pp. 228–32. 'Old' in this case meant those aged sixty and above.
143. A.M. Carr-Saunders, D. Caradog Jones and C.A. Moser, *A Survey of Social Conditions in England and Wales* (Oxford, 1958), p. 252.
144. Zweig, *Labour, Life and Poverty* pp. 38–9.
145. *1953–54 Household Expenditure Enquiry*, p. 27; *1963 Family Expenditure Survey*, p. 31.
146. Rowntree and Lavers, *English Life and Leisure*, p. 199 calculated that 80 per cent of expenditure on tobacco was taxed.
147. M. Young and P. Willmott, *Family and Kinship in East London* (London, 1957), pp. 116–27.
148. Halsey, *Trends in British Society*, pp. 549–52.
149. Stacey, *Tradition and Change*, p. 108.
150. Young and Willmott, *Family and Kinship*, p. 114.
151. *Hansard*, vol. 444 (24 Nov. 1947), col. 1635.
152. *Hansard*, vol. 444 (24 Nov. 1947), col. 1636.
153. C. Steedman, 'Landscape for a Good Woman', in L. Heron, *Truth,*

Dare or Promise (London, 1965), pp. 118–19. The reference is to G. Stedman Jones, 'Why is the Labour Party in a Mess?' in *Languages of Class* (Cambridge, 1983), p. 246.

154. P. Goldman, 'Preface', in Conservative Political Centre, *The Future of the Welfare State* (London, 1958), p. 9.

155. A. Briggs, 'The Welfare State in Historical Perspective', *Archives Européennes de Sociologie*, **2** (1961), p. 222.

156. Abel-Smith and Townsend, *The Poor and the Poorest*, pp. 57–8.

157. R.M. Titmuss, *Income Distribution and Social Change* (London, 1962), pp. 169-86; J. Saville, 'Labour and Income Redistribution', *Socialist Register 1965* (London, 1965), pp. 159–60; P. Townsend, 'A Society for People', in N. Mackenzie (ed.), *Conviction* (London, 1958), p. 101.

158. Hood, *Room at the Bottom*, p. 55.

159. See Titmuss, *Income Distribution* pp. 141–2 for a full list of tax-free allowances, payments, receipts and benefits in 1960. On the regressive nature of National Insurance and indirect taxation see J. Saville, 'The Welfare State', *New Reasoner* (Winter, 1952–53), p. 22.

160. B. Abel Smith, 'Social Security', in M. Ginsburg (ed.), *Law and Opinion in England in the Twentieth Century* (London, 1959), p. 362. 'Social Security' in this context meant all forms of outdoor relief, family allowances and insurance benefits.

161. B. Abel-Smith, 'Whose Welfare State?' in N. Mackenzie (ed.), *Conviction* (London, 1958), p. 69.

162. For a consensus-based view of change, see I. Macleod, 'The Political Divide', in Conservative Political Centre, *The Future of the Welfare State* (London, 1958); for a radical approach, M. Fogarty, 'Social Welfare', in A. Seldon (ed.), *Agenda for a Free Society* (London, 1961)

163. Goldman, 'Preface', p. 9.

164. G. Howe, 'Reform of the social services', in D. Howell and T. Raison (eds), *Principles in Practice* (London, 1961), pp. 65–7.

165. Fogarty, 'Social Welfare', p. 123; N. Bosanquet, *After the New Right* (London, 1983), pp. 136–45.

166. For a strong defence of the 'anti-capitalist' ethos of the welfare state, see. D. Thompson, 'The Welfare State', *New Reasoner*, **4** (Spring, 1958), pp. 127–30.

167. D. Wedderburn, 'Facts and Theories of the Welfare State', *The Socialist Register 1965* (London, 1965), p. 142.

168. Stedman Jones, 'Why is the Labour Party in a Mess?', p. 245.

CHAPTER FOUR

Poverty and Growth 1964–90

INTRODUCTION

By 1964 the rising tide of criticism of the post-war poverty legislation had forced the Labour Party to commit itself to a major reform of the structure it had created. Its successful election manifesto drew attention to the shortcomings of the insurance scheme: 'Social security benefits – retirement and widows' pensions, sickness and unemployment pay – have been allowed to fall below minimum levels of human need. Consequently one in four of National Insurance pensioners are today depending upon means-tested National Assistance benefits. Labour will reconstruct our social security system.'[1] During the succeeding quarter of a century every political party has at some stage promised to undertake a complete overhaul of the means by which the state seeks to combat Beveridge's giant of want. Parliament has inquired and enacted with almost as much vigour as the inter-war governments, but whereas the cumulative adjustments which began in 1918 transformed the scale and form of state intervention, the more recent sequence of reforms and proposals have made relatively little impact on a system which all agreed was ill-suited to changing needs and aspirations.

At the heart of this combination of a constant search for effective reform and a persistent failure to attain it, was the issue of economic growth. From the Edwardian period onwards, the expansion of the economy and the rising standard of living of those in work, sustained the programmes of state relief and compensated for their many limitations. Just as increasing tax revenues emboldened the last Liberal Government to tackle the long-standing problem of old age pensions, so Beveridge's optimistic verdict on the performance of the inter-war economy encouraged the first majority Labour Government to take the risk of a huge expansion of social expenditure in the midst of post-war dislocation. And just as the resentment of the means-tested unemployed was contained by the growing prosperity of the majority of the working class who kept their jobs, so the failings and contradictions of the new welfare state were confined by the continued progress of the economy and the unprecedented victory over unemployment. Townsend may have exaggerated the case when he claimed in 1958 that, 'Full employment and not social insurance has been responsible for the reduction in poverty since the war',[2] but there was no doubt that the legacy of Keynes was greatly enhancing the bequest of Beveridge. If inflation and rising expectations were raising new difficulties, all sides assumed that further growth would supply the means for their resolution. For the Left it would make genuine redistribution politically feasible, for the Right it would make a serious contraction of state support relatively painless.

From 1964 onwards, the relationship between the performance of the economy and the perceived adequacy of the welfare system became more complex and less benign. Most years still saw a growth in most real incomes, and as before this did much to ease the political and social tensions engendered by the incidence and relief of poverty. But as the Wilson Administrations of 1964 and 1966 plunged into financial difficulties, so the need for a response to the inadequacies of the Beveridge system became more urgent, and the freedom to manoeuvre became more limited. It was not just that many of the reforms which the Left might wish to make required money which was no longer forthcoming. More fundamentally, major change in any direction by any party raised problems of consent which in times of deepening crisis seemed virtually insoluble. Whether or not every individual and vested interest knew what they were agreeing to, or were consciously agreeing to the same thing, the breadth of support Beveridge achieved for his plan, and the range of material benefits which it spread across the population gave the scheme the effect of a flywheel which appeared more irresistible the more attempts were made to alter its direction. It became extremely difficult to conceive of a reform which would be at once radical and cost-free to all those involved, or to devise a strategy of legislation which could negotiate the conventions of what was still a nineteenth-century parliamentary system. At the same time the almost complete absence of direct participation by the poor themselves rendered impossible a cumulative programme of small-scale modifications to an ever more expensive and cumbersome structure.

ADJUSTMENT

Labour had waited a long time to regain office, and despite its tiny majority in the 1964 General Election, it moved with great speed to honour its commitments to the poor. Within a month, legislation was introduced to provide the largest ever single increase in pensions and other social benefits. Wilson owed his reputation as a left-winger to his resignation from the last Attlee Administration over the introduction of prescription charges, and these were immediately abolished. This much was straightforward, if expensive; structural reform required more planning, and a more comfortable margin of seats. By the time this was achieved in 1966, the pressures for and against effective action were becoming increasingly difficult to reconcile.

On the one hand, the re-establishment of poverty as a major political issue had been confirmed by the publication late in 1965 of *The Poor and the Poorest*, which not only emphasised the failure of National Insurance to cope with the problem of old age, but provided persuasive evidence that poverty amongst families was a real and growing problem. With the associated launching of the Child Poverty Action Group, the poor gained a separate public voice for the first time since the disappearance of the Family Endowment Society in 1949. The Group's extremely successful press campaign played upon Labour's carefully nurtured identity as the party of the dispossessed. It had come into being to represent the outsiders, it had risked everything in defence of the unemployed in 1931, it had achieved a revolution on behalf of the poor after the war, and now its response to the rediscovered and redefined problem of poverty would be a touchstone of the use it could make of its renewed tenure of office.

At the same time, the money that had paid for the initial benefit increases was no longer available, and, more important, the party leadership did not believe that a constituency existed for raising further taxes to fund additional expenditure. The key question was, as it always had been, the party's perception of its political strength. To maintain its vital, hard-won foothold in the expanding middle-class electorate, it had to demonstrate its competence as the manager and moderniser of a clearly troubled economy. Faced with a serious balance of payments crisis after the 1966 election, this demanded emergency controls on collective bargaining, which in turn risked alienating Labour's support amongst organised labour. The one action calculated to make a difficult situation impossible would be to increase the tax burden on those who believed themselves to be already overtaxed, or on those whose standard of living was under growing pressure from a statutory incomes policy.[3] In this situation, the newly formed poverty lobby had no means of forcing an alternative strategy on the Government. Its combination of emotive language and hard statistics made for powerful journalism, but it did not get the poor out on to the streets, nor, crucially, did it get the trade unions demanding action at party conferences.[4] If the rhetoric of radical social reform deliberately raised echoes of the heroic era of the Beveridge Report, the political calculations produced quite different answers. Now public pressure for a new deal for the poor seemed eminently resistable, whilst the risks of precipitate action appeared impossible to ignore.

The only solution to this dilemma was to maximise the appearance of reform whilst minimising the departure from existing assumptions and practices. The proposed 'Incomes Guarantee' which would have provided a form of negative income tax for the elderly was scrapped, partly because of Treasury opposition to the expense, and partly because the Inland Revenue was implacably hostile to the conflation of taxation and welfare. In its place Labour passed the 1966 Ministry of Social Security Act which renamed the benefits and reorganised their administration but left the basic structure of relief and its attendant problems virtually unchanged. The Insurance and means-tested systems were brought together in a single Ministry, and 'National Assistance' became 'Supplementary Benefit', with a fresh specification of entitlement, a simplified claims procedure, an increase in the basic scales together with a new long-term addition for the elderly, and an extensive publicity campaign to encourage take-up.[5]

From the point of view of the Government, the reform secured the worst of both worlds. The cosmetic treatment given to the means test embodied a public admission that the problem of stigma had survived into the welfare state, but offered nothing in the way of a long-term solution. There was an immediate 20 per cent increase in payments, but subsequent research has indicated that the bulk of the extra claims were a product of the enhanced rates rather than the diminished obstacles to application, and by the end of the Wilson Administration the proportion of those eligible for assistance who exercised their rights may have fallen below the level of 1966.[6] In the same way the attention which the new Supplementary Benefits Commission began to pay to the destructive operation of the wage stop highlighted the difficulties but provided only superficial remedies. Its inquiry confirmed that in most cases large families were both the cause and the victims of the reduction in benefit, but the easing of the regulations in 1968 produced merely a marginal reduction in the number of wage-stopped households.[7] Not only was the Government unable to break out of the liberal orthodoxy that a rational man would prefer charity to work if the former offered even a marginal cash advantage, in the same year it capitulated to a press campaign against scrounging by the rising number of unemployed and introduced a new rule under which the Supplementary Benefit of a single unemployed man under forty-five would be suspended after four weeks, on the assumption that he was not trying hard enough to re-enter the economy.[8] Both the principle and the practice of means-tested payments were as vulnerable to criticism as they had been when the Conservatives left office, and their range had actually increased, as rent and rate rebates were introduced, school meals became more expensive, and finally prescription charges were reimposed as part of the 1967 devaluation package.

The Government gained little credit for its reforms, and saved less money. Even the one cost-free innovation of the period, the 1968 ten-shilling rise in family allowances paid for by a 'claw-back' from child tax allowances, increased the ostensible cost of public welfare as expenditure was transferred from the Inland Revenue to the budget of the Ministry of Social Security. Although James Callaghan at the Exchequer had decided as early as the 1966 sterling crisis that restoring the balance of payments and promoting growth took precedence over transferring resources to the poor, by 1970 social security spending had climbed from 7.2 to 9.3 per cent of the GNP. The bulk of this increase was accounted for by the paper transfer from the tax system and the enforced extra expenditure caused by a doubling of the rate of male unemployment. Less than a third of it was devoted to the real improvement in the treatment of the elderly.

An administration which had set out to placate the poverty lobby and restrict the cost of welfare, ended up with a substantial increase in spending, and damaging accusations from the Child Poverty Action Group in the midst of the 1970 election campaign that the poor had become worse off under Labour. In terms of the narrow issue of whether claimants had been adequately protected from inflation, the criticism may have been overstated. Whilst the impact of the 1965 increase in the scales had been gradually eroded, over the period as a whole those dependent on welfare probably fared marginally better than those in work, whose wages were subject to an incomes policy which only in its final phase contained an element of downward redistribution. Non-tax-paying families certainly made real gains from the doubling of family allowances, even if these began to be undermined by rising National Insurance contributions and a continuing fall in the tax threshold.[9] The real failing was a matter not of the value of individual benefits, but rather of the structural weaknesses of the Beveridge system which had become increasingly apparent during the long period of Conservative rule.

The second – and at the time of writing last – Labour Government possessed of a comfortable parliamentary majority was too much a part of the political system to escape from its restrictions, and too committed to the thinking embodied in the welfare state to challenge its shortcomings. It could not and would not resist the long-standing antipathy of organised labour to subsistence-level family allowances, or the traditional hostility to the undeserving poor, who were moving towards the centre of the debate over welfare policy as the era of low unemployment began to come to an end. Despite the important innovation of the Equal Pay Act on the eve of the 1970 Election, it remained committed to Beveridge's view that in the long run poverty would be solved by the uninterrupted labour of adult males in an expanding market economy. Although voices were now heard urging a fundamental redistribution of privilege and resources, this was seen by ministers as an optional goal rather than a precondition for any effective reform. The sterling crisis and the requirement to maintain relations with the organised representatives of both sides of industry demanded the indefinite postponement of larger objectives.

The nearest the Government came to an assault on the failings of the labour market was the establishment in 1967 of an inter-departmental committee to consider the ancient shibboleth of a minimum wage. Its report in 1969 concluded that such a scheme would be inflationary, and would be 'a less efficient means of relieving poverty than selective social benefits related to individual needs'.[10] The fraught attempt to intervene in wage settlements was conceived solely as a response to what was hoped would be a passing economic crisis. It was a telling comment on the continuing gulf between fiscal and social policy that the low paid did best in the brief return to free collective bargaining in 1969 and early 1970.[11] Poverty had been rediscovered as a problem, but not as a political imperative. The poor themselves were seen as a collection of minorities indirectly represented by middle-class pressure groups, rather than 'our people' whose votes or violence could seriously endanger the election prospects of a Labour Government. Those who had power lacked imagination, those who had imagination had no battalions.

In the field of poverty legislation, the subsequent Conservative Government of 1970–74 was in many ways the mirror image of the administration which unexpectedly lost office in 1970. As with Labour in the early sixties, it had used its time in opposition to develop a more distinctive approach to welfare policy, but once faced with the practical obstacles to large-scale reform, it found itself unable to do much more than multiply the existing difficulties. The one major departure from Beveridge, and indeed from the party's own election manifesto, was the rapid introduction of the Family Income Supplement (FIS). Working heads of families whose income was below a set scale were to have half the difference made up in the form of a benefit payable for a six-month period. The scheme was devised as an alternative to the general uprating of family allowances which the poverty lobby had been urging, and presented as a significant manifestation of the Conservative commitment to abandon universality for selectivity.[12] It was also the first direct subsidy of full-time earnings since the 1834 Poor Law had brought the Speenhamland system to an end.

However, despite the presence at the Ministry of Social Security of Sir Keith Joseph – a central figure in the intellectual reaction against the interventionist state – both the reasons for the innovation and its consequences belonged squarely to the now established practice of modifying rather than transforming the treatment of poverty. The Tories accepted the Labour view that as much as possible had to be done for poor children for the least overall increase in expenditure. The 1968 solution of the clawback was no longer feasible, as tax thresholds had fallen to the point at which a cut in child tax allowances would harm the families most in need of assistance. At the same time there was available a fully worked out plan for an income supplement which the Labour Administration had prepared but finally abandoned. In one sense FIS merely constituted a formal recognition that the family allowances which Labour had administered through four governments would never be capable of achieving Beveridge's original objective of meeting the full subsistence costs of raising children.

The hope that the benefit might represent the flagship of a new approach to the relief of poverty was confounded by a serious shortfall in applications. Instead of a projected 85 per cent take-up, the Government only managed to attract claims from just under half those eligible, in spite of a vigorous and expensive advertising campaign.[13] In fact FIS was neither the first nor the last means-tested benefit to encounter such difficulties, but its failure acquired great symbolic importance because it was so obviously an alternative to a universal allowance which from the outset had always reached virtually all of its target.[14] The harder Joseph tried to improve the take-up, the more hostages he gave to his critics. Not only did the innovation confirm everything that had been said in the previous decade about the resistance of the poor to selective assistance, it also brought into focus for the first time the phenomenon of the poverty trap. The subsidisation of low wages was compounding the tendency of means-tested relief to imprison the poor at or just below subsistence level, penalising every increase in earnings by a corresponding loss of benefits. A Government supposedly committed to more efficient public spending and the promotion of the work ethic was seen to be wasting money through the high launch costs of the new supplement and to be discouraging the poor from improving their condition by their own efforts.

Family Income Supplement was at least an attempt to unite radical thinking with innovative legislation; for the remainder of the Heath Administration, theory and practice were kept well apart. Ministers with responsibilities for poverty pursued the now traditional course of pressing for increases in their budgets, and introducing *ad hoc* and mostly selective schemes to deal with newly identified problems. The only consistent change in emphasis was to expand services rather than benefits, which resulted in rapid growth in the number of social workers.[15] Otherwise, Labour's rent and rate rebate schemes were tidied up and extended, bringing a substantial section of the respectable working class into the sphere of means-tested benefits. An invalidity benefit was introduced for the long-term sick, and an attendance allowance for disabled adults and children who needed care for more than six months. The 1973 Social Security Act provided for a long-term growth in earnings-related pensions schemes, but did nothing to resolve the problems of the existing generation of pensioners. The scope of existing means tests was widened by increases in prescription charges and the price of school meals, and by the abolition of cheap welfare milk. The campaign against the able-bodied poor, which had been re-launched in 1968, was continued through the appointment of the Fisher Committee on the abuse of social security benefits.[16] This found that public fears about 'the work-shy', and 'layabouts who prefer to live on supplementary benefit rather than do an honest day's work', were exaggerated, and that 'the great majority of long-term unemployed on supplementary benefit (who are predominantly older men) are unemployed because they cannot get work.'[17] Nonetheless it recommended an increase in the number of special investigators and some tightening of the regulations.

Yet whilst the Government was busy making an already confused system still more complex, it was also at work planning a major rationalisation of the administration of public welfare. In 1972 it published a green paper on a tax credit scheme which set out 'to simplify and reform the whole system of personal tax collection, and, at the same time, to improve the system of income support for poor people'.[18] Every individual in the scheme would be allocated a credit based on family circumstances, which would be set against his or her tax liability; if the credit exceeded the tax, the difference would be paid as a weekly benefit. The reform was presented as a direct response to the mounting body of criticisms of the post-war legislation and its later additions. It would be easier to understand, it would extend tax allowances to those presently below the threshold, it would 'relieve hundreds of thousands of pensioners from the need to claim supplementary benefit', and would 'prove of great help to hard-pressed families of working age – especially those with children – many of whom cannot be helped effectively through FIS and other means-tested schemes.'[19] Although it would not abolish the poverty trap, the combination of a comprehensive cash benefit and a constant rate of tax would greatly diminish its effect.

The proposals were attacked for institutionalising means-tested relief and weakening the insurance principle, and the poverty lobby argued that the likely cost of the exercise would be better spent on up-rating the existing benefits, particularly family allowances and National Insurance pensions, and extending the widowed mother's benefit to all single-parent families.[20] There were also doubts about whether the Inland Revenue was yet capable of taking on such additional responsibilities. Nonetheless the Government remained committed to what is still the only serious plan by a party in power to challenge the basic features of the Beveridge system, and announced in the 1973 Queen's Speech that the scheme would come into operation in five years' time.

The defeat in the election of February 1974 put paid to such a prospect, and brought in a Labour Administration pledged, to its subsequent embarrassment, 'to eliminate poverty wherever it exists'.[21] The strategy which it had developed during the period in opposition was in its way as radical as the tax credit proposal which was now abandoned. Little fundamental change to the basic features of the welfare structure was envisaged. Even FIS, which had evoked so much hostility on its introduction, was retained, and in 1979 extended to assist single-parent families.[22] Instead the Government proposed to tackle for the first time the relationship between the management of the economy and the relief of poverty, which required in turn, the creation of a new partnership between the power of organised labour and the needs of the disorganised poor. The 'social contract' which was drawn up between the TUC and the Labour Party in 1973 was an attempt to achieve radical ends by conservative means. The goal of a constructive integration of wages policy and welfare spending had escaped every post-war administration and was the most striking indicator of the welfare state's failure to achieve the kind of systematic pursuit of social justice that Beveridge had once envisaged. At the same time the agency of this transformation was to be the re-establishment of the co-operation between the state and the unions which had been undermined by recent attempts by both Labour and the Tories to subject aspects of collective bargaining to legal control.

The agreement covered government action on prices, food subsidies, rents, taxes and the repeal of industrial relations legislation, in return for union restraint on pay claims and support for higher public spending.[23] At the heart of the contract was the notion of the 'social wage', an attempt to break down the conceptual barriers that still existed after a quarter of a century of the Beveridge revolution between income gained from work, and direct and indirect benefits derived from the state, which were calculated to amount to £1,000 a year for every worker. The ultimately disastrous failure of the strategy to achieve almost all of its objectives was the consequence of the inability of both sides to deliver their undertakings.

The initial difficulty was that neither partner possessed nor was willing to acquire sufficient coercive powers to impose alternative ways of thinking and behaving. Despite all the authority the union leaders still exercised, with their immunity from regular re-election and their easy access to Downing Street almost irrespective of the complexion of the Government, they lacked the means to force their members to adopt a new attitude towards their wage packets. An apparent change of heart by the TUC did not mean an automatic change of mind on the shop floor.[24] There is little evidence that after 1974 wage demands were in practice modified or recast to take into account actual or potential gains from the welfare system.[25] On its side, the Government, which possessed an ever more tenuous parliamentary majority, reluctantly introduced a mildly redistributive statutory pay policy in 1975,[26] but had to rely on a series of increasingly difficult negotiations to establish the annual level of settlement.

The Government's capacity to keep the unions to their side of the contract was further undermined by its own inability to deliver what it had promised. It was able to increase the value of pensions by an eighth,[27] but thereafter its freedom of manoeuvre was increasingly restricted. The combination of growing unemployment and even more rapidly rising prices which it had inherited from the Heath Administration placed intensifying pressure on its financial strategy, which culminated in the imposition of widespread public expenditure cuts as a condition of the granting of a loan from the International Monetary Fund early in 1976.[28] Although an attempt was made to protect the welfare budget from the full effects of the retrenchment, there was no longer any prospect of a substantial, planned expansion of spending on the poor. The state had little left to offer the unions other than the avoidance of still worse inflation and unemployment; the social contract no longer had any other purpose but the achievement of consensual pay restraint.

The joint endeavour was replaced by mutual recrimination as each side accused the other of bad faith. What was left was a further sequence of unco-ordinated modifications to the existing welfare system, which, taken together with the remorseless rise in the jobless, whose numbers more than doubled to one and a quarter million, extended the scope and compounded the problems of means-tested relief. The long-standing grievance of the wage stop was abolished in 1975.[29] Greater concern about the needs of the disabled resulted in a non-contributory invalidity pension in the same year and an invalid care allowance in 1976, which, although advances in themselves, were set too low to lift their recipients above the supplementary benefit level. In 1975 the national rent and rate rebate schemes were unified, and their qualifying levels standardised, which resulted in a jump in rate rebates from 910,000 to 2,300,000.[30] There was also a large increase in means-tested free school meals as a consequence of the phasing out of subsidies.

The only substantial, clearly worked out innovation was the introduction in 1978 of the State Earnings Related Pension Scheme, which on its maturity twenty years later would guarantee a benefit equivalent to a quarter of the prevailing average earnings.[31] Beveridge's intention of relieving the elderly from humiliating and inadequate discretionary relief would be achieved half a century late, which was little credit to the governments of the era, and less help to those growing old in the 1970s, few of whom would live to see this belated triumph. The other radical and carefully planned reform of the period, the guaranteed maintenance allowance for one-parent families recommended by the 1974 Finer Committee,[32] was not implemented. Instead the problems of this growing sector of the poor were dealt with by extensions to FIS, family and tax allowances, and by the provision of a new entitlement to Supplementary Benefit.[33] The long process of piecemeal accumulation meant that by the mid-seventies at least forty-five separate means tests were in operation, with those administered at the local level subject to many variations in conditions and procedure.[34]

Nothing more graphically illustrated the way in which the social contract came to represent the lowest rather than the highest common denominator of its constituent elements than the troubled introduction of child benefits. Worried about inflation and increasing strains with its Liberal partner, the Government tried to renege on its commitment to complete the integration of family and child tax allowances for fear of the supposedly entrenched opposition of male trade unionists to transferring money from their pay packets to their wives' purses. The Child Poverty Action Group, which had long campaigned for the change, obtained leaked Cabinet documents and was able to shame the trade unions into forcing the ministers to implement the scheme on a reduced basis.[35] The Government gained little political credit for a potentially valuable reform, and then proceeded to erode its impact by failing to index-link the benefit and allowing more poor families into the tax system. By the end of the decade, child benefits were worth little more in real terms than family allowances in the mid-fifties.[36]

In their different ways, the major political parties had run out of time. They had both come too late to a recognition that major structural alterations were required to the treatment of poverty. The succession of escalating economic crises had denied them the freedom of action which they now required. The Beveridge system was no longer susceptible to fine tuning, and the political process was no longer capable of generating a consensus for major reform. The social contract might have provided the basis for the emergence of a new approach, but in the absence of coercion, it required a lengthy period of mutual re-education which was not available. A vehicle for social justice became a device for crisis management, and as a consequence both the poor and their problems became more numerous.

SURVIVAL

The failure of the larger visions of reform in the 1960s and 1970s left the landscape of poor relief looking very familiar. The inability of the National Insurance system to marginalise discretionary help was confirmed by a continuing growth in means-tested benefits. Renaming National Assistance did nothing to halt the long-term rise in payments, which reached almost three million in 1971, nearly three times the level of 1948.[37] For the remainder of the decade the figure fluctuated around that level, before beginning to increase again as mass unemployment once more became a feature of the British economy. After thirty years of growing concern about the exposure of the elderly to the means test, the proportion of pensioners amongst National Assistance/Supplementary Benefit claimants had only fallen two points to 61 per cent. The most that had been achieved was a containment of the problem as the numbers of old people in the population continued to grow. Ever since their plight had become an issue in the 1959 election, they had received better protection from the effects of inflation than other categories of claimants. If the sequence of modifications and up-ratings had not been sufficient to remove pensioners from means-tested relief altogether, it had brought real improvements to their benefits, especially with the introduction of the long-term supplement in 1966.

The survival of the basic outlines to some extent concealed important changes which were taking place in the composition of the dependent population, but these were not so much resolving as recreating older difficulties. In particular, family poverty which had been rediscovered in the early sixties, was beginning to arouse as much concern as it had before the war. Although there were almost as many pensioners amongst the individual claimants as ever, their numbers as a proportion of the overall number of those dependent on National Assistance/Supplementary Benefit (NA/SB) fell from 61 to 44 per cent between 1955 and 1978 because more and more parents with children applied for relief. The doubling and redoubling of unemployment in the seventies resurrected the phenomenon of the able-bodied poor on a scale which had been unknown in the early years of the welfare state. Whereas in 1948 there had been 51,000 Supplementary Benefit payments to individuals registered for work, by 1979 there were just over half a million.

At the same time the single-parent family, barely visible at the outset, was an increasing cause of poverty. In common with other problems, official recognition, which in this case came with the Finer Report of 1974, represented not a turning point but merely a milestone in its progress. There were 570,000 such domestic units when the inquiry began in 1969, three-quarters of a million five years later, and nearly a million by the mid-eighties, by which time they comprised 13 per cent of all families and 11 per cent of all children.[38] Two-thirds of these families, mostly headed by divorced or lone mothers, were living on or below the Supplementary Benefit level. In common with the jobless, the first three decades of the welfare state saw a ten-fold increase in the volume of claims for means-tested benefits. By 1986 nearly half of all families with children claiming Supplementary Benefits were headed by single parents.[39]

As in Rowntree's York of 1901, the old and the young were disproportionately vulnerable to hardship. The original poverty-cycle was not perfectly reproduced as the causes of poverty amongst those below pension age were more varied than once they had been. There were fewer very large families and wholly inadequate incomes than at the turn of the century. Nonetheless in the 1970s as in the 1900s, an individual born into the working class would typically progress through alternating periods of greater or lesser exposure to material hardship, with the troughs occurring as a young child, as the parent of a young family, and in old age.[40] Manual incomes still reached a plateau in early manhood, making it difficult to make adequate provision for marriage and starting a family, and virtually impossible to save for retirement. Children were more likely to be poor than the population as a whole, with those below school age, or with four or more siblings, or in a household which had lost its main breadwinner, particularly at risk. In the mid seventies, a third of all children living at or below the Supplementary Benefit level belonged to single-parent families.[41] Improvements in life expectancy had an ambiguous effect. They encouraged smaller families and permitted more couples to survive together into the relatively sunny uplands of late middle age, but by the same measure they condemned ever larger numbers of men and particularly women to long years of straightened circumstances beyond the age of retirement.

The same conclusions could be drawn from the modern as from the original poverty-cycle. Its presence indicated the inability of the market economy to provide manual workers with the opportunity to secure themselves against the inevitable transitions of their lives, and the failure of public relief to provide adequate compensation. The recent innovations of Family Income Supplement and Child Benefit were not managing to ensure that parents could meet the full cost of raising their children, and the general short-fall of insurance benefits meant that those unable to support themselves were still exposed to the uncertainties of means-tested assistance. It also indicated that, as in 1900, estimates of the total proportion of the population in poverty at any one time underestimated the number who would be exposed to deprivation at some point in their lives, and that those most at risk were least able to bear the physical strain.

What had changed absolutely since the beginning of the century was the intensity of the relationship between the state and poverty. Whereas Rowntree's families only encountered bureaucratic welfare *in extremis*, the modern poor were engaged with the state at every age and in virtually every condition. Although low pay was still an underlying cause of many forms of poverty, and specifically responsible for the plight of about a third of those struggling below the Supplementary Benefit level, the large majority of those who received cash benefits had no main income of their own. This meant that the Government now directly determined the level at which a substantial minority of the population lived, and by extension was also principally responsible for establishing in the public mind what the poverty line was.[42] By the late eighties, the Income Support scales were responsible for setting the standard of living of one in seven of the UK population.[43] Despite occasional attempts to follow in Rowntree's footsteps by defining an independent measure of poverty, most of the published estimates, and much of the debate that surrounded them were founded on the scales of the prevailing basic means-tested benefit. Calculating the volume of poverty over time was still complicated by the adoption of different periods for comparison and the inclusion of varying components of a changing scale, but the official figures suggested that between 3 and 4 per cent of the population in the sixties and the seventies were living below the basic Supplementary Benefit level, and that between a fifth and a quarter were subsisting on or below the full benefit entitlement.[44] There were distinct though small rises under Labour in the late sixties and from 1976 onwards, and then a rapid growth under the Conservatives. Between 1979 and 1987, the last year for which official statistics are available, the proportion below the basic S.B. level rose from four to five per cent, with the percentage on or below full entitlement increasing from twenty-two to twenty-eight.[45] The sharpest change of all since 1979 was in the numbers living on or below the basic S.B. level, which jumped from twelve to nineteen per cent of the population.

Between the first, and, to date, last Labour Governments, the social security budget grew in real terms at an average rate of 4.9 per cent a year, and from a lower base, the personal social services increased by 5.7 per cent. By 1977 the cost of the former was twenty times higher than it had been in 1950, and the latter forty-five times higher, and the two categories were together absorbing 26.1 per cent of all public expenditure.[46] The performance of the economy during the history of the welfare state thus had a paradoxical effect on the treatment of poverty. On the one hand the escalating financial crises from the mid sixties onwards both exacerbated the need for reform and prevented its implementation. On the other hand the continuing expansion of the economy, which in spite of all the troubles did not stop growing until the return of the Conservatives in 1979, sustained a real advance in the value of the principal welfare benefits. Although by the mid seventies social expenditure in the UK represented the lowest proportion of GNP of all the Common Market Countries except Eire,[47] in relation to the early years of the welfare state there had been a significant improvement. In the three decades which followed the introduction of National Assistance, the basic NA/SB scale went up by almost exactly double the retail price index.[48] Whilst the shortcomings of the economic record raised the issue of whether the welfare state could ever abolish want, its achievements were causing doubts about whether there was any meaning left in the very concept of poverty.

It could now be argued that not only were means tests but a pale reflection of the inquisition which faced the jobless in the thirties, the value of their benefits was so much greater in real terms that to use the scales as a modern poverty line was a misuse of language. In 1977 a major study by the National Institute of Economic and Social Research concluded that

> . . . there has been a substantial fall in absolute poverty. Real incomes of the poor increased by about 60–70 per cent over the past twenty years and, more significantly still, when measured by a (1971) living standard held constant over time, the proportion of individuals thus defined fell from about a fifth of the population in 1953 to about a fortieth in 1973.[49]

This meant that over the two decades the standard of living of the median household had become the standard of the bottom tenth.[50] For all the difficulties the Callaghan Government encountered during its later years there was no serious reversal of this trend, and for all their avowed intention of overhauling the welfare state, the Conservatives after 1979 refrained from following the example of the National Government by radically altering the basis of entitlement or imposing major across-the-board reductions in benefits.

However, as a close reading of Rowntree's *Poverty* indicates, the term had in the twentieth century properly referred not just to a basic lack of income, but to an inability to achieve the prevailing minimum standards of living. The question of whether after so long a period of economic growth the term still had meaning outside the protests of academics and agitators can only be resolved by an examination of relativities. Here the NIESR findings were less conclusive. The value of the standard NA/SB rates as a proportion of gross average earnings had remained virtually unchanged throughout the first thirty years of the welfare state.[51] More generally, in 1979 the lowest decile of manual workers still earned almost exactly the same percentage of average manual wages as in the first calculations in 1886.[52] Yet to demonstrate that Britain was still unequal was not to show that the poor were still present. The central issue was whether there existed a sector of the population excluded by their lack of resources from what contemporary society considered to be a basic way of life.

In this context the efficacy of state action had to be measured in terms of how far it enabled the most vulnerable members of society to conduct their campaign for survival. As in earlier periods, this was a matter of both the volume of money that was made available, and its mode of distribution. The key question in either case was the extent to which the strategies of the state and the dispossessed were aligned with each other. The extent and the consequences of the continuing conflict were most readily apparent in the realm of administration. Those threatened with destitution had three interdependent requirements of their sources of assistance. Firstly it should be accessible on the basis of shared knowledge. Those in need should have full information about their rights, those to whom they applied should take decisions on the basis of the necessary information about their circumstances. Secondly, its provision should strengthen rather than undermine the dignity of the claimant. Independence and privacy were as they always had been mutually reinforcing objectives.[53] Thirdly, its receipt should be on the basis of equal status. To ask for help was not to surrender common membership of society.

The initial obstacle to an effective flow of information was the sheer volume of paperwork generated by the basic means test. The changing character of those claiming benefits caused an exponential rise in the work-load of those charged with meeting their needs. Between 1965 and 1971 the number of claimants increased by 150 per cent, but the number of officers by only half as much.[54] The pensioners were still there, and, as before, were comparatively well treated.[55] It was those below retirement age who posed the real challenge. Their problems were far more complex, and changed much more frequently. The unemployed and the single parents came into the office bewildered or offended at their sudden reversal of fortune, embarrassed by having to queue with tramps and alcoholics, and prone to give vent to their resentment of the detailed interrogation of their financial or sexual arrangements with which they were then faced.

Although the levels of verbal and physical abuse never reached prewar levels, the clerks and inspectors worked in an environment far removed from the palmy days of the National Assistance Board and their patient pensioners.[56] Not only were the staff exposed to intimidation across the counter, they were under constant pressure from the Government to save money, and from sections of the press convinced that they were wasting it. Finally as subordinate members of the public sector, they were in the front line of the attempts by successive governments to curtail pay. One angry but perceptive claimant explained their resulting behaviour: 'a lot of their antagonism and hostility stems from the fact that they invariably work in the most humble of offices, their environment is absolutely deplorable, and also that there is this psychological . . . call it blow-back, which comes from giving out to some of the claimants more money than they themselves receive in wages.'[57]

It was not surprising therefore that a series of studies dating back to the closing years of the National Assistance Board found that requests for help frequently received inadequate attention, especially where they involved discretionary judgements on emergency needs payments. So complex and overburdened a system made widespread human error almost inevitable. There was never enough time to give proper consideration to individual claims. As one office manager admitted: 'We have to make snap decisions on single payment requests in almost every case, with no evidence.'[58] In the press of business, suspected fraud was dealt with by cutting benefit and reading the papers later if the claimant protested.[59] Details were misrecorded, files were mislaid, sums were miscalculated, giro cheques were delayed or lost in the post. In every case maladministration threatened malnutrition as few applicants had cash reserves to tide them over until the problems were resolved.

The greater work-load posed by the able-bodied claimants, coupled with the multiplication of the other means-tested benefits to which a family might be eligible, also destroyed the NAB's dream of becoming the co-ordinating agency of the entire welfare state, advising the poor of everything that was on offer throughout the system, and ensuring that all their needs were met. Now it was unlikely that the counter-staff would be able or willing to guide the applicant through the increasingly complex body of qualifications and additions within the Supplementary Benefit structure itself, let alone map out a course through the entire labyrinth of national and local authority means tests. A study in 1982 found that as in the seventies, interviews, especially with those under pension age, were a means of gathering information about the claimant's shortcomings, not of imparting knowledge about the welfare state's resources.[60] This role was gradually being assumed by welfare rights officers appointed by social service departments or pressure groups, but the spasmodic growth of this service was seen by many Supplementary Benefit officials as both a criticism of their work, and a threat to their attempts to reduce expenditure.

Such inadequacies could only deepen the long-standing reluctance of those in need to claim their full entitlement. Poor take-up had begun to worry the National Assistance Board in the later years of its existence, but the body which had been created to attack this problem was by 1979 faced with even worse difficulties. Three in ten of all those eligible for supplementary benefits were failing to make a claim, forgoing an average of £5.60 a week and saving the state £350 million a year. Only 65 per cent of pensioners were receiving their full entitlement, and 63 per cent of the sick and disabled. Despite constant publicity, Family Income Supplement was reaching only half of its targeted audience at the end of the seventies, as were rate rebates. Some of the smaller schemes were operating at derisory levels. Less than one in twenty were claiming the school uniform grants they were due, and less than one in fifty were getting free welfare milk.[61]

Research into low take-up gathered momentum after the unhappy introduction of the Family Income Supplement. It was established that the low level of applications for this and other benefits could not be attributed to either a lack of need or to the generalised phenomenon of stigma, a concept which concealed as much as it described. More weight was attached to the failure of another part of Beveridge's welfare state to slay the giant of ignorance, leaving at least two million adults functionally illiterate and therefore incapable of coping with the notices and forms which now lay between every would-be applicant and the successful completion of a claim. The nominally literate fared little better. As the Fisher Report observed in 1973, 'the leaflets' instructions and conditions are so complicated that even if they read them many claimants would not understand them'.[62] As in the Depression, the proliferation of means tests brought forth plain guides to the system. The CPAG began publishing its *National Welfare Benefits Handbook* in 1970, the Supplementary Benefits Commission (SBC), under pressure to reveal the 'A Code' which controlled the discretionary judgements of local officers, compromised by producing the *Supplementary Benefits Handbook* in the same year, and there were other voluntary and commercial ventures, most notably the regularly revised *Penguin Guide*. The volume of detail required in even the most basic account of the system, meant that these publications were far bulkier than the pioneering manuals issued by the National Unemployed Workers Movement between the wars, and they were used not so much by the claimants as by the agencies which were coming into being to give advice on entitlement.[63]

By the mid-seventies, the failure of the system to meet its designated responsibilities was beginning to cause serious concern to those who managed it. In the words of its new chairman, David Donnison, the SBC was faced with problems of 'excessive complexity, poor take-up of benefits, poor morale among staff, confused relations with neighbouring social services, the misuse of discretion, and the danger of a general breakdown of the system'.[64] The process of the bureaucratisation of welfare which had begun with the New Poor Law of 1834 had now reached nightmare proportions. In 1975 alone the Commission issued 10,000 pages of new and revised instructions. It employed 35,000 staff to administer a vast body of regulations which Parliament could not change and the public could not know. As its discretionary powers had become more extensive, so its efficiency had declined. By this time the administrative costs of Supplementary Benefits were running at just over ten pence in the pound, compared with a penny in the pound for retirement pensions.[65]

In order to prevent the anticipated general breakdown of the system, Donnison persuaded the Labour Government to launch a review of Supplementary Benefits, which led to a white paper and the 1980 Social Security Act.[66] The exercise was constrained by the lack of a broader study of the full range of income support systems and the relationship between them, and by the condition that any reforms should be at nil cost. All that could be attempted was a reversal of the decline in some areas of the system. The complexity was reduced by a simplification of the emergency-needs payments which had proliferated during the seventies. As in the 1966 Act there was an attempt to shift the emphasis from discretion to rights. In future the decisions of officers were to be guided not by secret instructions from the SBC but by rules drawn up and published by the Secretary of State. Some response was made to the requirements of individual claimants by the appointment of trained 'special case officers' who would possess the time and expertise to give constructive guidance on the options which were available.

At best it was a move in the right direction, but by the time the Act was passed, the tide was flowing strongly against its main objectives. A Conservative Government was in power, armed with a fresh set of priorities. The attempt to alleviate the pressure on means-tested relief was confounded partly by further legislation which reduced the real value of insurance benefits, and partly by a dramatic rise in unemployment, which was principally responsible for a growth in claims for Supplementary Benefit from just under three million in December 1979, to a little over four million three years later.[67] These developments coincided with and reinforced a decisive shift in the balance of power away from those who wished to maintain the momentum of change. During the previous Administration, the SBC itself had become an agency for reform, opening up channels of communication with its critics, attempting to shape opinion through the publication of annual reports, and encouraging a wide debate of the review of its work. The new ministers recognised that both the SBC and the campaigning pressure groups had been acting in the absence of rather than in response to an effective movement of the poor themselves, and thus they felt free to replace the SBC by the weaker Social Security Advisory Committee and to deny the pressure groups the access to Government they had begun to enjoy.

Those in need of relief from the state were exposed to conflicting official strategies. The efforts to liberalise the operation of means tests were undermined by renewed attacks on 'scrounging' as the able-bodied poor became ever more numerous and a Government committed to reducing expenditure found itself spending ever larger sums on their relief. Whatever good the 'special case officers' may have achieved was overshadowed by the increasing use of special investigators to detect and prosecute fraud. Greater openness about the regulations was met by increased publicity given to those suspected of breaking them, which soured the atmosphere in the benefit offices, and imposed greater strain on both sides of the counter. Constant attempts to save money exposed the latent contradiction between simplification and economy. Less discretion meant more expenditure, less expenditure meant more rules.

In areas where unemployment was low, and in places where the slow process of modernising the offices and their procedures had taken effect, the gains may have held, elsewhere the increasing numbers of claimants exacerbated all the problems the 1980 Act had tried to resolve.[68] It was symptomatic of the tensions that part of the much-needed programme of refurbishing waiting rooms and counters included the installation of plate-glass barriers to protect staff from attacks by claimants.[69] At its worst, the process of obtaining assistance was reminiscent not just of the Depression but of the convergence of the penal and welfare systems which had characterised the Poor Law. A survey of Hackney in the early eighties revealed long queues in poor buildings for humiliating treatment: 'It is like a high-security prison visit, with just as little dignity and just as little privacy. The most intimate questions, the most insulting allegations, are put and answered in the full gaze and hearing of upwards of a couple of dozen spectators.'[70]

No amount of revising the training manuals could prevent officers causing at best embarrassment and at worst humiliation to their clients. Means tests demanded a full disclosure not just of the household's material conditions, but of sexual relations in the case of single parents,[71] and of occupational failings and intentions in the case of the unemployed.[72] Whatever the national regulations, junior staff in local offices retained extensive powers of discretion, particularly in respect of additional single payments.[73] Working in a bureaucratic culture which distrusted the motives and morality of able-bodied claimants, they were more concerned to ensure that public money was not wasted than that the private citizens were not denied their full entitlement. Claimants were categorised as deserving or undeserving on the basis of appearance and demeanour, and the officers were no more immune to racial prejudice than the population from which they were drawn.[74] At all stages in the process of decision and appeal, the burden of proof rested with the applicant, not with the state. Those who through some combination of pride and uncertainty failed to make a claim, lost their chance of a basic income, those who did undergo a test of their means sacrificed the dignity which a basic income was designed to protect.

Many of the shortcomings in the relations between claimant and bureaucrat could be ascribed to pressures under which each was operating. However, conflict was also the consequence of the deliberately constructed hierarchy of authority which the welfare state had inherited from the thirties and which became more apparent as unemployment began to reach pre-war levels. The system embodied the view that those who received official assistance were to have no practical influence over its provision. Although Supplementary Benefit, the most important source of relief, was subjected to greater parliamentary scrutiny by the 1980 Act, the prospect of claimants themselves exercising any general control via their MPs was remote in the extreme. Only in cases of severe maladministration was it sometimes possible for persistent victims to use their MPs to obtain redress.[75] Nothing came of the attempts made by Donnison at the SBC in the late seventies to set up a new system of consultative groups of claimants and local officers.[76]

Even in local government, where direct democracy was in theory more feasible, the professionalisation of the social services and housing management had consolidated the separation between provider and client. The major reorganisation in 1974 had done nothing to bring authorities nearer their voters.[77] On the council estates, tenants were almost as impotent as they had been under the private landlords. If the conditions were better, and the administration less arbitrary, the rules controlling occupancy were more pervasive and restrictive. Tenants had duties rather than rights, and whereas in the old private sector it had been possible to escape the consequences of transgression by flitting to another landlord, there was virtually no alternative to the often vast housing authorities.[78] At the local level the late seventies and early eighties saw the beginnings of a reaction, as the social services started to sanction or promote tenants' committees and other self-help groups. However, the Conservatives' increasing attempts to centralise the control over the volume and form of council spending, together with their growing indifference to the representations of pressure groups at the national level, meant that individual or collective participation by the poor was at best confined to the detail of their assistance.

The substance of the rules and conditions further reduced the recipients' influence over their own circumstances. In housing, the restrictions ranged from nominally trivial but often important issues, such as permissible pets or decorations, to fundamental questions about where on the estate the family was allowed to live, and how many of its members could occupy the accommodation. Those requiring financial assistance found that officially designated misconduct in the management of their occupational or domestic affairs could expose them to a reduction or loss of benefit, or, at worst, to legal sanctions. Those dependent on means-tested relief had less effective control over their way of life than any other sector outside total institutions such as prisons or hospitals. They lacked sufficient knowledge, dignity and power to function as active citizens. If the claimants did not regard themselves as set apart from their neighbours by reason of their poverty, the system was failing in its intention.

Defenders of the system would, however, argue that at least in respect of the able-bodied poor, an element of less eligibility was desirable. The Beveridge plan had been founded on a commitment to supply no more than a minimum standard of living, and on an expectation that those below retirement age would shortly resume their place in the labour market or in the household of a male worker. What mattered was whether the value of benefits was high enough to prevent material deprivation yet small enough to avoid the destruction of the work ethic.

The latter question was easier to answer than the former. Despite renewed bouts of press-induced public concern from the late sixties onwards, all the evidence indicated that those forced by unemployment to rely on the state had every incentive to re-enter the labour market. Setting aside the indignities visited upon the 52 per cent of the jobless who in the early eighties had to supplement or supplant their National Insurance with means-tested benefit, the sums available from public sources were too small to overcome the powerful social pressures to resume work. The only group to gain from the abolition of the wage stop in 1975 were the handful of claimants with large families and a record of low-paid employment. A DHSS cohort study of unemployed men found that benefits exceeded previous net earnings in no more than 6 per cent of cases. For nearly 50 per cent of the sample, state support replaced less than half the former disposable income.[79] The common experience for the mounting numbers of unemployed was a sharp and unwelcome fall into poverty.[80]

For the most part, the role of the state in assisting the jobless to assist themselves can best be described as one of malevolent neutrality. Its positive initiatives were limited in their effect. Only one in four of those finding work as unemployment reached its peak did so through job centres. The unskilled who were most vulnerable to spells out of work still tended to rely on personal contact. Only in the mid–eighties did the Government begin to make a serious attempt to integrate its training and relief schemes, and even so these initiatives appeared to have a larger impact on the official numbers than the real skills of the unemployed. More consistent effort went into discouraging the forms of private endeavour to which those who had lost their principal source of income had always turned. This struggle had been waged ever since the first unemployment benefit had been paid, and, as had always been the case, the state received its most effective assistance not from its inspectors, but from long-term changes in the economy. The personal service sector was now much smaller than in the thirties, and the units of production and distribution much larger. It was now even more difficult to start businesses with no capital or take up trades with no experience. The crevices in the economy had become narrower and more difficult to find. Caught between declining opportunity and increasing pressure from fraud investigators, the unemployed rarely revealed the possession of significant income outside their state benefits.[81] Some earnings remained hidden, but in towns hit by high unemployment, there was a limit to how many taxis could be driven unseen by inspectors, or windows cleaned unreported by neighbours.[82]

In men's labour, changes in the economy made them more dependent on the state. However, in the realm of women's work, the reverse appeared to be happening. The most important contribution to the alleviation of family poverty in the modern period was not collective provision but the rapid rise in dual-income households.[83] Once their offspring reached school age, mothers were increasingly able to find jobs, the proportion of those with two children in paid employment rising from a quarter to a half between 1961 and 1979. Where work had once taken place between school and motherhood, now motherhood occurred in an interval between school and work.[84] The additional income was usually far larger than Child Benefit and providing the husband retained his employment was sufficient to guarantee the family's basic prosperity.[85] The Royal Commission on the Distribution of Income and Wealth concluded in 1978 that 'whether a wife works is a crucial determinant of whether a family is financially speaking poor. Even when the husband has very low earnings, only 18 per cent of families have incomes below 140 per cent of the supplementary benefit level if the wife works, compared with 76 per cent if she does not.'[86]

Yet the female workforce remained poorly paid. In 1979 there were three times as many women as men whose wages were below the poverty level, and a recent survey of couples found that only five per cent of husbands had incomes below half the income support level, compared with fifty per cent of wives.[87] If the state was relieved of some of its welfare responsibilities by the labour of so many more mothers, it did little to help in return. Little attempt was made to improve child-care facilities to ease the strain on working mothers and their families. The limited impact of the 1970 Equal Pay Act was outweighed by the absence of full safeguards against the inadequate rates in women-only occupations, particularly those which were part-time. Because there was no longer any direct correlation between low pay and poverty, the arguments for effective minimum wage legislation were weakened, despite the fact that more and more individual earners were taking home pay packets which were insufficient to keep a family.[88] The growth of wage protection under successive governments of both parties was reversed after 1979.[89] In particular, the wages councils which had been mainly intended to deal with female sweated labour, became less effective after 1979 as first the inspectorate was reduced and then coverage was removed from workers under twenty-one by the 1986 Wages Act.[90] The deepening recession made it less easy for women to find full-time work. By 1989 they constituted nearly ninety per cent of the part-time sector, where National Insurance benefits were rarely available, and much of the employment protection legislation did not apply.

The tendency of the state to withdraw rather than extend its assistance meant that the increased economic activity of women was not matched by a parallel growth in their financial security. Because of the continuing limitations of the Child Benefit and Family Income Supplement schemes, many were compelled to work to keep their children above the poverty line, but because of the persistent inadequacy of their own wages, many knew that the loss of the male breadwinner through unemployment, sickness or marital breakdown would force them below the line whether or not they continued to earn.[91] Indeed the earnings regulations of the basic means tests often meant that it was pointless for the wife to remain in her own ill-paid job once her husband's wage had disappeared.[92] As the number of single-parent families rose above a million between 1979 and 1983, so the proportion either in receipt of Supplementary Benefit/Income Support or living below 140 per cent of the basic scales rose from a half to two thirds.[93]

The issue of women's work was in several ways representative of the impact on poverty of developments in the state and the economy and in the relationship between them. The expansion in the range of benefits since 1948, and the increase in their real value, despite some reductions in the eighties, meant that absolute destitution was far less common than it had been before the war. The growth in the economy and in dual-earner families ensured that an adequate standard of living was more readily attainable. Yet the inability of successive governments to halt the increasing use of means tests, or to promote a redistribution of privilege and rewards in the market, meant that the material and normative gap between sufficiency and poverty was as real as it ever had been, as was the danger of crossing it. In a timeless way, the burden of failure rested most heavily on women, whether as managers of over-stretched family economies, or as widowed pensioners living below the levels of ease and comfort they had a right to expect.

Two major studies conducted by Townsend in 1969, and by Mack and Lansley in 1983 confirmed that, notwithstanding the general rise in living standards, it was possible to identify a range of expenditure required to meet customary expectations of a basic standard of living. The latter study in particular suggested that in the 1980s as in the 1900s, the poor were divided from the non-poor not by different wants and values, but by their economically determined capacity to realise them.[94] If those at the bottom of the income tables were, usually with good reason, less optimistic than those above them, they had very similar notions of what constituted the necessities of life. And whilst the chances of being unable to afford at least one of the goods or services were distributed across 50 per cent of the population, the studies discovered that there was a point between one and a third and one and a half times the basic Supplementary Benefit scales below which the capacity to meet the prevailing standards began to decline very sharply.[95]

The poorer the family, the more likely it was that the wife would be sent out to work, and the more likely that she would be left in charge of managing the family's resources.[96] To her fell the principal responsibility for managing the consequences of male unemployment.[97] In essence her task was the same as her grandmother's. She would take as many critical financial decisions in the course of a week as the wealthiest entrepreneur, and manipulate as elaborate a pattern of income and debt. The continuing simplificaton of family structure and the disappearance of the household Means Test reduced the complexity of monetary transactions within the domestic economy, but the strategic dispersal of inadequate resources still required unceasing mental effort.

In high and low finance alike, timing was everything. If a bill was paid too soon, the budget might not survive until the next pay packet or giro cheque, if it was paid too late, long-term recovery might never be achieved.[98] Since the thirties the pattern of borrowing and repayment had become less intricate but in many ways more dangerous. It was still possible to raise occasional bridging loans from better-placed relatives, or gain extended credit by avoiding bills from the milkman or other small tradesmen. But the local structures of lending centred on the pawnbroker and the corner shop had decayed, partly because of the post-war disappearance of mass unemployment, which began to make poverty more an individual than a community phenomenon, and partly because of the emergence of new forms of debt, which were easier to incur and more difficult to escape. Although street money-lenders could still be found in hard-pressed neighbourhoods, they had to compete with more commercial ventures with better means of ensuring repayment of their high interest rates. The national mail-order catalogues were twice as widely used by the poor in the eighties as the older system of clothing cheques,[99] and hire-purchase outbid the tally man, offering the possession of a much wider range of goods, and threatening their total loss in the event of a default on payments. Although there had been concern about the misuse of this type of lending since it was first introduced, its perils paled into insignificance beside the later refinement of the credit card, which in the absence of adequate controls over the resources of the holder, offered instant solutions in return for permanent insolvency.

In the field of borrowing, as in other aspects of budget management, the poor at once shared in and were excluded from the behaviour patterns of the more prosperous. After two decades of steady growth, consumer credit expanded rapidly from the mid-seventies, by which time its use had lost any association with deprivation.[100] Only pensioner households showed a consistent disinclination to engage in deferred spending. However, there were marked contrasts in both the causes and consequences of indebtedness. The bulk of transactions by the poor were for mail-order purchases, or for raising small sums of money from relatives and other non-commercial sources.[101] Credit was sought to meet immediate family needs or to postpone imminent domestic insolvency. Food, fuel and children's clothing were the most frequent causes of borrowing.[102] It was not extravagant spending but inadequate or unreliable income which led over a quarter of low-income non-pensioner households to incur problem debts. Families with children and without savings were most at risk. Three-quarters of those in trouble had no reserves to fall back on when a sudden decline in resources threatened an already overstretched family economy.[103] As had been the case in the thirties, very few of the unemployed had any money put by.[104] Most had been in low-paid jobs beforehand, and any redundancy payments soon dwindled away. Ninety-five per cent of those declaring assets to the DHSS in the late seventies had savings of less than £150.[105] Amongst a sample of sixty-seven long-term unemployed families with children in Tyne and Wear in 1987, only three had savings of more than £100, whereas the average level of indebtedness was £440, with the repayments consuming 11 per cent of weekly income.[106]

Debts could be incurred both by borrowing and by failure to pay existing bills. For those at the bottom of the income scale in the eighties, the most intractable problems were caused not by furnishing homes, but by the more basic requirement to meet the costs of rent, gas and electricity.[107] The greatest pressure was exerted by public rather than private creditors. The clearance of the slums and the increasing domination of the rented sector by local authorities meant vastly improved facilities in return for much higher financial commitments. As a proportion of their total income, the poor spent more on housing and related costs than earlier generations and their wealthier contemporaries.[108] Whereas in the pre-war terraces it had always been possible, if often difficult or uncomfortable, to make emergency compromises on heating and lighting expenses, and to engineer enforced subventions from the landlord by departing in the night to a new address, now the rent, electricity and gas bills mounted remorselessly, with disconnections and eviction a real threat. The most thorough survey of fuel debts suggested that the more than 100,000 households a year who were losing their electricity supply were unable rather than unwilling to pay their bills.[109] At the end of the eighties, just over a million households in Britain had rent debts.[110] Early evidence suggests that the introduction of the Community Charge (poll tax) in Scotland in 1989, and a year later south of the border, has exacerbated the difficulties previously presented by rates. It has been calculated that in spite of rebates and transitionary arrangements, the tax has penalised four-fifths of poor families.[111]

Although it is not possible to establish a proper basis for comparison with the pre-war period, there is reason to suppose that the problem of indebtedness may have improved during the first period of the welfare state, and taken a turn for the worse in the early seventies. The post-war reforms had removed the often lethal threat of medical bills, and provided a more secure and hence more manageable source of income for many of those on the breadline. If wives still shouldered a disproportionate burden of responsibility, their right to Family Allowance/Child Benefit had been maintained. Pensioners who in the fifties and sixties constituted by far the largest group of National Assistance recipients less frequently incurred consumer credit, and were more leniently treated if they ran into trouble with their housing costs. The Gas and Electricity Boards, for instance, very rarely disconnected their elderly customers. However, households with one parent or no wage-earner had always had recourse to devices for spreading their expenditure over time, and as their numbers grew, so too did the difficulties caused by unpaid bills. County Court proceedings for debt rose from 1.5 million in 1978 to 2.2 million in 1983, double the number in the years before the first welfare reforms of the century.[112] Households with children under eleven years of age featured in half of all fuel disconnections. Four single-parent families in ten had at least one problem debt at the end of the eighties, and one in seven were in serious trouble, with three or more outstanding commitments.[113]

As families fell into financial difficulties, so they were further exposed to the decisions of central government. The attempts by successive administrations to reduce the size of public deficits had the effect of increasing the vulnerability of their less prosperous citizens to the risk of insolvency. Less borrowing by the state meant more borrowing by the poor. In the field of housing, the curtailment of subsidies led to a persistent upward pressure on rent and fuel costs, and a corresponding growth in dependency on means tests with their attendant problems of take-up and disincentives. The Conservatives' programme of selling council houses and privatising utilities threatened a shift back to market values in determining housing costs and coping with their non-payment. Although the more prosperous sections of the working class gained unprecedented opportunities to acquire real assets, few of the poor could buy their own homes, and those who did found it increasingly difficult to avoid falling behind with their mortgage payments as interest rates rose sharply at the end of the decade.

At the same time the state began to move away from providing direct assistance to poor debtors by replacing the lump sums available for fuel debts by the 'fuel direct' scheme, under which contributions to outstanding bills were deducted from Supplementary Benefit at source.[114] By this means the insolvency of the poor was to be reduced not by increasing their resources but by diminishing their control over them. A more widespread menace to domestic financial strategies was posed by the Social Fund, introduced early in 1988. Those who received the new form of assistance would be impeded from re-floating their budgets by newly incurred debts to the state; those judged too poor to repay such loans would instead be forced onto the rocks of private credit.

In the struggle to make ends meet there was a greater prospect of comfort, but less freedom of manoeuvre. The gap between dependence and independence was becoming more difficult to bridge. The total dislocation of home life caused by the disconnection of gas or electricity was symptomatic of the new vulnerability. There were always devices of the last resort, but paraffin heaters were a major health and fire hazard, and reading by candlelight a pitiful alternative to adequate lighting and the television. At such times of crisis, the prospects of turning to the neighbourhood for effective assistance were smaller than they had ever been.[115] The completion of the post-war slum-clearance programme, the growth of women's employment away from the home, and the increase in more private forms of recreation after work, together dispersed the body of shared knowledge and interests which had bound the localities together.[116] Even in the last of the old poverty-stricken communities, such as the much studied St Ann's district of Nottingham in the mid-sixties, informal sources of relief were of limited value. As had always been the case, families struggled to maintain their privacy for as long as possible, and found that when they sacrificed their pride, help was inconsistent and insubstantial. Constant population movement, tensions between over-stretched men and women now compounded by racial divisions, meant large variations in the level of contact, with half those questioned never calling on their neighbours, and a quarter regularly doing so.[117]

In some respects the return of large-scale, locally specific unemployment began to reverse the trend away from the enclosed communities bound together by shared adversity, but in the midst of the new Depression it was difficult to recreate the way of life which had been founded on generations of collective deprivation. The state was now too large a provider, and also, as it had been in the thirties, a source of division. Like the PACs before it, the SBC received extensive information from the resentful or mistrusting neighbours of the poor.[118] The 1973 Fisher Report on benefit fraud discovered that 'an appreciable proportion of abuse which is detected comes to light through anonymous letters'.[119] It accepted that 'public-spirited citizens' had a duty to report their suspicions, but drew back from officially encouraging the creation of a society of informers. Even amongst the claimants themselves, lack of knowledge about entitlement and assessment sowed the seeds of jealousy and discord. It always seemed possible that someone else in the queue had privileged information or was receiving favourable treatment. Where rumours ruled they could trust neither their neighbours nor each other.[120]

Kinship support networks, long subject to the increasing separation of the generations, were also hit by the break-up of old-established neighbourhoods. In inner London, the proportion of the elderly who had a child living within five minutes walk, halved between the late fifties and the late seventies.[121] Yet this still left more than a third who could maintain regular contact, and surveys indicated that where it was physically possible, extensive use was still being made of relatives by those in need of help.[122] Amongst a sample of pensioners over the age of seventy-five, for instance, almost three-quarters of those with surviving children saw them at least once a week.[123] There remained a wide range of small but significant services which the poor could render the poor. With an increase in working mothers and no compensatory growth in child-care facilities, the time-honoured functions of grandmothers and aunts as stand-in parents often became more rather than less important. Where employment had been lost, relatives were the source of much of the small-scale but essential borrowing which carried hard-pressed family economies through periods of crisis.[124] The bulk of financial support now came from the state, but it was estimated that in spite of the dramatic growth in the personal social services in the late sixties and early seventies, nine-tenths of the care of those who could not fend for themselves was still rendered by 'spouses, parents, children and other kin'.[125]

The strength of kinship support was the continuing element of reciprocity. Those who needed cash returned favours in kind. Its weakness was its vulnerability to time and distance. The longer a period of unemployment lasted, the less tolerant relatives became of repeated requests for assistance.[126] The further away the relatives lived, the more difficult it became to exchange services on a regular basis, particularly if one side no longer possessed a margin of surplus cash to spend on transport. For many families, the onset of trouble deprived them of the only means they had of finding their own solution. Less than a quarter of households on means-tested benefit had access to a car, and amongst single-parent families only one in twenty had their own means of transport.[127] The more a car became an affordable possession of an increasing proportion of the working class, the more serious became the consequences of its absence. Those who could no longer afford to own or run one found greater difficulty in finding new sources of income, or making the most efficient use of such resources as they possessed. As factories, like people, had also been dispersed from central locations, making enquiries, getting to interviews, undertaking new journeys to work – all were frequently tasks beyond the most tireless and determined pedestrian or cyclist. Problems of communication were further compounded if a telephone had never been installed, or had been cut off.[128]

Luxuries became necessities at just the point when it was impossible to afford them, and necessities became more expensive when it was essential to economise. There is little evidence that those reduced to living on or below the levels of state benefit consistently and wilfully wasted their limited resources, but like earlier generations of poor households, they were forced by their circumstances to live less efficiently.[129] There was only marginally more room for manoeuvre than there had been in the early years of the welfare state. A fall in the proportion of low-income budgets spent on food had been partially compensated for by rises in fuel and housing, so that inescapable necessities still accounted for more than half of all outgoings.[130] Low-income families were more likely to be living in the poorer quality council flats and houses[131] or still worse in privately rented rooms, which cost proportionately more to heat than better built, centrally heated and double-glazed accommodation. Credit purchases were more costly than those paid for by cash, and the forms of borrowing employed by the poor carried higher rates of interest than those available to households with mortgageable property or secure and rising incomes.[132] The corner shop had never been the cheapest source of goods, but the introduction of the out-of-town supermarket and bulk frozen foods placed an increasing penalty on the budgets of those unable to do their shopping by car, or make use of a freezer on their return home.[133] One careful survey concluded that the poor paid 11 per cent more than average families to obtain equivalent goods and services.[134] The consumer revolution blessed families whose means kept pace with economic growth, but punished the ones whose fall in income forced them to live behind the times.

If there was a familiarity about the dilemmas faced by women managing a budget financed by the state, this was because benefit scales remained incapable of meeting the full range of socially established necessities, particularly when there were children or when the period of dependency lasted any period of time.[135] Although the levels of

physical deprivation were less acute, resources still had to be husbanded from day to day rather than from week to week. Compared
with the casual labourer's household before 1914, there may have been
more certainty about the weekly giro cheque or Family Allow-
ance/Child Benefit, but the exhausting task of endless calculation and
re-calculation had not disappeared. As one housewife put it, the problem was 'always having to think about how to stretch the money
through the week'.[136] 'Mentally it is a constant drain', complained
another. 'I worry from Friday to Tuesday [Family Allowance day] that
I'll run out of money.'[137]

In terms of specific items, recent studies suggest that those living on
or below the state benefit levels faced restrictions in their diet, serious
clothing shortages, and complete shortfalls in a wide range of basic
household possessions and domestic expenditure.[138] Above all, survival
continued to be a matter not just of generally cutting back but of
constantly choosing amongst a range of competing necessities. There
was a timeless quality to Marsden's description of the financial
strategies forced upon the unemployed: 'the families we saw had budgets which differed markedly from those of the rest of the population,
in that it seemed as though they could put the emphasis on one basic
essential only at the expense of another'.[139]

The absence of an adequate income imposed a progressive withdrawal from the way of life enjoyed by the majority of the community.
The first victim of a re-ordered domestic economy was expenditure
on all entertainment outside the home.[140] As in shopping, so in
leisure, an exploitation of the fruits of progress increasingly depended
on an ability to travel and to spend substantial sums of money at the
destination. The inability to run a car was both loss of an amenity in
itself and a major impediment to the enjoyment of many others. Engagement in new participatory or spectator activities declined in direct
proportion to disposable wealth. Although the distinctions between
middle-class and working-class patterns of social exchange were becoming less marked, the latter were still more likely to maintain
friendships outside the home, in contexts where it was difficult to
avoid incurring travel, refreshment and other expenses. Even those
who had begun to depart from traditional ways and entertain at home
would be deterred from continuing the practice by the difficulty of
sustaining reciprocal hospitality with friends or relatives who still possessed sufficient margins of surplus income to afford the outlay on food
and drink.[141] Only the consolation of smoking remained relatively immune to the retrenchment demanded by poverty.

The single mother, the middle-aged unemployed man, the elderly widow, saw more public officials and fewer private individuals than any other sector of society. With the replacement of the twice or thrice weekly signing-on ritual by the weekly and then fortnightly visit to the benefit office, and the widespread use of giro cheques to make payments, the able-bodied poor also saw less of each other than once they had, although from the late seventies onwards, 'drop-in' centres for the jobless started to appear in towns and cities hardest hit by unemployment. At the same time self-help bodies for other categories of claimants began to make some attempt to break down the isolation caused by dependency on welfare or low incomes.[142] For the most part, however, the principal alternative to the benefit officer or the social worker was the television screen. Unlike the early years of the welfare state, this was now an almost universal possession. By 1981 only 3 per cent of homes were without a receiver, and many of these lacked one from choice. Whilst the licence fee was still a threat, the second-hand and rented markets were now large enough to eliminate the problem of capital outlay, and those who finally managed to get hold of a video recorder lost any remaining interest in visiting the cinema whose collectively enjoyed fantasies had helped an earlier generation to survive hard times. Thus modern technology eased the desolation but intensified the isolation of those excluded from its economic rewards.

IMPASSE

In 1958, Ian Macleod contributed an essay to a Conservative Political Centre symposium on 'The Future of the Welfare State', in which he surveyed the growing concern about its shortcomings and reviewed the prospects for reform:

> One thing seems clear. Whether our proposals or those of the Socialist Party, or some combination of them, prove most acceptable to the people of this country, it will not be possible to change the system every time there is a change of Government. There is, therefore, every advantage in putting on the Statute Book proposals which will command general support.[143]

Partly by intention, and partly by force of circumstance, this consensus-based approach dominated attempts to deal with the shortcomings of the Beveridge System throughout the following two decades. Even the Heath Government's attempt to engineer a radical shift in the balance between contributory and means-tested relief had fizzled out after the marginal innovation of the Family Income Supplement, which Labour subsequently retained in spite of its earlier opposition. However, the final collapse of the social contract in the winter of 1978 led to the election of a Conservative Administration which saw no advantage whatever in enacting proposals which would command general support. In its view, progress on such a basis was no longer possible nor desirable. The relationship between the poor and the state had become so mutually destructive that it was necessary to launch a full-scale attack on the structures of self-deception and self-interest which had grown up around it.

The Tories derived much of their confidence in this field from the fact that some of their most implacable critics were working with them to undermine the edifice which had been erected by the post-war Labour Government. For the first time since 1945, elements on the Left were mounting a serious challenge to the balance of power between the state and its citizens. The passivity of the poor was beginning to be seen as both a consequence and a condemnation of the bureaucratisation of public welfare. The prospects of either side engineering an escape from the impasse which the system presented were dependent on the extent to which the old divisions of opinion and power were breaking down under the pressure of economic crisis. Those who wished to transfer responsibility from the state to the market saw the chance of creating a new alliance of middle-class and working-class voters brought together by their desire to protect their material progress against importunate unions and irresponsible claimants. Those who wished to broaden the attack on the inequalities of authority and privilege hoped to exploit the breadth of shared interests engendered by the thirty-year history of the welfare state.

The attempt to encourage the beneficiaries of assistance from central or local government to take a more active part in its provision was faced by a number of time-honoured difficulties. Politics in all its dimensions had always overlapped with recreation. In practice there might be little difference between an evening at the pub in which grievances were occasionally aired, or a couple of hours at a meeting which ended with a round of drinks. The real question was whether the money and energy could be found to maintain any social contacts outside the home. Regular, secure employment provided the basis for association and supplied the means for developing it. Exclusion from the workplace and from the prevailing basic standards of living set up a mutually reinforcing process of physical isolation and political pessimism. The less it seemed possible to take part in organised protest, the less likely it appeared that protest would achieve its ends.

In some respects these obstacles were growing larger rather than smaller. In politics as in leisure, the dispersal of inner-city populations made collective action more conditional on expensive cars or unreliable public transport. The unemployed tended to be scattered across towns rather than confined to single neighbourhoods.[144] As entertainment became more dependent on costly technology, so protest groups made greater use of modern devices for conducting their business. Meetings and committees had always generated expenditure, but the word-processor required more capital outlay than the hand-written minute book. And whereas the growth of television and other domestic recreation might be seen as merely an alternative to more sociable forms of recreation, it was directly hostile to attempts to attract audiences to distant halls.

At the same time there were important countervailing tendencies. Once the cost of new forms of communication was overcome, it was much easier than it had been to operate independently of older and larger organisations. Posters, newsletters and correspondence could be produced with an ease and a style hitherto confined to established parties and trade unions. Equally, once allowance for the divorce between the workplace and the home had been made, there were new opportunities for collective endeavour. Many of the housing estates were far larger than the factories and offices to which their tenants travelled, and offered untapped possibilities for joint action against distant bureaucracies. Furthermore, the rapid expansion of means-tested rent and rate rebates from the mid-sixties onwards exemplified the way in which the changing characteristics of the welfare system and its clients were helping to break down some of the old barriers between the haves and the have-nots. It was no longer just those on the edge of destitution who were exposed to intrusive enquiries into their circumstances. By the late eighties, a quarter of all parents were claiming some form of income-related benefit. And it was no longer just the ill-educated and inarticulate who were living on the breadline. Whilst a curtailed and unproductive schooling was still a reliable indicator of future poverty, modern categories of claimants such as single parents displayed a more varied range of qualifications and experience than the poor of the pre-war era.

The success of new forms of participatory democracy in many ways depended on the particular conjunction of gains and losses. Tenants' associations were first into the field in the late sixties, and until the programme of council house sales began to undermine the basis of their operation, achieved the largest changes in relations between the providers and the receivers.[145] Amongst those who relied on state support for the bulk of their income, it was organisations such as Gingerbread which developed the most effective forms of self-help. Where there was no clearly defined single interest or physical community, the task of mobilisation proved more difficult.

As the unemployed began to reappear, attempts were made to recreate the NUWM, which despite its failings remained by far the most impressive representative body of the dispossessed the century had produced. Following initiatives by Birmingham students and a former Barnsley miner and NUWM member Joe Kenyon, the Claimants' Union emerged in 1970.[146] Like its predecessor it sought to improve the individual and collective entitlement of the jobless and to provide alternative centres of economic and recreational activity.[147] In its desire to establish self-help as both its end and its means, the loosely federated body avoided the danger of dependency on an authoritarian Communist Party, but also lacked some of the advantages enjoyed by Hannington's organisation. The unemployed, who as in the thirties tended to be at the beginning or the end of their working lives, were more likely to be found at home watching soap operas than standing around outside Labour Exchanges listening to agitators.[148] The administration of relief was now so centralised that there was much less opportunity for local pressure, although the better appeals procedures allowed greater scope for personal representation.[149] Whilst the emphasis on local autonomy provided real opportunities for participation, it hampered the development of an effective national movement, and the Union failed in its ambition to provide a powerful rallying point for all the dispossessed in the welfare state.[150] Later attempts to replicate the hunger marches, such as the 1983 People's March for Jobs, were more reminiscent of past defeats than past victories.[151]

The efficacy of the new organisations at the national level also depended on the variable susceptibility of civil servants and politicians. Those representing causes with a high emotional appeal and a low potential for disruption, such as the disabled or the pensioners, enjoyed a better hearing than those claiming to speak for large numbers of the able-bodied poor. Whilst in theory, participatory associations should have displaced the role of the older middle-class pressure groups, in practice Whitehall doubted the capacity of such bodies to deliver their membership, and in so far as it still listened to any voices outside the Government, was more attentive to the well-researched, carefully presented arguments of the professional lobbyists.[152] In the end the key question, as it always had been, was the relationship between the

poor and the traditional structures of organised labour. The road towards a redistribution of power to the dispossessed could not by-pass
the organisations which claimed to represent them. Here it may be
argued that the prospects of new forms of democratic action were
both undermined and enhanced by the weakness and uncertainty of
the trade unions and the Labour Party.

In several respects the proliferating forms of collective self-help
were swimming against the tide. The fall of the Labour Government
in 1979, followed by a rapid rise in unemployment and further electoral defeats, exposed the most direct victims of the recession to many of
the traditional shortcomings of the labour movement. The trade
unions, which in spite of all the deficiencies of the social contract had
given some protection to pensioners and later to families during the
row over the introduction of Child Benefit, were now on the defensive. As in the thirties they were able to do little for unemployed men,
and were ill-equipped to deal with the problems of low-paid or casual
women workers who frequently bore the brunt of the 'shake-out' of
British industry. With membership falling sharply and long-standing
legal rights under attack, they were too preoccupied with holding their
ground to advance into fresh areas of activity or develop new forms of
representation. As in the thirties they were deeply suspicious of extra-
union organisations of the unemployed, such as the Claimants Union.
Moreover, the series of public-sector strikes in the 'winter of discon-
tent' had reinforced their popular image as the defenders of the produ-
cers rather than the customers of the social services. It was not difficult
for the Conservatives to present them as an obstacle to the necessary
modernisation of the machinery of welfare.

The demoralised Parliamentary Labour Party was in some ways
even less able to render assistance to the cause of the rapidly increasing
numbers of claimants. The wave of 'scrounger-phobia' which the incoming Tory Government was successfully exploiting had in fact been
gathering momentum throughout the last Labour Administration. The
increasing volume of lurid accusations about the abuse of the social
security system stemmed from the greater visibility of the able-bodied
poor and the remorseless rise in the social security budget at a time of
deepening economic crisis. The growing domination of large sections
of the popular press by right-wing proprietors was also a factor. But
the descendants of the men who had brought the welfare state into
being also had to bear some of the responsibility for the ever-more
strident disparagement of those now dependent on it. They had never
shaken off their distrust of those who turned to the state for assistance
instead of keeping their families by their own efforts. The more blatant

forms of discrimination, such as the four-week rule and the wage stop had only been repealed after prolonged pressure-group campaigns,[153] and comfort was given to the enemies of the Supplementary Benefit system by well-publicised increases in the powers of the fraud inspectors. Although an attempt was made to protect the welfare budget from the 1976 cuts, the argument that state expenditure was too large for the private sector to sustain had been conceded long before the party lost office. It was in this context that some explanations of the crisis gained authority over others. Despite their genuine hostility to the press stories and to the Tory propaganda, Labour was deeply implicated in the verdict that unprincipled claimants were responsible for the expansion of social security spending, and that uncontrolled spending was responsible for the malaise of the economy as a whole.

Both the established pressure groups and the more recently formed self-help bodies were thus at a double disadvantage. Central to the thesis of 'Government overload' which was rapidly gaining currency in the upper reaches of the Conservative Party, was the argument that the spokesmen of the poor were directly responsible for upsetting the balance between the public and private sectors through the constant escalation of their demands. It became a positive duty to ignore their advocacy and deny them any role in the decision-making process.[154] And as the by now officially inspired press campaign became yet more hostile, so the prospect of gaining any sort of parliamentary redress disappeared. Only at the local level where individual Labour authorities were able for a few years to mount a successful guerilla struggle against attempts to curtail their welfare services, was it possible to combine the strengths of the old party with the vigour of the new protest organisations.

The forms of politics which began to emerge in the inner cities were a product of the evident decay of both the structure and the ideology of the Labour Movement. The local parties were frequently moribund, as detached from the communities they claimed to represent as the communities were alienated from the welfare system which earlier Labour Governments had brought into being. By mobilising the wide range of minority groups which were threatened by the newly liberated market forces it appeared possible to revitalise the constituency organisations, and to begin the long process of re-educating the national party, which since the war had rarely paid more than lip-service to local democracy.[155] Through the development of new modes of direct action embracing not just the unemployed and the low paid, but all those categories of citizens who by reason of their race, gender, sexual preference, or economic, physical or domestic circumstances either made use of the social services or required access to them, a new coalition of committed supporters could be called into being to replace the shrinking base of the traditional, male-dominated working class. At the same time the campaigns to win a role in the provision and delivery of assistance would provide a model for the development of a broader programme of egalitarian, participatory democracy. The attacks on the excessive powers of the bureaucrats and professionals would raise questions about the division of labour throughout the political process, and the attempts to break down the barriers between salaried suppliers and passive receivers would force a reconsideration of such long taboo issues as the place of voluntary workers in the promotion of social justice.

By these means it was hoped to turn a source of weakness into a means of theoretical and practical strength, but it was a fraught undertaking. The more successful local forms of resistance were, the more hostile became the attacks through the media and the law. The Labour leadership was caught between conflicting pressures. As the 1979 defeat was repeated in 1983, and again in 1987, it was obvious enough that the party needed to modernise its organisation and reformulate its philosophy, yet it was all too easy to believe that the now embattled community groups represented not so much the answer to all its problems as the destruction of all its hopes of ever regaining power.

The Labour Party was aware that whilst some sections of the underprivileged could evoke broad public sympathy, opinion polls indicated a widespread antagonism to able-bodied claimants which stretched well down into the social groups upon which Labour had always based its support. An influential survey of the EEC nations in 1976 had concluded that the British were most prone to blame the poor for their own misfortunes, and whilst the subsequent leap in unemployment began to shift some of the attention to structural factors, the collective capacity of the minority organisations to overcome the orchestrated press campaign against them remained open to doubt. What turned apprehension into outright rejection was the growing incidence of conflicts with an increasingly rigid legislative structure. If noisy demands for direct democracy caused embarrassment, outright defiance of the law brought instant condemnation from the party. When faced with the choice, it instinctively backed the authority of Parliament, whether it was confrontation with central government in Liverpool or more dispersed calls for rent strikes. Most recently it has had to disown attempts to defy poll tax legislation which may result in the *de facto* disenfranchisement of at least a proportion of the poor for the first time since the abolition of pauper disqualification in 1918.[156]

At the heart of Labour's dilemma was their historic sensitivity to the Conservative charge that the demands and behaviour of their supporters rendered them unfit to govern. As in the previous period of mass unemployment, they were more frightened by the prospect of direct action than were the agencies against which it might be directed. They were increasingly worried that the new breed of articulate, well-educated activists might alienate the much larger body of middle-class voters upon whom any electoral recovery depended. By the time Neil Kinnock set in motion a full-scale policy review in the aftermath of the third successive election defeat in 1987, the attempts to generate new forms of democratic politics were in danger of achieving the reverse result. Although the party had taken on board the rhetoric of decentralisation and accountability, in practice its new programme revealed a scant departure from the traditional model of parliamentary sovereignty.

The welfare programme outlined in its 'new agenda for Britain' consists largely of a set of 'back-to-Beveridge' proposals. The role of the means test would be reduced to the level envisaged in 1942 by an uprating of insurance benefits and pensions and a substantial increase in Child Benefit. There are commitments to repeal the harsher aspects of the 1986 Social Security Act, to restore earnings-related benefits and the full SERPS scheme, and at last to introduce a minimum wage. As in the case of the original Beveridge Report, the strong element of retrospection is a form of both ambition and retreat. A serious attempt to return to the original blueprint would cause profound changes to the well-being of millions, and with the modern Labour Party's greater concern for the rights of women, the gains would be spread more evenly between the sexes. There is an even clearer recognition that policies to reduce unemployment should be an integral part of a poverty programme. But as in the post-war legislation, the political process, the line of authority from the state to those citizens still dependent upon it, remains unaltered. The Labour Party merely undertakes to make the welfare bureaucracy 'user friendly', which as the terminology implies, largely means the introduction of new technology to speed the administration.[157] Power is to be given not to the people but to computers.

So much for the future. The start of the nineties, however, still belongs to the Conservatives who have enjoyed more than ten years of power at Westminster. The party has won three elections in succession as the most radical of the major contestants. In 1979 it came into office equipped with a right-wing critique of the welfare system which had been gaining in coherence and force since the early sixties.[158] The state and the poor, it was argued, were enmeshed in a mutually destructive relationship. The demands of the claimants and their spokesmen had become so insatiable that the state could only respond with levels of taxation which were undermining both economic and political stability. A meaningless insurance system and an uncontrollable structure of means-tested benefits were in turn undermining the moral and material well-being of ever larger sections of the population. State welfare was extending rather than diminishing poverty. As one of its most persistent critics, Ralph Harris, wrote in *Beyond the Welfare State* in 1988: 'In Britain, I have no doubt that improved social benefits have increased the incentive for people to make some kind of a living out of being poor. . . . Likewise, the dramatic increase in unmarried mothers a good deal to the special payments and subsidised housing priority won by pressure groups for the biological curiosity of "single-parent families".'[159]

Not since the 1945 Labour Government had a party possessed so much opportunity and so clear an idea of what to do with it. And not since the 1929 Labour Government did a party so completely achieve the opposite of its intentions in respect of those dependent on the state. Rather than declining, the social security budget went up in real terms by 39 per cent in the decade from 1978/89, and the number of people dependent on Supplementary Benefit/Income Support rose from six to nine million.[160] Although it was extensively reviewed and renamed, the basic structure of the Beveridge system survived intact. This failure at once confounded and endorsed the arguments of right-wing commentators. They had always maintained that the malaise lay deep in the political system, and it may be argued that it was indeed the persistence of post-war structures of influence and opinion which frustrated radical change.

When faced with cuts, the principal beneficiaries of the welfare state mounted a determined and largely effective defence. As had long been observed, it was not the shrinking working class, but the ever larger and wealthier middle class which had made the greatest use of Beveridge's innovations, particularly in health and education. Recent research indicates that the more articulate and influential sections of society enjoyed considerable success in dissuading the party which claimed to represent them from making lasting reductions in the services they enjoyed.[161] To the extent that the wealthier lived longer, their vested interest also played a part in protecting pensions, however the relentless growth in the remainder of the social security budget requires a broader explanation. In the long run, the evasions and shortfalls of the Beveridge system, which had been causing growing concern in the sixties and seventies, turned out to be its greatest strengths in its hour of need. The most English of revolutionaries had through compromise and caution created a general consensus for his principles and mechanisms which, as opinion polls consistently indicated, was capable of surviving the apparently seismic upheavals in the economic and political landscape.[162] The radical reformer in Mrs Thatcher had to give way to the pragmatic politician. The frontiers of the state could be rolled back only an inch at a time. Despite her secure parliamentary majorities, she lacked the constituency for a wholesale dismantling of the system she had inherited.

Instead the Conservatives' room for manoeuvre was confined to exploiting two further assumptions inherent in the post-war settlement, that beyond the adjustments required to establish a national minimum the pursuit of economic equality was not a necessary objective of the state, and that in granting public assistance it remained possible to distinguish between the deserving and the undeserving poor. In the first instance it was possible to embark on a deliberate policy of widening differentials. The richest fifth's share of post-tax and benefit income rose from forty to forty-five per cent between 1979 and 1989, whilst the poorest fifth's fell from 6.1 to 5.1.[163] Tax cuts were weighted heavily towards the better off, with two-thirds of the concessions between 1979 and 1986 going to the top fifth of earners, whilst from 1980 benefits were no longer uprated in line with earnings, but only with prices. Thus although the real value of the basic scales actually rose by 5 per cent against the retail price index, they fell sharply against the standard of living enjoyed by those able to keep themselves without state support. Between 1978 and 1987 the ordinary Supplementary Benefit payable to a married couple dropped from 61 to 53 per cent of personal disposable income per capita.[164]

At the same time the long-standing lack of public sympathy for the able-bodied poor[165] became a more potent force as they came to dominate the work of the supplementary benefits system. If the basic cost of supporting the poor could not be reduced, it was possible to undermine their status and dignity. The severity of the recession during the first Thatcher Administration meant that for the first time since 1948, unemployed families overtook pensioners as recipients of means-tested relief. With the number of single-parent families also continuing to grow, the field was left open for an intensification of the official campaign against those who could be held responsible for their own plight. The abolition of the SBC in the midst of an expansion in the number of claimants from three to five million between 1979 and 1983 checked the programme of humanising the treatment of applicants, and in areas worst hit by unemployment, threw it into reverse. Whilst increased resources were committed to the prevention and detection of fraud, the quality of the counter service declined as the provision of staff failed to keep pace with the growth in business. A series of rule adjustments made the procedures for claiming more difficult, and the interaction with other means-tested assistance was rendered more complex by reductions in subsidies, most seriously in the field of local authority housing, where a 60 per cent cut in state support led to increases in rents at twice the rate of inflation.[166]

Prevented by rising unemployment and immovable public opinion from halting the growth in the social security budget, the Government was finally forced to settle for a programme of reform which did little more than tilt the scales from justice to simplicity, and from the poor to the very poor. A review launched in 1984 led to the 1986 Social Security Act which came into operation in 1988. What had once been called National Assistance now became Income Support. The tangled structure of special rates was replaced by basic additions for the broad categories of families with children, lone parents, pensioners, the long-term sick and the disabled. The system of emergency needs payments, was translated into the separate Social Fund, under which a smaller number of requirements would be met, for the most part, not by grants but by cash-limited loans, repayable by deductions at source from Income Support. Finally, Family Income Supplement – still only reaching 50 per cent of its target – was renamed Family Credit with increased eligibility and payments re-routed through employers in an attempt to reduce the problem of take-up. The precise impact of the changes on individual families depended on their circumstances. Improvements in some scale rates were offset by reductions elsewhere and by a general requirement that in the interests of local accountability, all claimants should meet a fifth of their housing costs. In general it was estimated that there were twice as many losers as gainers, with most of the beneficiaries concentrated amongst the very needy.[167] During the first three years of the operation of the reforms, pressure on poor families was further intensified by a freezing of the value of Child Benefit.

In several respects, the new Social Fund exemplified the impasse in which the Conservatives now found themselves. Although it was intended to save money, the sum involved – an anticipated £160 million in the first year – was trifling compared with the overall social security budget of £46.5 billion in 1986/7.[168] The Government felt itself driven to make the reform by its inability to control the growth of dependent families who were making disproportionate demands on the existing system of discretionary payments. By 1987 the number of children being supported on Supplementary Benefits had passed two million. In spite of the commitment to reduce the powers of bureaucrats, the Social Fund increased the discretion of officials and abolished the right of appeal against it. All that the reform achieved was to focus attention on the basic contradiction in its approach to poverty.

On the one hand ministers argued that the terminology imported into the political discourse by Rowntree in 1901 was now redundant. It was no longer possible to reach a consensus about the subsistence level, there was no longer any justification for using basic means test scales as a poverty line, and therefore the concept of poverty had lost all meaning. The word itself appeared once in the 1979 Tory manifesto, and not at all in those of 1983 and 1987. Official calculations of individuals subsisting below Supplementary Benefit levels, which showed an increase from 2.09 to 2.89 million between 1979 and 1987, were discontinued in favour of a measure of households below average income, which did not contain an obvious poverty line.[169] On the other hand, the underlying justification for an innovation which, as soon became apparent, was causing real distress to hard-pressed families who were either denied help or gained it in exchange for a cut in their Income Support, was that there did indeed exist a section of the population separated from the rest of society by the strategies it adopted to manage its resources. There was a positive gain in making the outcome of applications conditional on the funds held by the local office that month, and in making the fortunate recipients incur further debts. They needed, it was argued, to learn what those independent of state assistance already knew, that it was an uncertain world, and that money had to be husbanded from week to week. So complete a failure to understand the experience of poverty served only to confirm its existence.

POOR CITIZENS

In 1952 *The Times* carried out one of the earliest reviews of the Beveridge scheme in operation. Amidst the compromises and shortcomings, a clear objective was visible: 'The strengthening of civic solidarity by provision of services on the footing of common citizenship seems a fundamental aim of the welfare state.'[170] The association of citizenship with the post-war legislation had first been made by T.H. Marshall in an influential paper three years earlier.[171] At the time it was a means of identifying the success of the new system. The granting of equal legal and then political rights had finally been complemented by the establishment of full social rights through the granting of equal access to education, health care and a minimum level of income. However, as subsequent research began to qualify the optimism of the initial verdicts such as that of Rowntree in 1951, it became possible to doubt the nature of the achievement. There remained a significant minority of the population who were in a double sense, poor citizens. Despite the structure of National Assistance and National Insurance, they lacked the resources to enjoy a minimum standard of living, and at the same time they were still incapable of fully exercising their associated legal and political rights.

Placing the Beveridge reforms in the context of the evolving relations between the poor and the state this century, emphasises the extent to which the twin failures have been mutually reinforcing. This is partly the consequence of a convergence of definition. Ever since the Liberal certainties about political freedom and pauperism were first questioned, the concepts of citizenship and poverty have increasingly partaken of each other.[172] The more poverty was seen as a relative rather than an absolute condition, the more weight was placed on the ability to participate in the community; the more citizenship was viewed as not just a legal or political process, the more attention was paid to the quality of the individual's membership of the social group.[173] David Donnison, the last in the line of academic critics who had the opportunity to play a direct role in the administration of the system of relief, has recently argued that 'poverty means the exclusion from the living standards, the life styles and the fellowship of one's fellow citizens'.[174] Properly understood, a poor citizen is a contradiction in terms.

The sense in which one term has become almost the mirror image of the other is also a consequence of a fundamental structural connection between them. Although Marshall was more aware of the possible conflicts between the several categories of citizenship than some of his later critics have allowed,[175] he did regard the granting of social rights as the culmination of the struggle for political freedom which had been virtually completed by 1918. The Liberal welfare reforms had been devised in anticipation of universal suffrage, their extension was a product of the votes of the underprivileged, and their completion was guaranteed by the sense of common citizenship engendered in the struggle against Hitler. It is now more evident, however, that whilst the growth of the modern democratic state has deeply influenced the experience of poverty since 1900, the relationship between them has been less consistently beneficial than once was hoped.

The founding of the welfare state required not only innovation but destruction. The structure of contributory and non-contributory benefits was built at the expense of older forms of mutual support. Growing public expenditure was accompanied by an erosion of formal and informal democratic processes which culminated after 1945 in the creation of one of the most centralised systems in Western Europe.[176] Much that was lost could not be preserved in the face of rising aspirations and increasing life expectancy. But the gains in security were not matched by a refurbishment of obsolete forms of participation and control. The more the state gave in the name of the poor, the more it denied the poor control over its disbursement. There was little sense of reciprocity in relations between bureaucrats and claimants.[177] 'It is no accident', observed Ignatieff, 'that the citizenship ideal of post-war liberals and social democrats stressed the passive equality of entitlements at the expense of the active equality of participation. The entitled were never empowered, because empowerment would have infringed the prerogatives of the managers of the welfare state.'[178] The inability of the recipients to mount an effective challenge to their exclusion arose partly from the lack of morale and resources contingent on their position, and partly from their prior and continuing exclusion from the agencies of organised labour which alone could have provided a vehicle for their protests. Lacking the means to give voice to their political citizenship, they were exposed to a form of bureaucratic welfare which denied them the dignity and status essential to their social citizenship.

It has been the misfortune of the poor that the income support sections of the welfare state were designed only to deal with poverty. Whereas elsewhere in Europe, the interruption or cessation of occupation was conceived as a problem of efficiency, in Britain it was seen principally as a problem of deprivation. In the long run, Rowntree the Quaker triumphed over Rowntree the chocolate manufacturer. The ruling problem became one of morality rather than economic performance. This not only made the welfare budget consistently vulnerable to industrial recession, it also meant that its beneficiaries were permanently identified as a distinct and dependent section of society, despite the myth of the insurance principle. On the one hand the recipients were exposed to renewed criticism and hostility as the ancient category of the able-bodied and hence undeserving poor became more salient from the mid-sixties, on the other, spending failed to keep pace with the rest of Europe. In the early fifties, Britain's initial lead in the field was still reflected in the table of social security spending as a proportion of GDP; by 1974 it had fallen from fourth to eleventh out of twelve.[179] In the following decade, the UK displayed much the sharpest increase in poverty in the European Community, rising from eleventh to seventh place in the league of poverty rates.[180]

Citizenship, like freedom, tends to be regarded as an absolute condition, but the history of poor citizens in Britain demonstrates the fundamental relativity of the term. Despite and in some respects because of the welfare state, many degrees of citizenship have survived or developed. Wealthier householders are more effective citizens than those with less certain sources of income, and indeed are frequently able to make better use of the common services of the welfare system. White householders are more resilient citizens than black, with a lower incidence of unemployment and a smaller exposure to mistreatment by benefit officers; within threatened households, husbands are more successful citizens than their wives, and wives more successful if they still have husbands. And always poor children are the least of all citizens.[181]

In response to the evident impasse into which relations between the poor and the state have fallen in recent years, the major political parties have begun to turn their attention to the concept of the active citizen. The Liberal Democrats, whose leader is the author of the recent *Citizens' Britain: A Radical Agenda for the 1990s*,[182] see the figure as the pivot of their ambition to decentralise power in all its forms. The Tories are trying to awaken a sense of duty amongst the impoverished citizenry, and a feeling of responsibility amongst the more prosperous. A fresh role is being developed for the citizen as philanthropist, acting privately or preferably through organised charities, giving help which the state can no longer afford to pay for, setting examples which bureaucrats were never capable of providing. The 1988 Social Fund was partly designed to bring the clothing and furniture charities into a closer relationship with the state, and has been accompanied by tax reforms intended to encourage private donations. Even the Left, which historically has had the greatest mistrust of voluntary provision, has begun to explore ways of using official action to enhance rather than destroy informal means of support in the community. It is coming to recognise that the rights of the poor have to be guaranteed both by and against the state. 'Democracy can only exist on the basis of "free and equal citizens"', write Hall and Held: 'But citizenship requires some specification, and some institutional and political protection, separate from and beyond the extension of democracy. In short, in the relationship between citizenship and democracy is entailed a new balance – a new settlement – between liberty and equality.'[183]

The outcome of such endeavours is for the nineties. The past is full of citizens condemned to passivity, and as a consequence forced to be more active in the management of their daily lives than any other sector of society.

REFERENCES

1. Craig, *British General Election Manifestos*, p. 239.
2. Townsend, 'A Society for People', p. 100.
3. M. McCarthy, *Campaigning for the Poor* (London, 1986), pp. 72, 84.
4. K.G. Banting, *Poverty, Politics and Policy* (London, 1979), pp. 76–8, 152–3.
5. For a full account of the reform see, A. Webb, 'The Abolition of National Assistance', in P. Hall et al., *Change, Choice and Conflict in Social Policy* (London, 1975).
6. A.B. Atkinson, *Poverty in Britain and the Reform of Social Security* (Cambridge, 1969), pp. 61–77.
7. Atkinson, *Poverty in Britain*, pp. 93–6.
8. M.J. Hill, 'Selectivity for the Poor', in P. Townsend and N. Bosanquet (eds), *Labour and Inequality* (London, 1972), p. 239.
9. A.B. Atkinson, 'Inequality and Social Security', in P. Townsend and N. Bosanquet (eds), *Labour and Inequality* (London, 1972), p. 24.
10. Department of Employment and Productivity, *A National Minimum Wage* (London, 1969), p. 51.
11. J. Hughes, 'The Low Paid', in P. Townsend and N. Bosanquet (eds), *Labour and Inequality* (London, 1972), pp. 172–3.
12. On the development of this policy see A. Gamble, *The Conservative Nation* (London, 1974), p. 135; Banting, *Poverty, Politics and Policy*, pp. 75–6.
13. A. Deacon and J. Bradshaw, *Reserved for the Poor* (London, 1983), p. 80; J.E. Meade, 'Poverty in the Welfare State', *Oxford Economic Papers*, XXIV, 3 (1972), p. 298.
14. J.C. Brown, *Family Income Support Part 1. Family Income Supplement* (London, 1983), p. 75.
15. B. Abel-Smith, 'The Welfare State: Breaking the Post-War Consensus', *Political Quarterly*, **51**, 1 (Jan.–Mar. 1980), p. 18.
16. T. Lynes, 'Policy on Social Security', in M. Young (ed.), *Poverty Report 1974* (London, 1974), pp. 78–9.
17. *Report of the Committee on Abuse of Social Security Benefits* (*Fisher Report*), Cmnd 5228 (London, 1973), p. 225. For a summary of subsequent

research on the persistent desire of unemployed men to find work, see S. Allen and A. Waton, 'The Effects of Unemployment: Experience and Response', in S. Allen et al., *The Experience of Unemployment* (London, 1986), p. 9.

18. *Proposals for a Tax Credit System* (London, 1972), p. 1.

19. *Proposals for a Tax Credit System*, p. 28.

20. Lynes, 'Policy on Social Security', pp. 92–3.

21. J. Mack and S. Lansley, *Poor Britain* (London, 1985), p. 229.

22. Brown, *Family Income Support*, p. 114.

23. G.C. Peden, *British Economic and Social Policy* (Deddington, 1985), pp. 213–6; S. MacGregor, *The Politics of Poverty* (London, 1981), pp. 120ff.

24. For an account of the TUC's inability to impose its authority, particularly from 1977 onwards, see D. Healey, *The Time of My Life* (London, 1989), p. 399. On the instability of relations between union leaders and their members in this process of centralised bargaining, see I. Gough, *The Political Economy of the Welfare State* (London, 1979), pp. 146–52.

25. R. Klein, 'The Welfare State: A Self-Inflicted Crisis', *Political Quarterly*, **51**, 1 (Jan.–Mar., 1980), p. 28.

26. For an assessment of these, see C. Trinder, 'Incomes Policy and the Low Paid', in M. Young (ed.), *Poverty Report 1974* (London, 1974).

27. Abel-Smith, 'The Welfare State: Breaking the Post-War Consensus', pp. 18–19.

28. D. Coates, *Labour and Power* (London, 1980), p. 50.

29. M. Clark, 'The Unemployed on Supplementary Benefit: Living Standards and Making Ends Meet on a Low Income', *Journal of Social Policy*, **7**, 4 (Oct. 1978), p. 392.

30. F. Field, 'How the Poor Fared', in K. Coates (ed.), *What Went Wrong* (Nottingham, 1979), p. 150.

31. A.W. Dilnot, J.A. Kay and C.N. Morris, *The Reform of Social Security* (Oxford, 1984), p. 26.

32. *Report of the Committee on One-Parent Families (Finer Report)* Cmnd 5629 (London, 1974), **I**, pp. 289–314.

33. J. Millar, *Poverty and the Lone-parent: the Challenge to Social Policy* (Aldershot, 1989), pp. 27–8.

34. National Consumer Council, *Means-Tested Benefits* (London, 1976), pp. 30–2.

35. Field, 'How the Poor Fared', p. 154; M. McCarthy, *Campaigning for the Poor* (London, 1986), pp. 269–77.

36. MacGregor, *The Politics of Poverty*, p. 149; D. Piachaud, *Family Incomes Since the War* (London, 1982), p. 10.

37. For a convenient survey of the work of the National Assistance and Supplementary Benefit systems between 1948 and 1971, see F. Field, *Inequality in Britain* (London, 1981), p. 48.

38. *Finer Report*, I, p. 22.; M. McIntosh, 'The Welfare State and the Needs of the Dependent Family' in S. Burman (ed.), *Fit Work for Women* (London, 1979), p. 165; Field, *Inequality in Britain*, p. 76; Millar, *Poverty and the lone-parent*, pp. 7–9.

39. J. Millar, 'Lone Mothers' in C. Glendinning and J. Millar (eds), *Women and Poverty in Britain* (Brighton, 1987), pp. 159–60.

40. G.C. Fiegehen, P. Lansley and A.D. Smith, *Poverty and Progress in Britain 1953–73* (Cambridge, 1977), pp. 114–5; P. Townsend, *Poverty in the United Kingdom* (London, 1979), p. 898.

41. R. Layard, D. Piachaud and M. Stewart, *The Causes of Poverty* (London, 1978), p. 132.

42. *Ibid.*, p. 133.

43. J. Bradshaw and H. Holmes, *Living on the Edge* (London, 1989), p. 131.

44. W. Beckerman and S. Clark, *Poverty and Social Security in Britain since 1961* (Oxford, 1982), p. 22; J. Bradshaw and A. Deacon, 'Social Security' in P. Wilding (ed.), *In Defence of the Welfare State* (Manchester, 1986), p. 92. 'Full benefit entitlement' indicates up to 140% of the Supplementary Benefit Scale.

45. Townsend, *Poverty in the United Kingdom*, p. 908; C. Oppenheim, *Poverty, the Facts* (London, 1990), pp. 21–3.

46. F. Gould and B. Rowerth, 'Public Spending and Social Policy: The United Kingdom 1950–1977', *Journal of Social Policy*, **9**, 3 (1980), p. 341–3.

47. 'Social expenditure' here follows the EEC definition, which excludes education and housing. Abel-Smith, 'The Welfare State: Breaking the Post-War Consensus', p. 22.

48. Field, *Inequality in Britain*, p. 61.

49. Fiegehan et al., *Poverty and Progress*, p. 31.

50. *Ibid.*, p. 91.

51. *Ibid.*, pp. 25–7.

52. Brown, *Family Income Support*, p. 51.

53. M. McNay and C. Pond, *Low Pay and Family Poverty* (London, 1980), p. 2.

54. M. Meacher, *Scrounging on the Welfare* (London, 1974), p. 86.

55. E. Briggs and A.M. Rees, *Supplementary Benefits and the Consumer* (London, 1980), pp. 43–4.

56. B. Jordan, *Paupers: the Making of the New Claiming Class* (London, 1973), p. 20.

57. T. Gould and J. Kenyon, *Stories from the Dole Queue* (London, 1972), p. 151.

58. S. Cooper, *Observations in Supplementary Benefit Offices* (London, 1985), p. 8.

59. M.J. Hill 'The Exercise of Discretion in the National Assistance Board', *Public Administration*, **47** (Spring, 1969), p. 82.

60. L.E.A. Howe, 'The "Deserving" and the "Undeserving": Practice in an Urban, Local Social Security Office', *Journal of Social Policy*, **14**, 1 (January, 1985) pp. 53–6.

61. Deacon and Bradshaw, *Reserved for the Poor*, p. 130; Dilnot et al., *Reform of Social Security*, p. 49; Townsend, *Poverty in the United Kingdom*, p. 892; National Consumer Council, *Means-Tested Benefits*, pp. 25–8.

62. *Fisher Report*, p. 230. Also Briggs and Rees, *Supplementary Benefits and the Consumer*, pp. 155.

63. M.J. Hill, *The State, Administration and the Individual* (London, 1976), p. 66.

64. D. Donnison, *The Politics of Poverty* (Oxford, 1982), p. 215; O. Stevenson, *Claimant or Client* (London, 1973), pp. 172–5.

65. Dilnot et al., p. 46; K. Judge, 'Beveridge: Past, Present and Future' in C. Sandford, C. Pond and R. Walker (eds), *Taxation and Social Policy* (London, 1980), p. 180.

66. D. Donnison, *The Politics of Poverty* (Oxford, 1982), pp. 140–83. Also National Consumer Council, *Means-Tested Benefits,* p. 63 for a comparable proposal.

67. Deacon and Bradshaw, *Reserved for the Poor,* p. 111.

68. On the variability of the atmosphere of supplementary benefit offices in this period, see D. Marsden, *Workless* (London, 1982), pp. 81–4; Briggs and Rees, *Supplementary Benefits and the Consumer,* pp. 43–5.

69. Cooper, *Observations in Supplementary Benefit Offices,* p. 27.

70. P. Harrison, *Inside the Inner City* (Harmondsworth, 1983), p. 137.

71. Millar, 'Lone Mothers', p. 171.

72. Gould and Kenyon, *Stories from the Dole Queue,* pp. 11, 21–2, 129–30.

73. For the basic continuity of attitude from the closing years of the NAB through to the mid-eighties, see, Hill, 'The Exercise of Discretion in the National Assistance Board', pp. 81–6; Hill, 'Selectivity for the Poor', p. 244; Briggs and Rees, *Supplementary Benefits and the Consumer,* pp. 47–9; Cooper, *Observations in Supplementary Benefit Offices,* pp. 8–25, 57–60; Howe, 'The "Deserving" and the "Undeserving"', pp. 50–9.

74. Cooper, p. 69.

75. For examples of how MPs could achieve what protests to the local officials could not, see Gould and Kenyon, *Stories from the Dole Queue,* pp. 29, 114, 126.

76. Department of Health and Social Security, *Social Assistance* (London, 1978), p. 101.

77. L. Smith, 'A model for the development of public participation in local authority decision-making', in L. Smith and D. Jones (eds), *Deprivation, Participation and Community Action* (London, 1981), p. 10.

78. C. Holmes, 'Housing' in F. Williams (ed.), *Why the Poor Pay More* (London, 1977).

79. S. Moylen, J. Millar and R. Davies, *For Richer, for Poorer? DHSS Cohort Study of Unemployed Men* (London, 1984), p. iv.

80. J. Bradshaw, K. Cooke and C. Godfrey, 'The Impact of Unemployment on the Living Standards of Families', *Journal of Social Policy,* **12**, 4 (October, 1983), pp. 438–41; A. Sinfield, 'Unemployment in an Unequal Society', in B. Showler and A. Sinfield (eds), *The Workless State* (Oxford, 1981), p. 158.

81. M. Clark, 'The Unemployed on Supplementary Benefit: Living Standards and Making Ends Meet on a Low Income', *Journal of Social Policy,* **7**, 4 (Oct. 1978), p. 390; Bradshaw and Holmes, *Living on the Edge,* p. 137.

82. Marsden, *Workless,* pp. 138–44.

83. Piachaud, *Family Incomes Since the War*, pp. 14–19; Brown, *Family Income Support Part I*, pp. 123–4.

84. *Finer Report*, p. 37.

85. M. Jones, *Life on the Dole* (London, 1972).

86. Layard et al., *The Causes of Poverty*, p. 129.

87. McNay and Pond, *Low Pay and Family Poverty*, p. 2, cited in Oppenheim, *Poverty*, p. 85.

88. Meade, 'Poverty in the Welfare State', p. 231. The continuing operation of FIS also deflected attention from the minimum wage. Brown, *Family Income Supplement*, p. 125.

89. Allen and Waton, 'The Effects of Unemployment', p. 10.

90. A. and C. Walker (eds), *The Growing Divide. A Social Audit 1979–1987* (London, 1987), p. 28.

91. Millar, 'Lone Mothers', pp. 162–6; Oppenheim, *Poverty*, p. 96.

92. Moylan et al., *For Richer, for Poorer*, pp. 132–4; D. Marsden, *Workless* (London, 1982), pp. 92–4.

93. A. and C. Walker, *The Growing Divide*, pp. 50–1.

94. A conclusion also reached by Bradshaw and Holmes, *Living on the Edge*, pp. 138–9.

95. Townsend, *Poverty in the United Kingdom*, pp. 268–70; Mack and Lansley, *Poor Britain*, p. 193.

96. G. Parker, 'Making Ends Meet: Women, Credit and Debt' in C. Glendinning and J. Millar (eds), *Women and Poverty in Britain* (Brighton, 1987), pp. 247–8; A. and C. Walker, *The Growing Divide*, p. 60; McNay and Pond, *Low Pay and Family Poverty*, p. 10.

97. Allen and Waton, 'The Effects of Unemployment', p. 12; Bradshaw and Holmes, *Living on the Edge*, p. 136.

98. Harrison, *Inside the Inner City*, p. 158.

99. Clark, 'The Unemployed on Supplementary Benefit', p. 399.

100. Parker, 'Making Ends Meet', p. 249.

101. B. Campbell, *Wigan Pier Revisited* (London, 1984), p. 14; R. Berthoud and E. Kempson, *Credit and Debt in Britain* (London, 1990), p. 6.

102. L. Burghes, *Living from Hand to Mouth* (London, 1980), p. 19.

103. Berthoud and Kempson, *Credit and Debt*, pp. 7–13.

104. Moylan et al., *For Richer, for Poorer*, p. iii.

105. Clark, 'The Unemployed on Supplementary Benefit', p. 395.

106. Bradshaw and Holmes, *Living on the Edge*, p. 136.

107. Mack and Lansley, *Poor Britain*, p. 160.

108. Fiegehan et al., *Poverty and Progress*, pp. 71–2.

109. R. Berthoud, *Fuel Debts and Hardship* (London, 1981), p. 127. In Burghes' sample of sixty-five families on supplementary benefit, 60 per cent had fuel debts. Burghes, *Living from Hand to Mouth*, p. 39. See also Parker, 'Making Ends Meet', pp. 241–2.

110. Berthoud and Kempson, *Credit and Debt*, p. 7.

111. K. Andrews and J. Jacobs, *Punishing the Poor* (London, 1990), p. 287.

112. Parker, 'Making Ends Meet', p. 241. On the incidence of County Court judgements in a specific community, see K. Coates and R. Sil-

burn, *Poverty: The Forgotten Englishmen* (Harmondsworth, 1970), p. 61.

113. Berthoud and Kempson, *Credit and Debt*, pp. 10–11.
114. Berthoud, *Fuel Debts*, pp. 89–91.
115. N. Johnson, *The Welfare State in Transition* (Brighton, 1987), pp. 89–90.
116. B. Jordan, *Paupers: the Making of the New Claiming Class* (London, 1973), p. 28; A. Friend and A. Metcalf, *Slump City* (London, 1981), p. 142; Harrison, *Inside the Inner City* p. 265; P. Willmott, *Friendship Networks and Social Support* (London, 1987), p. 13.
117. Coates and Silburn, *Poverty*, pp. 93–118.
118. Donnison, *Politics of Poverty*, pp. 108, 112.
119. *Fisher Report*, p. 198; Gould and Kenyon, *Stories from the Dole Queue*, p. 85.
120. Marsden, *Workless*, p. 97.
121. Friend and Metcalf, *Slump City*, p. 129.
122. For a recent summary of research findings see Willmott, *Friendship Networks*, p. 14.
123. M. Abrams, *Beyond Three-Score and Ten* (London, 1978), p. 8.
124. Clark, 'Unemployed on Supplementary Benefit', p. 403.
125. M. Bulmer, *Neighbours: The Work of Philip Abrams* (Cambridge, 1986), p. 233.
126. Clark, 'Unemployed on Supplementary Benefit', p. 404.
127. Bradshaw and Holmes, *Living on the Edge*, p. 134; Millar, *Poverty and the Lone Parent*, p. 81. Also Clark, 'Unemployed on Supplementary Benefit', p. 396; Burghes, *Living from Hand to Mouth*, p. 45.
128. In response to this problem the Government eventually created 'job clubs' for the unemployed which provided free use of telephones to contact employers.
129. Mack and Lansley, *Poor Britain*, pp. 118–26.
130. Piachaud, *Family Incomes Since the War*, p. 18. Figures from Family Expenditure Surveys. Other case studies found the proportion still as high as 60 per cent. See Bradshaw and Holmes, *Living on the Edge*, p. 17; Millar, *Poverty and the Lone Parent*, p. 74.
131. This was especially likely to be true of single-parent families. Millar, 'Lone Mothers' p. 169; Friend and Metcalf, *Slump City*, p. 131.
132. Parker, 'Making Ends Meet', p. 230.
133. Campbell, *Wigan Pier Revisited*, p. 17; Harrison, *Inside the Inner City*, p. 159.
134. A. Aird, 'Goods and Services' in F. Williams (ed.), *Why the Poor Pay More* (London, 1977), p. 22.
135. Bradshaw and Deacon, 'Social Security', p. 92; Mack and Lansley, *Poor Britain*, p. 112.
136. Burghes, *Living from Hand to Mouth*, p. 14.
137. *Ibid.*, p. 14.
138. M. Brown and N. Madge, *Despite the Welfare State* (London, 1982), p. 162; Mack and Lansley, *Poor Britain*, pp. 99–170; Clark, 'Unemployed on Supplementary Benefit', p. 397; Bradshaw and Holmes, *Living on the Edge*, p. 178.

139. Marsden, *Workless*, p. 102.

140. Mack and Lansley, *Poor Britain*, p. 153; Jones, *Life on the Dole*, p. 109.

141. Clark, 'Unemployed on Supplementary Benefit', p. 400; Jordan, *Paupers*, p. 27.

142. Gould and Kenyon, *Stories from the Dole Queue*, p. 175.

143. I. Macleod, 'The Political Divide', in Conservative Political Centre, *The Future of the Welfare State* (London, 1958), p. 18.

144. Jordan, *Paupers* p. 28.

145. Smith, 'A model for the development of public participation', pp. 7–8.

146. H. Rose, 'Up against the Welfare State: the claimant unions', in R. Miliband and J. Saville (eds), *The Socialist Register 1973* (London, 1973), pp. 183–6.

147. Gould and Kenyon, *Stories from the Dole Queue*, pp. 169–77.

148. Campbell, *Wigan Pier Revisited*, p. 208.

149. On the success of the Claimants Union tribunal work, see Jordan, *Paupers*, pp. 20, 48–9.

150. For a perceptive critique of organisational problems, see Rose, 'Up against the Welfare State', pp. 197–9.

151. Campbell, *Wigan Pier Revisited*, pp. 212–3.

152. P.F. Whiteley and S.J. Winyard, *Pressures for the Poor* (London, 1987), pp. 132–5.

153. Clark, 'The Unemployed on Supplementary Benefit', p. 392.

154. Donnison, *Politics of Poverty*, pp. 132–3; McCarthy, *Campaigning for the Poor*, p. 285.

155. D. Blunkett and G. Green, *Building from the Bottom. The Sheffield Experience* (London, 1983), p. 8.

156. S. Miller, 'Thatcherism, Citizenship and the Poll Tax' in M. Brenton and C. Ungerson (eds), *Social Policy Review 1988–9*, (London, 1989), pp. 85–101; R. Lister, *The Exclusive Society* (London, 1990), p. 41.

157. Labour Party, *Meet the Challenge, Make the Change* (London, 1989), pp. 29–39.

158. N. Bosanquet, *After the New Right* (London, 1983), pp. 136–45.

159. R. Harris, *Beyond the Welfare State* (London, 1988), pp. 21–3.

160. Andrews and Jacobs, *Punishing the Poor*, p. 287.

161. R.E. Goodwin and J. Le Grand, *Not Only the Poor* (London, 1987), pp. 147–68; J. Le Grand and D. Winter, *The Middle Classes and the Welfare State* (London, 1987), *passim*.

162. P. Taylor-Gooby, 'Attitudes to Welfare', *Journal of Social Policy*, **14**, 1, (Jan. 1985), pp. 77–9; N. Johnson, *The Welfare State in Transition* (Brighton, 1987), p. 50.

163. Peden, *British Economic and Social Policy*, p. 231, HMSO, *Economic Trends* (London, 1990).

164. D. Piachaud, 'The growth of poverty', in A. and C. Walker (eds), *The Growing Divide* (London, 1987), pp. 21–2.

165. Whiteley and Winyard, *Pressure for the Poor*, p. 126.

166. Peden, *British Economic and Social Policy*, p. 230.

167. Andrews and Jacobs, *Punishing the Poor*, pp. 45–9.

168. Social Security Consortium, *Of Little Benefit, An Update* (London, 1987), pp. 16–19.
169. House of Commons Social Services Committee, *Families on Low Income: Low Income Statistics* (London, 1988), p. iv. Debate about the substance and implications of this latest measure continues. The most recent study of official figures by the Institute of Fiscal Studies suggests that the number of people living on less than half the average income has increased from 4.9 million to 10.5 million in the decade from 1979.
170. *The Times*, 25 February, 1952, p. 7.
171. T.H. Marshall, *Citizenship and Social Class* (Cambridge, 1950). The central essay in this collection appeared in 1949.
172. D.S. King and J. Waldron, 'Citizenship, Social Citizenship and the Defence of Welfare Provision', *British Journal of Political Science*, **18**, 4 (October, 1988), pp. 419–31.
173. Harris, *Justifying State Welfare* (Oxford, 1987), pp. 145–65.
174. Donnison, *Politics of Poverty*, p. 226.
175. See, for instance, R. Mishra, *The Welfare State in Crisis* (Brighton, 1984), p. 171.
176. D.E. Ashford, *The Emergence of the Welfare States* (Oxford, 1986), p. 299; W.A. Robson, *Welfare State and Welfare Society* (London, 1976), p. 177.
177. J. Parker, *Social Policy and Citizenship* (London, 1975), pp. 146–54
178. M. Ignatieff, 'Citizenship and Moral Narcissism', *Political Quarterly*, **60**, 7 (January, 1989), p. 68.
179. P. Flora, *State, Economy and Society in Western Europe 1815–1975. Vol. 1, The Growth of Mass Democracies and Welfare States* (London, 1983), p. 456. 'Social security' here refers to public assistance, family allowances, public health, and insurance for health, pensions, occupational injuries and unemployment.
180. Oppenheim, *Poverty*, pp. 122–3. 'Poverty' here means numbers below 50 per cent of average income for each country.
181. Lister, *The Exclusive Society*, pp. 27–8, 52–62.
182. London, 1989.
183. S. Hall and D. Held, 'Left and Rights', *Marxism Today* (June, 1989), p. 21.

Glossary

ANOMALIES	1931	*Anomalies Act.* Designed to remove 'anomalies' whereby some categories of claimants, specifically intermittent, short-time and seasonal workers, and married women, could receive more insurance benefit than others. Discouraged married women from remaining in the labour market by disqualifying insurance contributions made before marriage.
BEVERIDGE PLAN REPORT	1942	*Report on Social Insurance and Allied Services.* Produced by the Inter-Departmental Committee on Social Insurance and Allied Services; led to the 1944 White Paper on Social Insurance. Blueprint of modern welfare system.
BOARDS OF GUARDIANS		*See* Poor Law.
BMA		British Medical Association.
CHILD BENEFIT		*See* Family Allowances.
CHILD TAX ALLOWANCES		Income tax allowances for all children of tax payers. Finally merged with Family Allowances (q.v.) to form Child Benefit in 1978.
CHILD WELFARE	1906	*Education (Provision of Meals Act).* LAs permitted to supply non-pau-

perising school meals, and encouraged to seek funding from parents or charities.

1907 *Education (Administrative Provisions) Act.* Established medical department within Board of Education to supervise inspection of health of school children.

1908 *Children Act.* Set out a clear definition of children's rights, imposed penalties on parents who neglected their children.

1914 *Education (Provision of Meals) Act.* Compulsory where 1906 Act was permissive. Government subsidy made available, eligibility based on assessment of child's health.

1918 *Maternity of Child Welfare Act.* LAs compelled to set up committees on maternity and child welfare, and enabled to support ante-natal and child welfare clinics.

1933 *Children and Young Persons Act.* Deprived Poor Law of remaining responsibilities for children in care.

1944 *Education Act.* School meals service made comprehensive and compulsory.

1948 *Children Act.* Brought all child care under LA supervision.

1963 *Children and Young Persons Act.* Enabled local authorities to give financial assistance to families faced with break-up.

1980 *Education (No. 2) Act.* LEAs no longer required to provide school meals except for families in receipt of welfare benefits.

CLAIMANTS UNION Loosely federated body of claimants' organisations, partly modelled on the inter-war NUWM. Committed to encouraging self-help

		amongst claimants, providing advice and advocacy and campaigning for welfare reform.
CLAWBACK		The device of reclaiming increases in benefits through the tax system, applied to the up-rating of family allowances (q.v.) in 1968.
COS		Charity Organisation Society.
CPAG		Child Poverty Action Group.
CPGB		Communist Party of Great Britain.
DHSS		Department of Health and Social Security.
DISABLED		*See* Invalidity.
DSS		Department of Social Security.
ENP		Emergency Needs Payment
ERS		Earnings Related Supplement.
EXTENDED BENEFIT		*See* Income Support.
FAMILY ALLOWANCES	1945	*Family Allowances Act.* Provided non-contributory benefit of 5s for second and subsequent children, payable to the mother through post offices.
	1968	Ten shilling rise in allowances (worth 8s since 1952), offset by the introduction of the clawback (q.v.).
	1975	Child tax allowances abolished, payments merged with family allowances to form Child Benefit, now payable to all children (from 1977).
FAMILY CREDIT		*See* Low Pay.
FES		Family Endowment Society.
FIS		Family Income Supplement. *See* Low Wages.
FOUR-WEEK RULE		Suspension of supplementary benefit for four weeks if it was judged there were good local employment prospects.
FOWLER REVIEW	1984	Large-scale review of welfare system undertaken by the then Secretary of State for Health and Social Security Norman Fowler. Led to

		Green Paper June 1985, White Paper Dec. 1985, reforms of 1986.
GEDDES AXE	1922	Emergency programme of retrenchment in social expenditure in Feb. 1922, on advice of committee of businessmen headed by Sir Eric Geddes.
GENUINELY SEEKING WORK TEST		Regulation introduced in 1921 to disqualify applicants for uncovenanted benefit who could not prove their intention to find employment. Extended to insured in 1924, abolished in 1930.
GINGERBREAD		Pressure group for one-parent families.
GUARANTEED MAINTENANCE ALLOWANCE		Non-contributory benefit for single parent families, tapered against income. Central proposal of 1974 Finer Committee. Not implemented. *See instead*, Child Benefit.
HOUSING	1909	*Housing and Town Planning Act*. LAs encouraged to build houses and demolish slums and engage in urban planning.
	1915	*Increase of Rent and Mortgage Interest (War Restrictions) Act*. Statutory control of war-time rises in housing costs.
	1919	*Housing and Town Planning Act* (Addison's). LAs required to prepare rebuilding plans and given subsidies to finance gap between costs and rents of new housing.
	1919	*Rent Act*. Renewed 1915 Act. Extended and modified by further Acts in 1920, 1923, 1933, 1939.
	1923	*Housing Act* (Chamberlain's). Flat rate subsidy for private builders, and for LAs if the former could not cope.

1924   *Housing (Financial Provisions) Act* (Wheatley's). Shifted focus of state subsidy from private to public sector.

1930   *Housing Act* (Greenwood's). Compelled LAs to plan slum clearance, and subsidised their schemes.

1933   *Housing Act.* Suspended previous subsidies; established programme of slum clearance.

1935   *Housing Act.* LAs further encouraged to clear slums and to be prosecuted if own housing substandard; council rents forbidden to undercut private sector.

1949   *Housing Act.* Provided subsidies for LAs which acquired houses for improvement or conversion, and for private owners to improve their property.

1954   *Housing Repairs and Rent Act.* Restarted slum clearance.

1957   *Rent Act.* Relaxed rent controls.

1965   *Rent Act.* Established security of tenure for unfurnished lets, and fair rents.

1974   *Rent Act.* Extended 1965 Act to furnished lets.

1975   *Housing Rent and Subsidies Act.* National rent and rate rebate schemes united; qualifying levels standardised.

1980   *Housing Act.* Council tenants given right to buy; state given more power over LA expenditure.

1982   *Social Security and Housing Benefit Act.* Housing benefit payable instead of rent and rate rebates.

ILP   Independent Labour Party.

IMF   International Monetary Fund.

INCOME GUARANTEE   Labour Party proposal of early 1960s to respond to the shortfall in national insurance pensions by introducing a form of negative income tax (q.v.) for the elderly. Not implemented.

INCOME SUPPORT

1914   Separation Allowances. Non-pauperising relief payable to families of servicemen.

1918   Out-of-Work Donation. Temporary extension of above for unemployed servicemen and families.

1921   *Unemployment Insurance (Amendments I and II) Acts.* On expiry of Out-of-Work Donation, non-contributory extended or uncovenanted benefits payable to unemployed when insurance exhausted.

1922   Extended benefit means-tested.

1924   *Unemployment Insurance Act.* Means test removed from extended benefit. Period of benefit unlimited.

1927   *Unemployment Insurance Act.* Extended merged with standard benefit. Transitional benefit introduced for those with insufficient insurance.

1934   *Unemployment Act.* Brought most forms of support for jobless under central control of UAB. Divorced transitional benefit, now unemployment assistance, from unemployment scheme.

1935   *Unemployment Assistance (Temporary Provisions) Act* (Standstill Act). Suspended scales of 1934 Act for two years, allowed unemployed to receive either old PAC or new UAB scale, whichever was higher.

1941   *Determination of Needs Act.* Replaced household by family means test.

1948 *National Assistance Act.* Provided means-tested benefit of 40s per couple, plus allowances for children, and rent. To cater for what was expected to be a declining minority of claimants not covered by the new national insurance system.

1966 *Ministry of Social Security Act.* National assistance renamed Supplementary Benefit, with fresh specification of entitlement, simplified claims procedures, and increases in scales. NAB and MPNI merged to form Ministry of Social Security (DHSS from 1968, DSS from 1988). Supplementary Benefits Commission established to supervise means-tested system. Higher weekly rate introduced for pensioners and other claimants (not unemployed) on SB for two years.

1980 *Social Security Nos 1 and 2 Acts.* Severed link between earnings and uprating of benefits. Reduced complexity of ENPs (q.v.) and the claims procedure.

1986 *Social Security Act.* Replaced supplementary benefits by Income Support. Structure of separate rates simplified to basic additions for families with children, lone parents, pensions, long-term sick and disabled. Emergency Needs Payments replaced by the Social Fund, designed to meet a smaller number of needs, mostly by cash limited loans repayable through Income Support. FIS replaced by Family Credit. *See also* Low Wages, PACs, UAB, Poor Law, National Insurance.

INDUSTRIAL INSURANCE Commercially provided insurance, sold and collected door-to-door, most frequently providing benefits in return for penny-a-week contributions.

INFANT MORTALITY Mortality of children under one year of age.

INVALIDITY 1975 *Social Security Benefits Act.* Provided non-contributory invalidity pension for disabled non-insured men and women under retirement age, hitherto dependent on SB. *See also* National Insurance, Income Support.

IS Income Support.

LAs Local Authorities.

LCC London County Council.

LIVING WAGE Objective of trade union movement, especially in inter-war period. A wage large enough to support a worker and his family, independently of outside assistance.

LOW PAY 1909 *Trade Boards Act.* Provided wage protection for around 100,000 workers, mostly women, in sweated industries.

1918 *Wages (Temporary Regulation Act).* Extended for eighteen months war-time wage controls.

1921 War-time extension of trade boards consolidated. Now covered about 300,000 workers.

1970 *Equal Pay Act.* Designed to abolish the historic under-payment of women workers.

1971 *Social Security Act* Family Income Supplement. Working heads of families whose income fell below a set scale to have the difference made up in the form of a benefit payable for a six-month period. *See also* Speenhamland System.

1979 Increased entitlement for lone parents on FIS.

	1986	*Social Security Act.* FIS replaced by Family Credit, with increased benefits payable through the earner's pay packet.
	1986	*Wages Act.* Removes protection of wages councils from workers under twenty-one.
MATERNITY	1913	Maternity Benefit of 30s included in National Insurance scheme.
	1946	*National Insurance Act.* Weekly maternity benefit for insured women, lump sum maternity grant payable on husband's insurance.
	1986	*Social Security Act.* Maternity grant abolished. *See also* Child Welfare.
MAY COMMITTEE	1931	Committee of National Expenditure headed by George May, Secretary of Prudential Assurance Company, appointed March 1931, reported July, recommended 20 per cent cuts in unemployment benefit. Attempts to implement recommendations led to fall of the 1929–31 Labour Government.
MEANS TEST		Test of means associated with several pre-1914 reforms, and with eighteen benefits by 1939; major version was 1931 Household Means Test, which subjected transitional benefit to a test of the possessions and income of all co-residing relatives. Scope reduced from household to family by 1941 Determination of Needs Act. Remains basis of most forms of non-contributory relief.
MINIMUM WAGE		A mirage. *See* Low Pay.
MOSS		Ministry of Social Security.
MPNI		Ministry of Pensions and National Insurance.
NA		National Assistance.
NAB		National Assistance Board.

NATIONAL INSURANCE

1911   *National Insurance Act.* Compulsory insurance, provided fifteen weeks benefit for unemployed shipbuilders, engineering workers and building workers, with contributions from employers, employees and the state. Health Insurance on similar basis for all wage earners.

1920   *Unemployment Insurance Act.* Extended scheme to all workers earning under £250 p.a., except agricultural labourers and servants.

1921   *Unemployment Insurance (Amendments I and II) Acts.* Provided thirty-two weeks 'extended' or 'uncovenanted' benefit for those who had exhausted contributory relief. *See* Income Support.

1921   *Unemployed Workers' Dependants' (Temporary Provision) Act.* Dependants' benefits added to insurance scheme.

1924   *Unemployment Insurance Act.* Unemployment Insurance benefit unlimited in length.

1927   *Unemployment Insurance Act.* Merged standard and extended benefit, introduced transitional benefit for those who had paid less than thirty weeks' contributions.

1930   *Unemployment Insurance Act.* Cost of transitional benefits transferred from LAs to Treasury; twelve month time limit and genuinely seeking work test abolished.

1931   September budget cut unemployment benefit by 10 per cent, reduced benefit period, increased contributions.

1934   *Unemployment Assistance Act.* Set up Unemployment Insurance Statutory Committee to manage system on strict actuarial basis, with equal contributions from employers, employees and the state, and UAB to provide central control of means-tested relief. 1931 cuts restored. Transitional benefit separated from insurance scheme.

1946   *National Insurance Act.* Unified pre-war system. Single flat-rate weekly contribution gave entitlement to non-graduated sickness, unemployment, maternity and widows benefits, and retirement pensions.

1959   *National Insurance Act.* Facilitated contracting out from the scheme in response to growth of private schemes, and introduced wage-related pensions.

1966   *National Insurance Act.* Extended wage-related benefits to sickness, unemployment, industrial injury and widows' allowances. Extended benefit period to twelve months.

1966   *Ministry of Social Security Act.* Merged control of insurance and means-tested schemes into a single ministry.

1980   *Social Security (Nos 1 and 2) Acts.* Disconnected rise in benefits from rise in earnings; abolished earnings related supplements. *See also* Income Support.

NCSS   National Council for Social Services.

NEC   National Executive Committee of the Labour Party.

NEGATIVE INCOME TAX   Alternative to the Beveridge system: all receive a tax assessment, those above a line to pay tax, those below to be paid through the tax system. Not implemented. *See also* Social Dividend.

NHS		National Health Service.
NIESR		National Institute of Economic and Social Research.
NUW[C]M		National Unemployed Workers [Committee until 1929] Movement.
OUT-OF-WORK DONATION		*See* Income Support.
PACs		Public Assistance Committees. *See* Poor Law.
OLD AGE		*See* Pensions
PAUPER DISQUALIFICATION		The regulation which until 1918 disenfranchised those in receipt of poor law assistance.
PENSIONS	1908	*Old Age Pensions Act.* Provided non-contributory, non-pauperising pension, subject to behavioural conditions, paid through post offices, of up to 5s for those of seventy and above earning less than £31 10s a week.
	1919	*Old Age Pensions Act.* Repealed behavioural clauses 1908 Act; raised pension to 10s.
	1924	*Old Age Pensions Act.* Removed earnings limit.
	1925	*Old Age and Widows and Orphans Contributory Pensions Act.* Granted pensions to men and women aged sixty-five to sixty-nine under the National Health Insurance scheme. Coverage extended to widows and orphans.
	1929	*Widows, Orphans and Old Age Contributory Pensions Act.* Gave pensions to widows at fifty-five.
	1940	*Old Age and Widows Pension Act.* Pensionable age of women lowered to sixty.
	1946	*National Insurance Act.* Flat rate contributions gave entitlement to retirement pensions at sixty-five for men, sixty for women, of 26s (single), 42s (married).

1959   *National Insurance Act.* Introduced graduated pensions.

1975   *Social Security Pensions Act.* Introduced earnings related scheme from 1978 designed to yield a pension of a quarter of prevailing average earnings in twenty years.

1986   *Social Security Act.* Reduced scope of SERPS.

POOR LAW

1834   *Poor Law Amendment Act.* Parishes grouped into Unions administered by elected Boards of Guardians, providing relief in purpose-built workhouses whose conditions would be 'less eligible' than those outside. Outdoor relief discouraged, but still available. Recipients of relief disenfranchised.

1918   *Representation of the People Act.* Abolished pauper disqualification.

1921   *Local Authorities (Financial Provisions) Act.* Established machinery for transferring funds between richer and poorer boroughs and increased powers of Minister of Health to prescribe scales and conditions of relief.

1926   *Board of Guardians (Default Act).* Enabled governments to replace allegedly extravagant Boards of Guardians by Ministry of Health commissioners.

1929   *Local Government Act.* Administration of Poor Law transferred from Boards of Guardians to Public Assistance Committees of local authorities.

1930   *Poor Law Act.* Poor Law relief renamed public assistance. Workhouse test abolished.

1948   *National Assistance Act.* Stated that 'the existing Poor Law shall cease

	to have effect'. *See also* Income Support, Poplarism.
POPLARISM	Movement associated with the London borough of Poplar (and its leader, George Lansbury) which sought to use the possibilities for democratic control under the Poor Law to improve the treatment of the poor. This led to a series of conflicts with central Government before and after the First World War.
POVERTY TRAP	Where families are unable to escape poverty because an increase in income causes a commensurate loss of means-tested benefits.
RIGHT TO WORK MOVEMENT	Loose grouping of left-wing bodies which in the pre-1914 period strove to obtain legislation to attack unemployment, particularly by local job creation schemes.
SB	Supplementary Benefit.
SBC	Supplementary Benefits Commission.
SCHOOL HEALTH	*See* Child Welfare.
SCHOOL MEALS	*See* Child Welfare.
SEPARATION ALLOWANCES	*See* Income Support.
SOCIAL CONTRACT	Concept introduced by 1974 Labour Government, under which wage restraint was traded against increases in the 'social wage' or state welfare.
SOCIAL DIVIDEND	Alternative to the Beveridge system, put forward in various forms since 1942. Instead of welfare benefits, everyone receives a weekly social dividend, paid for by a graduated tax on all income. Not implemented. *See also* Negative Income Tax.
SOCIAL FUND	*See* Income Support.
SPEENHAMLAND SYSTEM	The device of subsidising wages of

men on the basis of a cost-of-living index. Introduced by Berkshire magistrates in 1795, abolished by the Poor Law Amendment Act of 1834, reintroduced in 1971 in the form of Family Income Supplement, now Family Credit.

SSAC	Social Security Advisory Committee.
SDF	Social Democratic Federation.
SERPS	State Earnings Related Pension Scheme.
SUPPLEMENTARY BENEFIT	*See* Income Support.
TAX CREDIT	Proposal to replace Beveridge structure by allocating every individual a credit based on family circumstances, which would be set against tax liability. If the credit exceeded tax a weekly benefit was payable. Embodied in particular in Tory 1972 Green Paper. Not implemented. *See also* Negative Income Tax, Social Dividend.
TRANSITIONAL BENEFIT	*See* Income Support.
TROUBLE	Man is born unto. *See* As the sparks fly upward.
TUC	Trades Union Congress.
UAB	Unemployed Assistance Board.
UNCOVENANTED BENEFIT	*See* Income Support.

UNEMPLOYMENT

1905 *Unemployed Workmen Act.* Sanctioned use of rates for work creation schemes and established machinery to co-ordinate efforts of official and volunteer organisations.

1934 *Special Areas (Development and Improvement) Act.* Set aside £2 for limited public works in specified areas. *See also* National Insurance, Income Support.

WAGE STOP — Regulation preventing the level of benefit exceeding the recipients' prior earnings in work.

WAGES	*See* Low Wages.
WORKHOUSE	Central device of 1834 Poor Law (q.v.). Survived between the wars as an institution for special categories of the needy.
WORK-SHY	*See also* fiddlers, layabouts, parasites, residuum, scroungers, undeserving, underclass, undergraduates. (Categories of abuse rather than analysis.)

Bibliography

Abel-Smith, B., 'Whose Welfare State?', in N. Mackenzie (ed.), *Conviction* (London, 1958)

Abel-Smith, B., 'Social Security', in M. Ginsberg (ed.), *Law and Opinion in England in the Twentieth Century* (London, 1959)

Abel-Smith, B., 'The Welfare State. Breaking the Post-War Consensus', *Political Quarterly* (January–March, 1980)

Abel-Smith, B. and Townsend, P., *The Poor and the Poorest* (London, 1965)

Abrams, M., *Beyond Three-Score and Ten* (London, 1978)

Abrams, P., 'The Failure of Social Reform 1918–20', *Past and Present*, **24** (1963)

Addison, P., *The Road to 1945* (London, 1975)

Aird, A., 'Goods and Services', in F. Williams (ed.), *Why the Poor Pay More* (London, 1977)

Allen, S. and Waton, A., 'The Effects of Unemployment: Experience and Response', in S. Allen et al., *The Experience of Unemployment* (London, 1986)

Andrews, K. and Jacobs, J., *Punishing the Poor* (London, 1990)

Ashdown P., *Citizen's Britain: A Radical Agenda for the 1990s* (London, 1989)

Ashford, D.E., *The Emergence of the Welfare States* (Oxford, 1986)

Astor, J.J. et al., *The Third Winter of Unemployment* (London, 1923)

Atkinson, A.B., *Poverty in Britain and The Reform of Social Security* (Cambridge, 1969)

Atkinson, A.B., 'Inequality and Social Security', in P. Townsend and N. Bosanquet (eds), *Labour and Inequality* (London, 1972)

Atkinson, A.B. and Trinder, C., 'Real Incomes of Other People', in M. Young (ed.), *Poverty Report 1974* (London, 1974)

Atkinson, A.B. and Trinder, C., 'Real Incomes of People at Work', in
  M. Young (ed.), *Poverty Report 1974* (London 1974)

Ayers, P., *The Liverpool Docklands* (Liverpool, 1988)

Ayers, P. and Lambertz, J., 'Marriage Relations, Money and Domestic
  Violence in Working-Class Liverpool, 1919–39', in J. Lewis (ed.),
  Labour and Love (Oxford, 1986)

Bailey, D.M., *Children of the Green* (London, 1981)

Bakke, F.W., *The Unemployed Man, A Social Study* (London, 1933)

Banting, K.G., *Poverty, Politics and Policy* (London, 1979)

Barnes, G.N., *From Workshop to War Cabinet* (London, 1923)

Barnes J., *Arthur and Me* (Bristol, 1979)

Barton, A., *Two Lamps in Our Street* (London, 1967)

Beales, H.L. and Lambert, R.S., (eds), *Memoirs of the Unemployed* (London, 1967)

Beaver, M.W., 'Population, Infant Mortality and Milk,' *Population
  Studies*, **27**, 2 (1973)

Beckerman, W. and Clark, S., *Poverty and Social Security in Britain Since
  1961* (Oxford, 1982)

Belloc, H., *The Servile State* (London, 1912)

Benson, J., *The Penny Capitalists* (Dublin, 1983)

Bentley, M., *The Climax of Liberal Politics* (London, 1987)

Berthoud, R., *Fuel Debts and Hardship* (London, 1981)

Berthoud, R. and Kempson, E., *Credit and Debt in Britain* (London, 1990)

Bevan, A., *In Place of Fear* (London, 1952)

Beveridge, W., *Power and Influence* (London, 1953)

Blake, J., *Memories of Old Poplar* (London, 1977)

Bloomberg, J., *Looking Back* (London, 1979)

Blunkett, D. and Green, G., *Building from the Bottom. The Sheffield
  Experience* (London, 1983)

Bosanquet, H., *The Standard of Life; and Other Studies,* (London, 1899)

Bosanquet, H., 'The Poverty Line', *Charity Organisation Society. Occasional Paper No. II, 3rd Series* (n.d.)

Bosanquet, H., *The Family* (London, 1915)

Bosanquet, N., *After the New Right* (London, 1983)

Bowley, A.L., *Prices and Wages in the United Kingdom, 1914–1920*
  (Oxford, 1921)

Bowley, A.L., *Wages and Income in the United Kingdom Since 1860*
  (Cambridge, 1937)

Bowley, A.L. and Burnett-Hurst, A.R., *Livelihood and Poverty* (London, 1915)

Bowley, A.L. and Hogg, M., *Has Poverty Diminished?* (London, 1925)

Bowley, M., *Housing and the State 1919–1944* (London, 1945)

Bradshaw, J. and Deacon, A., 'Social Security', in P. Wilding (ed.), *In Defence of the Welfare State* (Manchester, 1986)

Bradshaw, J., Cooke, K. and Godfrey, C., 'The Impact of Unemployment on the Living Standards of Families', *Journal of Social Policy*, **12**, 4 (Oct. 1983)

Bradshaw, J. and Holmes, H., *Living on the Edge* (London, 1989)

Braithwaite, C., *The Voluntary Citizen* (London, 1938)

Branson, N., *Popularism, 1919–1925* (London, 1979)

Brend, W.A., *Health and the State* (London, 1917)

Briggs, A., 'The Social Services', in G.D.N. Worswick and P.H. Ady, (eds), *The British Economy, 1945–50* (Oxford 1952)

Briggs, A., *Social Thought and Social Action. A Study of the Work of Seebohm Rowntree, 1871–1954* (London, 1961)

Briggs, A., 'The Welfare State in Historical Perspective', *Archives Européennes de Sociologie*, **2** (1961)

Briggs, A., 'The History of Changing Approaches to Social Welfare', in *Comparative Development in Social Welfare* (London, 1972)

Briggs, E. and Rees, A.M., *Supplementary Benefits and the Consumer* (London, 1980)

Brockway, A.F., *Hungry England* (London, 1932)

Brown, J.C., *Family Income Support Part I, Family Income Supplement* (London, 1983)

Brown, K.D., 'Conflict in Early British Welfare Policy: The Case of the Unemployed Workmen's Bill of 1905', *Journal of Modern History* XLIII, 4 (1971)

Brown, K.D., *Labour and Unemployment 1900–1914* (Newton Abbot, 1971)

Brown, M., *Stop This Starvation of Mother and Child* (London, c. 1935)

Brown, M. and Madge, N., *Despite The Welfare State* (London, 1982)

Bull, D., 'The Rediscovery of Family Poverty', in D. Bull (ed.), *Family Poverty* (London, 1971)

Bulmer, M., *Neighbours, The Work of Philip Abrams* (Cambridge, 1986)

Burghes, L., *Living from Hand to Mouth* (London, 1980)

Burnett, J., *Plenty and Want* (Harmondsworth, 1968)

Calder, A., *The People's War* (London, 1971)

Calder, A. and Sheridan, D. (eds), *Speak for Yourself* (London, 1984)

Callaghan, T., *A Long Way to the Pa'anshop* (Newcastle-on-Tyne, 1979)

Campbell, B., *Wigan Pier Revisited* (London, 1984)

Caradog Jones, D., *The Social Survey of Merseyside* (3 vols, Liverpool, 1934)

Carr-Saunders, A.M., Caradog Jones, D. and Moser, C.A., *A Survey of Social Conditions in England and Wales* (Oxford, 1958)

Chesterton, Mrs C., *I Lived in a Slum* (London, 1937)

Churchill, W.S., *Liberalism and the Social Problem* (London, 1909)

The Clarion

Clark, F.Le G., *Social History of the School Meals Service* (London, 1948)

Clark, F.Le G. (ed.), *National Fitness* (London, 1938)

Clark, M., 'The Unemployed on Supplementary Benefit: Living Standards and Making Ends Meet on a Low Income', *Journal of Social Policy*, **7**, 4 (October, 1978)

Clark, P., *Liberals and Social Democrats* (Cambridge, 1978)

Coates, D., *Labour in Power* (London, 1980)

Coates, K. and Silburn, R., *Poverty: The Forgotten Englishmen* (Harmondsworth, 1970)

Cohen, M., *I Was One of the Unemployed* (London, 1945)

Cole, D. and Utting, J.E.G., *The Economic Circumstances of Old People* (London, 1962)

Cole, G.D.H., *The Simple Case for Socialism* (London, 1935)

Collins, D., 'The Introduction of Old Age Pensions in Great Britain', *Historical Journal*, **8** (1965)

Connolly, J., *An Easy Guide to the New Unemployment Act* (London, c. 1935)

Conybeare, W., *Charity of Poor to Poor* (London, 1908)

Coombes, B.L., *These Poor Hands* (London, 1939)

Cooper, S., *Observations in Supplementary Benefit Offices* (London, 1985)

Copeman, F., *Reason in Revolt* (London, 1948)

Cowling, M., *The Impact of Labour, 1920–1924* (Cambridge, 1971)

Cox, B.D., et al., *Health and Lifestyle Survey* (Cambridge, 1987)

Craig, F.W.S., *British General Election Manifestos, 1918–1966* (Chichester, 1970)

Cripps, S., *Why This Socialism* (London, 1934)

Crosland, C.A.R., *The Future of Socialism* (London, 1956)

Croucher, R., *We Refuse to Starve in Silence* (London, 1987)

Crow, G., 'The use of the concept of "strategy" in recent sociological literature', *Sociology*, **23**, 1 (1989)

Crowther, M.A., 'The Later Years of the Workhouse 1890–1929', in P. Thane (ed.), *The Origins of Political Social Policy* (London, 1978)

Crowther, M.A., *Social Policy in Britain 1914–1939* (London, 1988)

Dalton, H., *Practical Socialism for Britain* (London, 1935)

Darby, A.S., *A View from the Alley* (Luton, 1974)

Daunton, M.J. (ed.), *Councillors and Tenants: Local Authority Housing in English Cities, 1919–1939* (Leicester, 1984)

Davies, M.L., *Maternity. Letters from Working-Women* (London, 1978; 1st edn 1915)

Dayus, K., *Her People* (London, 1982)

Deacon, A., 'Labour and the Unemployed: The Administration of Insurance in the Twenties', *Bulletin of the Society for the Study of Labour History*, **3** (1975)

Deacon, A., *In Search of the Scrounger* (London, 1976)

Deacon, A., 'Concession or Coercion: the Politics of Unemployment Insurance in the Twenties', in J. Saville and A. Briggs (eds), *Essays in Labour History, 3* (London, 1977)

Deacon, A., 'An End to the Means Test? Social Security and the Attlee Government', *Journal of Social Policy*, **11**, 3, (July, 1982)

Deacon, A. and Bradshaw, J., *Reserved for the Poor* (London, 1983)

Deacon, A. and Briggs, E., 'Local Democracy and Central Policy: The Issue of Pauper Votes in the 1920s', *Policy and Politics* **2**, 4 (June, 1974)

Deakin, N., *The Politics of Welfare* (London, 1987)

Dearle, N., *The Cost of Living* (London, 1926)

Department of Employment and Productivity, *A National Minimum Wage* (London, 1969)

Department of Health and Social Security, *Social Assistance. A Review of the Supplementary Benefits Scheme in Great Britain* (London, 1978)

Department of Health and Social Security, *Inequalities in Health* (London, 1980)

Dicey, A.V., *Lectures on the Relation between Law and Public Opinion in England during the Nineteenth Century* (2nd edn, London, 1914)

Dilnot, A.W., Kay, J.A. and Morris, C.N., *The Reform of Social Security* (Oxford, 1984)

Donnelly, P., *The Yellow Rock* (London, 1950)

Donnison, D., *The Politics of Poverty* (Oxford, 1982)

Donoghue, B., *Prime Minister, The Conduct of Policy under Harold Wilson and James Callaghan* (London, 1987)

Donoghue, B. and Jones, G.W., *Herbert Morrison: Portrait of a Politician* (London, 1973)

Drage, G., *The State and the Poor* (London, 1914)

Dwork, D., *War is Good for Babies and Other Young Children* (London, 1987)

Eder, N.R., *National Health Insurance and the Medical Profession in Britain, 1913–1939* (New York and London, 1982)

Edwards, I., *No Gold on My Shovel* (London, 1947)

Elias, S., *A Practical Guide to the Unemployment Acts including the Anomalies Regulations and the Means Test* (London, c. 1932)

Emy, H.V., *Liberals, Radicals and Social Politics, 1892–1914* (Cambridge, 1973)

Eyles, M.L., *The Woman in the Little House* (London, 1922)

Ezard, E., *Battersea Boy* (London, 1979)

Fiegehen, G.C., Lansley, P.S. and Smith A.D., *Poverty and Progress in Britain, 1953–73* (Cambridge, 1977)

Field, F., 'A Pressure Group for the Poor', in D. Ball (ed.), *Family Poverty* (London, 1971)

Field, F., 'Unemployment and Poverty', in F. Field (ed.), *The Conscript Army* (London, 1977)

Field, F., 'How the Poor Fared', in K. Coates (ed.), *What Went Wrong* (Nottingham, 1979)

Field, F., *Inequality in Britain* (London, 1981)

Field, F., *What Price a Child* (London, 1985)

Finn, R.L., *No Tears in Aldgate* (London, 1963)

Flora, P., *State, Economy and Society in Western Europe, 1815–1975* (2 vols, London, 1983)

Foakes, G., *My Part of the River* (London, 1974)

Fogarty, M.P., 'Social Welfare', in A. Seldon (ed.), *Agenda for a Free Society* (London, 1961)

Ford, P., *Work and Wealth in a Modern Port* (London, 1934)

Ford, P., 'Means Tests and Responsibility for Needy Relatives', *Sociological Review*, XXXIX (1937)

Fraser, D., *The Evolution of the British Welfare State* (London, 1973)

Freeden, M., *The New Liberalism* (Oxford, 1978)

Friend, A. and Metcalf A., *Slump City* (London, 1981)

Gamble, A., *The Conservative Nation* (London, 1974)

Gamble, R., *Chelsea Child* (London, 1979)

George, R.F., 'A New Calculation of the Poverty Line', *Journal of the Royal Statistical Society*, C (1937)

George, V., *Social Security: Beveridge and After* (London, 1968)

Gibney, J., *Joe McGarrigle's Daughter* (Kineton, 1977)

Gilbert, B.B., 'Health and Politics: The British Physical Deterioration Report of 1904', *Bulletin of the History of Medicine* XXXIX, (1965)

Gilbert, B.B., *The Evolution of National Insurance in Great Britain* (London, 1966)

Gilbert, B.B., *British Social Policy 1914–1939* (London, 1970)

Gilbert, B.B., *David Lloyd George, A Political Life. The Architect of Change 1863–1912* (London, 1987)

Gittins, D., *Fair Sex. Family Size and Structure 1900–39* (London, 1982)

Glynn S. and Booth A., 'Unemployment in Inter-war Britain: A Case for Re-learning the Lessons of the 1930s', *Economic History Review*, XXXVI, 3 (August, 1983)

Golding, P. and Middleton, S., *Images of Welfare* (Oxford, 1982)

Goldman, P., 'Preface' in Conservative Political Centre, *The Future of The Welfare State* (London, 1958)

Goldthorpe, H., *Room at the Bottom* (Bradford, 1959)

Goodwin, R.E. and Le Grand J., *Not Only The Poor* (London, 1987)

Gough, I., *The Political Economy of the Welfare State* (London, 1979)

Gould, F. and Roweth, B., 'Public Spending and Social Policy: The United Kingdom 1950–1977', *Journal of Social Policy*, **9**, 3 (1980)

Gould, T. and Kenyan, J., *Stories from the Dole Queue* (London, 1972)

Gourvish, T.R., 'The Standard of Living 1890–1914', in A. O'Day (ed.), *The Edwardian Age* (London, 1979)

Gray, N., *The Worst of Times* (London) 1985

Green, D.G., *Working-Class Patients and the Medical Establishment* (Aldershot, 1985)

Greene, F. (ed.), *Time to spare; what unemployment means. By eleven unemployed* (London, 1935)

Greenwood, W., *How the Other Man Lives* (London, 1939)

Greenwood, W., *There Was a Time* (London, 1967)

Griffiths, J., *Pages From Memory* (London, 1969)

Hair, P.E.H., 'Children in Society 1850–1980', in T. Barker and M. Drake, (eds), *Population and Society in Britain 1850–1980* (London 1982)

Hall, E., *Canary Girls and Stockpots* (Luton, 1975)

Hall, P., Land, H., Parker, R. and Webb, A., *Change, Choice and Conflict in Social Policy* (London, 1975)

Hall, S. and Held, D., 'Left and Rights', *Marxism Today* (June, 1989)

Halsey, A.H., *Change in British Society* (Oxford, 1978)

Halsey, A.H. (ed.), *Trends in British Society since 1900* (London, 1972)

Halstead, J., Harrison, R. and Stevenson, J., 'The Reminiscences of Sid Elias', *Bulletin of the Society for the Study of Labour History*, **38**, (Spring 1979)

Hannington, W., *The Insurgents in London* (London, 1923)

Hannington, W., *The Story of the National Hunger March* (London, 1929)

Hannington, W., *Ten Lean Years*, (London, 1949)

Hannington, W., *Never On Our Knees* (London, 1967)

Hannington, W. and Llewelyn, E., *How To Get Unemployment Benefit* (London, c. 1928)

Hansard

Harris, D., *Justifying State Welfare* (Oxford, 1987)

Harris, J., *Unemployment and Politics* (Oxford, 1972)

Harris, J., *William Beveridge* (Oxford, 1977)

Harris, J., 'Some Aspects of Social Policy in Britain During The Second World War', in W.J. Mommsen (ed.), *The Emergence of the Welfare State in Britain and Germany* (London, 1981)

Harris, J., 'Did British Workers Want the Welfare State? G.D.H. Cole's Survey of 1942', in J. Winter (ed.), *The Working Class in Modern British History* (Cambridge, 1983)

Harris, R.W., *National Health Insurance in Great Britain 1911–1946* (London, 1946)

Harrison, P., *Inside the Inner City* (Harmondsworth, 1983)

Harrison, T., 'Who'll Win?', *Political Quarterly*, XV, 1 (1944)

Harvey, A., *Casualties of the Welfare State* (London, 1960)

Hay, J.R., *The Origins of the Liberal Welfare Reforms 1906–1914* (London, 1975)

Hayburn, R., 'The Police and The Hunger Marchers', *International Review of Social History*, XVII, 3 (1972)

Healey, D., *The Time of My Life* (London, 1989)

Hennock, E.P., *British Social Reform and German Precedents* (Oxford, 1987)

Hennock, P., 'The Measurement of Urban Poverty: From The Metropolis to the Nation, 1880–1920', *Economic History Review*, 2nd Ser., XL, 2 (1987)

Hess, J.C., 'The Social Policy of the Attlee Government', in W.J. Mommsen (ed.), *The Emergence of the Welfare State in Britain and Germany* (London, 1981)

Hill, M.J., 'The Exercise of Discretion in the National Assistance Board', *Public Administration*, **47** (Spring, 1969)

Hill, M.J., 'Selectivity for the Poor', in P. Townsend and N. Bosanquet (eds), *Labour and Inequality* (London, 1972)

Hill, M.J., *The State, Administration and the Individual* (London, 1976)

Hill, M.J., Harrison, R.M., Sargeant, A.V. and Talbot, V., *Men Out Of Work* (Cambridge, 1973)

Hilton, J., *Rich Man, Poor Man* (London, 1938)

Hitchin, G., *Pit-Yacker* (London, 1962)

Hobbs, M., *Born To Struggle* (London, 1973)

Hobhouse, L.T., *Democracy and Reaction* (London, 1904)

Hobson, J.A., *Problems of Poverty* (6th edn, London, 1906)

Hoggart, R., *The Uses of Literacy* (London, 1958)

Holman, R., *Poverty, Explanations of Social Deprivation* (Oxford, 1978)

Holmes, C., 'Housing', in F. Williams (ed.), *Why The Poor Pay More* (London, 1977)

Holt, W., *I Haven't Unpacked* (London, 1939)

Hood, K., *Room At The Bottom* (London, 1960)

Hooley, J., *A Hillgate Childhood* (Stockport, 1981)

House of Commons Employment Committee, *The Problems of Low Pay* (London, 1985)

Howarth, E.G. and Wilson, M., *West Ham: A Study in Social and Industrial Problems* (London, 1907)

Howe, G., 'Reform of the Social Services', in D. Howell and T. Raison (eds), *Principles in Practice* (London, 1961)

Howe, L.E.A., 'The "Deserving" and the "Undeserving"': Practice in an Urban, Local Social Security Office', *Journal of Social Policy*, **14** (January, 1985)

Howkins, A. and Saville, J., 'The Nineteen Thirties: A Revisionist History', *Socialist Register 1979* (London, 1979)

Hughes, John, 'The Low Paid', in P. Townsend and N. Bosanquet (eds), *Labour and Inequality* (London, 1972)

Hurstfield, J., 'Women's Unemployment in the 1930s: Some Comparisons with the 1980s', in S. Allen et al., *The Experience of Unemployment* (London, 1986)

Hurt, J., 'Feeding The Hungry Schoolchild In The First Half Of The Twentieth Century', in D.J. Oddy and D.S. Miller (eds), *Diet and Health in Modern Britain* (London, 1985)

Ignatieff, M., 'Citizenship and Moral Narcissism', *Political Quarterly*, **60**, 7 (January, 1989)

James, R.R. (ed.), *Winston S. Churchill. His Complete Speeches Vol. II 1908–1913* (New York, 1974)

Jasper, A.S., *A Hoxton Childhood* (London, 1969)

Johnson, N., *The Welfare State in Transition* (Brighton, 1987)

Johnson, P., 'Credit and Thrift and The British Working Class, 1810–1939', in J. Winter (ed.), *The Working Class In Modern British History* (Cambridge, 1983)

Johnson, P., *Saving and Spending. The Working-Class Economy in Britain 1870–1939* (Oxford, 1985)

Jones, J., *Unfinished Journey* (London, 1938)

Jones, M., *Life on the Dole* (London, 1972)

Jones, S.G., *Workers at Play* (London, 1986)

Jordan, B., *Paupers: The Making of the New Claiming Class* (London, 1973)

Judge, K., 'Beveridge: Past, Present and Future', in C. Sandford, C. Pond and R. Walker (eds), *Taxation and Social Policy* (London, 1980)

Keith-Lucas, B. and Richards, P.G., *A History of Local Government in the Twentieth Century* (London, 1978)

Kincaid, J.C., *Poverty and Equality in Britain* (London, 1973)

King, D.S. and Waldron, J., 'Citizenship, Social Citizenship and the Defence of Welfare Provision', *British Journal of Political Science*, **18**, 4 (October, 1988)

Kirkman Gray, B., *Philanthropy and the State* (London, 1908)

Klein, R., 'The Welfare State: A Self-Inflicted Crisis', *The Political Quarterly* (Jan.–Mar., 1980)

Kuczynski, J., *Hunger and Work* (London, 1938)

Labour Party, *Meet The Challenge, Make The Change* (London, 1989)

Land, H., *Large Families in London* (London, 1969)

Land, H., 'The Introduction of Family Allowances: An Act of Historic Justice,' in P. Hall et al., *Change, Choice and Conflict in Social Policy* (London, 1975)

Langley, J., *Always a Layman* (Brighton, 1976)

Lansbury, G., *My Life* (London, 1928)

Layard, R., Piachaud, D. and Stewart, M., *The Causes of Poverty* (London, 1978)

Le Grand, J. and Winter, D., *The Middle Classes and the Welfare State* (London, 1987)

Lewis, J., *The Politics of Motherhood* (London, 1980)

Lewis, J., 'Dealing with Dependency: State Practices and Social Realities, 1870–1945', in J. Lewis (ed.), *Women's Welfare/Women's Rights* (London, 1983)

Lewis, J., 'Eleanor Rathbone', in P. Barker (ed.), *Founders of the Welfare State* (London, 1984)

Lewis, J., 'The Working-Class Wife and Mother and State Intervention 1870–1918', in J. Lewis (ed.), *Labour and Love* (Oxford, 1986)

Lewis, J. and Piachaud, D., 'Women and Poverty in the Twentieth Century', in C. Glendinning and J. Millar (eds), *Women and Poverty in Britain* (Brighton, 1987)

Lister, R., *The Exclusive Society* (London, 1990)

Llewellyn Smith, H., *The New Survey of London Life and Labour* (London, 1934)

Loane, M., *The Queen's Poor* (London, 1905)

Loane, M., 'Husband and Wife among the Poor', *Contemporary Review*, **87** (1905)

Loane, M., *From Their Point of View* (London, 1908)

Loane, M., *Neighbours and Friends* (London, 1910)

Lowe, R., 'The Erosion of State Intervention in Britain, 1917–1924', *Economic History* (May, 1978)

Lowe, R., 'Welfare Legislation and the Unions During and After The First World War', *Historical Journal*, xxv (1982)

Lyman, R.W., *The First Labour Government 1924* (London, 1957)

Lynes, T., 'Poverty in the Welfare State', *Aspect* (Aug., 1963)

Lynes, T., 'Policy on Social Security', in M. Young (ed.), *Poverty Report 1974* (London, 1974)

Lynes, T., 'Unemployment Assistance Tribunals in the 1930s', in M. Adler and A. Bradley (eds), *Justice, Discretion and Poverty* (London, 1975)

McBriar, A.M., *An Edwardian Mixed Doubles* (Oxford, 1987)

McCarthy, M., *Campaigning For The Poor* (London, 1986)

M'Gonigle, G.C.M. and Kirby, J., *Poverty and Public Health* (London, 1936)

MacGregor, S., *The Politics of Poverty* (London, 1981)

McIntosh, M., 'The Welfare State and the Needs of the Dependent Family', in S. Burman (ed.), *Fit Work for Women* (London, 1979)

MacIntyre. S., 'British Labour, Marxism and Working-Class Apathy in the Nineteen Twenties', *Historical Journal*, **20**, 2 (1979)

McKibbin, R., 'Social Class and Social Observation in Edwardian England', *Transactions of the Royal Historical Society*, **28**, (1978)

McKibbin, R., 'Working-Class Gambling in Britain 1880–1939', *Past and Present*, **82**, (1979)

McKibbin, R., 'The "Social Psychology" of Unemployment in Inter-war Britain', in P.J. Waller (ed.), *Politics and Social Change in Modern Britain* (Brighton, 1987)

McLachlan, H.V., 'Townsend and the Concept of "Poverty"', *Social Policy and Administration*, **17**, No. 2, (Summer 1983)

Macleod, I., 'The Political Divide', in Conservative Political Centre, *The Future of the Welfare State* (London, 1958)

Macleod, I. and Powell, E., *The Social Services. Needs and Means* (London, 1952)

MacMillan, H., *The Middle Way* (London, 1938)

McNay, M. and Pond, C., *Low Pay and Family Poverty* (London, 1980)

MacNicol, J., 'Family Allowances and Less Eligibility', in P. Thane (ed.), *The Origins of British Social Policy* (London, 1978)

MacNicol, J., *The Movement for Family Allowances 1918–45* (London, 1980)

Mack, J. and Lansley, S., *Poor Britain* (London, 1985)

Mallock, W.H., *Social Reform* (London, 1914)

Mannheim, H., *Social Aspects of Crime in England between the Wars* (London, 1940)

Marquand, D., *The Unprincipled Society* (London, 1986)

Marris, P., *Widows and Their Families* (London, 1958)

Marsden, D., *Mothers Alone* (London, 1969)

Marsden, D., *Workless* (London, 1982)

Marshall, T.H., *Citizenship and Social Class* (Cambridge, 1950)

Marshall, T.H., 'Poverty or Deprivation', *Journal of Social Policy*, **10**, 1, (January 1981)

Marwick, A., 'The Labour Party and the Welfare State in Britain, 1900–1948', *American Historical Review*, LXXIII, No. 2 (December, 1967)

Marwick, A., *British Society Since 1945* (Harmondsworth, 1982)

Mass-Observation, *War Begins at Home* (London, 1940)

Mass-Observation, 'Social Security and Parliament', *Political Quarterly*, XIV, 3 (1943)

Masterman, C.F.G., 'The Social Abyss', *Contemporary Review*, LXXXI (January 1902)

Maurice, F., 'National Health: A Soldier's Study', *Contemporary Review*, LXXXIII (January 1903)

Meacham, S., *A Life Apart. The English Working Class 1890–1914* (London, 1977)

Meacher, M., *Scrounging on the Welfare* (London, 1974)

Meade, J.E., 'Poverty in the Welfare State', *Oxford Economic Papers*, XXIV, 3 (1972)

Melling, J., 'Introduction', in J. Melling (ed.), *Housing, Social Policy and the State* (London, 1980)

Middlemas, K., *Politics in Industrial Society* (London, 1979)

Middlemas, K., 'Unemployment: The Past and Future of a Political Problem', *The Political Quarterly*, **51**, 4 (Oct.– Dec., 1980)

'Miles' (Maurice, F.), 'Where to Get Men', *Contemporary Review*, LXXXI (January 1902)

Miliband, R., 'Politics and Poverty', in D. Wedderburn (ed.), *Poverty, Inequality and Class Structure* (Cambridge, 1974)

Millar, J., 'Lone Mothers', in C. Glendenning and J. Millar, *Women and Poverty in Britain* (Brighton, 1987)

Millar, J., *Poverty and the Lone-parent: The Challenge to Social Policy* (Aldershot, 1989)

Miller, F.M., 'The Unemployment Policy of the National Government, 1931–1936', *Historical Journal*, XIX (1976)

Miller, F.M., 'The British Unemployment Assistance Crisis of 1935', *Journal of Contemporary History*, **14** (1979)

Ministry of Labour and National Service, *Report of an Enquiry into Household Expenditure in 1953–54* (London, 1957)

Ministry of Labour, *Family Expenditure Survey Report for 1957–59* (London, 1961)

Ministry of Labour, *Family Expenditure Survey Report for 1963* (London, 1965)

Mishra, R., *The Welfare State in Crisis* (Brighton, 1984)

Moggeridge, D., (ed.), *The Collected Writings of John Maynard Keynes* (London, 1978)

Money, C., *Riches and Poverty* (8th edn, London, 1908)

Morgan, K.O., *Consensus and Disunity* (Oxford, 1979)

Morgan, K.O., *Labour in Power 1945–1951* (Oxford, 1985)

Morgan, J., *Conflict and Order* (Oxford, 1987)

Morrison, H., *Herbert Morrison. An Autobiography* (London, 1960)

Mowat, C.L., 'The Approach to the Welfare State in Great Britain', *American Historical Review*, **58**, 1 (October, 1952)

Mowat, C.L., *Britain Between the Wars* (London, 1955)

Mowat, C.L., *The Charity Organisation Society 1869–1913* (London, 1961)

Moylan, S., Millar, J. and Davies, R., *For Richer for Poorer? DHSS Cohort Study of Unemployed Men* (London, 1984)

National Consumer Council, *Means-Tested Benefits* (London, 1976)

NUWM, *Guide to Unemployment Insurance* (c. 1939)

Nicholas, K., *The Social Effects of Unemployment in Teeside* (Manchester, 1986)

Noakes, G., *To Be A Farmer's Boy* (Brighton, 1977)

Oddy, D.J., 'A Nutritional Analysis of Historical Evidence: the Working-Class Diet, 1880–1914', in D.J. Oddy and D. Miller (eds), *The Making of the Modern British Diet* (London, 1976)

O'Mara, P., *The Autobiography of A Liverpool Irish Slummy* (Bath, 1968)

Oppenheim, C., *Poverty, the Facts* (London, 1990)

Oren, L., 'The Welfare of Women in Labouring Families: England 1860–1950', in M.S. Hartman and L. Banner (eds), *Clio's Consciousness Raised* (New York, 1974)

Orr, J.B., *Food, Health and Income* (London, 1936)

Orr, J.B., 'Nutrition and the Family', in J. Marchant (ed.), *Rebuilding Family Life in the Post-War World* (London, 1945)

Orwell, G. *The Road to Wigan Pier* (Penguin edn, London, 1989)

Owen, A.D.K., *A Survey of the Standard of Living in Sheffield* (Sheffield, 1933)

Owen, D., *English Philanthropy 1660–1960* (Cambridge, Mass., 1965)

Pakenham, F., *Born to Believe* (London, 1953)

Parker, G., 'Making Ends Meet: Women, Credit and Debt', in C. Glendenning and J. Millar (eds), *Women and Poverty in Britain* (Brighton, 1987)

Parker, J., *Social Policy and Citizenship* (London, 1975)

Paton, J., *Proletarian Pilgrimage* (London, 1935)

Paynter, W., *My Generation* (London, 1972)

Peacock, A.T. and Wiseman, J.V., *The Growth of Public Expenditure in the United Kingdom* (Oxford, 1967)

Peden, G.C., *British Economic and Social Policy* (Deddington, 1985)

Pelling, H., 'The Working Class and the Origins of The Welfare State', in *Popular Politics and Society in Late Victorian Britain* (2nd edn, London, 1979)

Philips, G. and Whiteside, N., *Casual Labour. The Unemployment Question in the Port Transport Industry, 1880–1970* (Oxford, 1985)

Piachaud, D., *Family Incomes Since the War* (London, 1982)

Piachaud, D., *Poor Children: A Tale of Two Decades* (London, 1986)

Pilgrim Trust, *Men Without Work* (Cambridge, 1938)

Pimlott, B., *Hugh Dalton* (London, 1985)

Pimlott, B., *Labour And The Left In The 1930s* (2nd edn, London, 1986)

Pinker, R., *The Idea of Welfare* (London, 1979)

P.E.P., 'Social Security and Unemployment in Lancashire', *Planning*, XIX (December, 1952)

Ponsonby, A., *The Camel and The Needle's Eye* (London, 1910)

Pope, R., Pratt, A. and Hoyle, B., (eds), *Social Welfare in Britain 1885–1985* (London, 1986)

Prochaska, F., *The Voluntary Impulse* (London, 1988)

Proposals for a Tax Credit System (London, 1972)

Pugh, M., *The Tories and The People* (Oxford, 1985)

Rathbone, E.F., *The Disinherited Family* (London, 1924)

Reeves, Mrs Pember, *Round About A Pound A Week* (2nd edn, London, 1914)

Rennie, J., *Every Other Sunday* (London, 1955)

Report of the Committee on Abuse of Social Security Benefits (Fisher Report), Cmnd 5228 (London, 1973)

Report of the Committee on One-Parent Families (Finer Report), Cmnd 5629 (London, 1974)

Report of the Inter-Departmental Committee on Physical Deterioration, Cmnd 2175 (London, 1904)

Report of the National Assistance Board for the year ended 31st December, 1951, Cmnd 8632 (London, 1952)

Report of the National Assistance Board for the year ended 31st December, 1954, Cmnd 9530 (London, 1955)

Report of the National Assistance Board for the year ended 31st December, 1955, Cmnd 9781 (London, 1956)

Report of the National Assistance Board for the year ended 31st December, 1959, Cmnd 1085 (London, 1960)

Report of the National Assistance Board for the year ended 31st December, 1964, Cmnd 2674 (London, 1965)

Report of the Royal Commission on the Poor Laws and the Relief of Distress (1909)

Riddell, Lord, *More Pages From My Diary 1908–1914* (London, 1934)

Robb, M., 'The Psychology of the Unemployed from the Medical Point of View', in A.L. Beales and R.L. Lambert, *Memoirs of the Unemployed* (London, 1934)

Roberts, E., '"Women's Strategies", 1890–1940', in J. Lewis (ed.), *Labour and Love* (Oxford, 1986)

Roberts, R., *A Ragged Schooling* (London, 1978)

Robson, W.A., 'The Beveridge Report: An Evaluation', *Political Quarterly*, XIV, 2 (1943)

Robson, W.A., *Welfare State and Welfare Society* (London, 1976)

Rose, H., 'Up Against The Welfare State: The Claimant Unions', in R. Miliband and J. Saville (eds), *The Socialist Register 1973* (London, 1973)

Ross, E., '"Fierce Questions and Taunts": Married Life in Working-class London 1870–1914', *Feminist Studies*, **8** (1982)

Ross, E., 'Survival Networks: Women's Neighbourhood Sharing in London', *History Workshop*, **15** (Spring, 1983)

Rowland, P., *The Last Liberal Governments* (London, 1968, 1971)

Rowntree, B.S., *Poverty. A Study of Town Life* (London, 1901)

Rowntree, B.S., *The Poverty Line; A Reply* (London, 1903)

Rowntree, B.S., *Poverty and Progress* (London, 1941)

Rowntree, B.S. and Kendall, M., *How the Labourer Lives* (London, 1913)

Rowntree, B.S. and Lavers, G.R., *Poverty and the Welfare State* (London, 1951)

Rowntree, B.S. and Lavers, G.R., *English Life and Leisure* (London, 1951)

Ryan, P.A., 'Poplarism 1894–1930', in P. Thane (ed.), *The Origins of British Social Policy* (London, 1978)

Rubinstein, D., 'Socialism and the Labour Party: The Labour Left and Domestic Policy, 1945–1950', in D.E. Martin and D. Rubinstein (eds), *Ideology and the Labour Movement* (London, 1979)

Runciman, W.G., *Relative Deprivation and Social Justice* (Harmondsworth, 1972)

Sarsby, J., *Missuses and Mouldrunners* (Milton Keynes, 1988)

Save The Children Fund, *Unemployment and the Child* (London, 1933)

Saville, J., 'The Welfare State', *New Reasoner*, **3** (Winter, 1957–58)

Saville, J., 'Labour and Income Redistribution', *The Socialist Register 1965* (London, 1965)

Seabrook, J., *The Unprivileged* (London, 1967)

Seabrook, J., *The Everlasting Feast* (London, 1974)

Seabrook, J., 'Living on Welfare', in M. Loney et al. (eds), *The State or the Market. Politics and Welfare in Contemporary Britain* (London, 1987)

Searle, G.R., *The Quest for National Efficiency* (Oxford, 1971)

Seldon, A., *Wither the Welfare State* (London, 1981)

Sharman, N., *Nothing to Steal* (London, 1977)

Sherard, R.H., *A Cry of the Poor* (London, 1901)

Sinfield, A., 'Unemployment in an Unequal Society', in B. Showler and A. Sinfield (eds), *The Workless State* (Oxford, 1981)

Sires, R.V., 'The Beginnings of British Legislation for Old-Age Pensions', *Journal of Economic History*, XIV, 2 (1954)

Skidelsky, R., *Politicians and the Slump* (London, 1967)

Slater, G., *Poverty and The State* (London, 1930)

Smith, L., 'A Model for the Development of Public Participation in Local Authority Decision-making', in L. Smith and D. Jones (eds), *Deprivation, Participation and Community Action* (London, 1981)

Snowden, P., *The Living Wage* (London, 1912)

Social Insurance, Cmnd 6550 (London, 1944)

'Social Security and Unemployment in Lancashire', *Planning*, XIX (1 December, 1952)

Social Security Consortium, *Of Little Benefit, An Update* (London, 1987)

Southgate, W., *That's The Way It Was* (London, 1982)

Spring Rice, M., *Working-Class Wives, Their Health and Conditions* (Harmondsworth, 1939)

Stacey, M., *Tradition and Change* (Oxford, 1960)

Stedman Jones, G., *Languages of Class* (Cambridge, 1933)

Stedman Jones, G., 'Why is the Labour Party in a Mess?', in *Languages of Class* (Cambridge, 1983)

Steedman, C., 'Landscape for a Good Woman', in L. Heron (ed.), *Truth, Dare or Promise* (London, 1985)

Stevenson, J., 'The Politics of Violence', in G. Peele and C. Cooke (eds), *The Politics of Reappraisal 1918–1939* (London, 1975)

Stevenson, J., 'The Making of Unemployment Policy 1931–1935', in M. Bentley and J. Stevenson (eds), *High and Low Politics in Modern Britain* (Oxford, 1983)

Stevenson, O., *Claimant or Client* (London, 1973)

Swenarton, M., *Homes Fit For Heroes* (London, 1981)

Tawney, R.H., *Equality* (London, 1964 edn)

Taylor-Gooby, P., 'Attitudes to Welfare', *Journal of Social Policy*, **14**, 1 (January 1985)

Tebbutt, M., *Making Ends Meet. Pawnbroking and Working-Class Credit* (London, 1983)

Thane, P., 'The Working Class and State Welfare 1880–1914', *Bulletin of the Society for the Study of Labour History*, **31** (1975)

Thane, P., 'Non-Contributory Versus Insurance Pensions 1878–1908', in P. Thane (ed.), *The Origins of British Social Policy* (London, 1978)

Thane, P., *The Foundations of the Welfare State* (London, 1982)

Thompson, D., 'The Welfare State', *New Reasoner*, **4** (Spring, 1958)

The Times

Thompson, F., *Lark Rise to Candleford* (Harmondsworth, 1973)

Titmuss, R.M., *Income Distribution and Social Change* (London, 1962)

Titmuss, R.M., 'Welfare "Rights", Law and Discretion', *Political Quarterly*, **42**, 2 (1971)

Titmuss, R.M., 'War and Social Policy', in *Essays on 'The Welfare State'* (3rd edn, London, 1976)

Tout, H., *The Standard of Living in Bristol* (Bristol, 1938)

Townsend, P., 'Poverty: Ten Years After Beveridge', *Planning*, XIX, 334 (1952)

Townsend, P., *The Family Life of Old People* (London, 1957)

Townsend, P., 'A Society for People', in N. Mackenzie (ed.), *Conviction* (London, 1958)

Townsend, P., 'Poverty is Relative Deprivation: Resources and Style of Living', in D. Wedderburn (ed.), *Poverty, Inequality and Class Structure* (Cambridge, 1974)

Townsend, P., *Poverty in the United Kingdom* (London, 1979)

Townsend, P. and Wedderburn, D., *The Aged in the Welfare State* (London, 1965)

Treble, J.H., *Urban Poverty in Britain, 1830–1914* (London, 1983)

Trinder, C., 'Incomes Policy and the Low Paid', in M. Young (ed.), *Poverty Report 1974* (London, 1974)

Trinder, C., 'The Social Contract and the Low Paid', in P. Willmott (ed.), *Sharing Inflation?* (London, 1976)

Valance, A., *Hire-Purchase* (London, 1939)

Veit-Wilson, J.H., 'Paradigms of Poverty: A Rehabilitation of B.S. Rowntree', *Journal of Social Policy*, **15**, 1

Veit-Wilson, J., 'Seebohm Rowntree', in P. Barker (ed.), *Founders of the Welfare State* (London, 1984)

Vincent, D., *Literacy and Popular Culture* (Cambridge 1989)

Vose, J.D., *Diary of a Tramp* (Zennor, 1981)

Wain, A.A., 'One Square Mile' TS Autobiography (University of Keele, n.d.)

Walker, A., 'The Social Construction of Dependency in Old Age', in M. Loney et al. (eds), *The State or the Market* (London, 1987)

Walker, A. and C. (eds), *The Growing Divide. A Social Audit 1979–1987* (London, 1987)

Webb, A., 'The Abolition of National Assistance', in P. Hall et al., *Change, Choice and Conflict in Social Policy* (London, 1975)

Webb, B., *My Apprenticeship* (Harmondsworth, 1938)

Webster, C., 'Healthy or Hungry Thirties', *History Workshop*, **13** (Spring, 1982)

Webster, C., 'Health, Welfare and Unemployment During The Depression', *Past and Present*, **109** (1985)

Wedderburn, D., 'Facts and Theories of the Welfare State', *The Socialist Register 1965* (London, 1965)

Westergaard, J., 'Social Policy and Class Inequality: Some Notes on Welfare State Limits', in R. Miliband and J. Saville (eds), *The Socialist Register 1978* (London, 1978)

White, J., *The Worst Street in North London* (London, 1986)

Whiteley, C.W., *A Manchester Lad/Salford Man* (University of Keele, n.d.)

Whiteley, P.F. and Wingard, S.J., *Pressure for the Poor* (London, 1987)

Whiteley, P.F., 'Public Opinion and the Demand for Social Welfare in Britain', *Journal of Social Policy*, **10**, 4 (October, 1981)

Whiteside, N., 'Welfare Legislation and the Unions during the First World War', *Historical Journal*, **23**, 4 (1980)

Wild, P., 'Recreation in Rochdale, 1900–1940', in J. Clarke, C. Critcher and R. Johnson (eds), *Working-Class Culture* (London, 1979)

Willmott, P., *Friendship Networks and Social Support* (London, 1987)

Wilson, E., *Women and the Welfare State* (London, 1977)

Wilson, T., *The Myriad Faces of War* (Cambridge, 1986)

Winter, J.M., 'The Impact of the First World War on Civilian Health in Britain', *Economic History Review*, **30** (1977)

Winter, J., 'Unemployment, Nutrition and Infant Mortality in Britain, 1920–1950', in J. Winter (ed.), *The Working Class in Modern British History* (Cambridge, 1983)

Withers, H., *Poverty and Waste* (London, 1914)

Woods, J., *Growin' Up – One Scouser's Social History* (Preston, 1989)

Wootton, B., *Remuneration in a Welfare State* (Liverpool, 1961)

Wynn, M., *Fatherless Families* (London, 1964)

Young, M., 'Distribution of Income Within The Family', *British Journal of Social Policy*, III, No. 4 (1952)

Young, M. and Willmott, P., *Family and Kinship in East London* (London, 1957)

Zweig, F., *Labour, Life and Poverty* (London, 1948)

Index